A *MAVERICK* LIFE: THE

STORY

Published in the USA by:
BearManor Media
PO Box 1129
Duncan, Oklahoma 73534-1129
www.bearmanormedia.com

ISBN 978-1-59393-678-5

Printed in the United States of America.
Book design by Brian Pearce | Red Jacket Press.

A *MAVERICK* LIFE: THE JACK KELLY STORY

LINDA ALEXANDER

Table of Contents

Jack Kelly as a young Bart Maverick. PHOTO COURTESY LINDA GALLO PRIVATE COLLECTION

Acknowledgments and Author's Notes

There was a day many moons ago when I sat in front of a black-and-white television set, as a very little girl, and fell in love with Western TV stars. I didn't know it then, but there would come a time when those handsome cowboys would literally inhabit nearly my every waking — and sleeping — moment. That time is now.

One handsome cowboy in particular caught my attention big-time, and this book is the result of extensive research into his life. Jack Kelly played Bart Maverick on TV from 1957 until the show rode off into the sunset in 1962. This is the role for which he is best known, but it most definitely was not his only role. He was in the movies as well as on TV. The second of four children born into an entertainment family, Jack knew what greasepaint was before he could write his name. Life for Jack Kelly was a never-ending effort to play another part…and he reinvented himself more than once.

When I put together a biography, there is nothing more important than doing my darnedest to get the story right. This is someone's life I'm writing about, and I don't take that fact lightly. I feel it is crucial to be as accurate as possible. Jack Kelly has never had a biography written about him. This means there was little collected information from which I could pull details and then research in-depth. I had to dig up every little bit of his life — from a childhood of which he rarely ever spoke, to a life in Tinseltown and on Broadway, and then into politics and fatherhood — and along the way I made some dear friends.

I have to first thank Peter Spatharis. If not for Peter, this book would never have happened. He and I met years ago, and after learning I was a writer, he suggested I speak with a friend of his, Jack Kelly's widow, Jo. Peter thought Jack would make a good subject for a book. He was right.

I met Jo, and then Nicole Kelly Garner, Jo's daughter with Jack, and the child Jack always wanted. Through these two wonderful women, I began the task of putting back together the pieces of a complicated life, the life of a man who deeply loved the women who loved him, a man who adored the stage — any stage — and a man who truly cared about the world around him and the people of his community. *You are special ladies, Jo and Nicole. Thank you for opening up your lives to my pen.*

It needs to be noted here that James Garner was contacted more than once for an interview but he respectfully declined, saying he had had a stroke and his memory wasn't what it used to be. His daughter, Gigi, did help with some details about the relationship between Jack and her dad. Mr. Garner has a book coming out this year, 2011.

Carol Kelly Maross, the only living Kelly family member at the time of the building of this book, also declined to be interviewed. Her son was kind enough to speak to me but he could shed very little light on family dynamics.

With that said, everyone else who was approached was more than happy to talk about Jack Kelly. He inspired, and continues to inspire, passion in most everyone who has ever had any knowledge of him. Besides Jo and Nicole, whom I now count as very dear friends, others opened their memory banks to tell me about Jack Kelly:

Donna Lee Hickey, known on movie screens as May Wynn, was Jack's first wife. I am grateful to her for trusting me with her recollections, and letting me see a side of Jack others never knew. *I appreciate everything you have offered this book, Donna. Your insights into Jack's world, the world he shared with you, gave me an awareness which I couldn't have had without your generous contribution. I enjoyed our conversations.*

Peggy Cantwell shared a number of years of her life with Jack, and her knowledge gave me evidence of a time when virtually no one else had access to the details of Jack's life. *I'm very grateful to you, Peggy.*

Tom Chevoor, one of Jack's best friends, along with his wife, Mary Ann, shared invaluable details. *Your help was tremendous, Tom and Mary Ann.*

Kelly Caro Rosenberg, daughter of Nancy Kelly and Jack's niece, offered recollections of what it was like for her mother to grow up on stage, and in doing so, gave insight into the Kelly family life. *Kelly, thanks for your memories, and a new friendship.*

Peter Economakis was a friend of Jack's in later years, kind enough to give me a look into parts of Jack's personality which, until we spoke, had remained elusive.

Bette Barilla was Jack's secretary on the Huntington Beach City Council, and they were friends as well as employer/employee.

Sir Roger Moore shared stories of his time on the *Maverick* set with Jack…extraordinarily helpful! Sir Moore's web assistant, Marie-France Vienne, runs his website and facilitated our interview.

James Drury was one of Jack's co-workers during his Western TV days. They crossed paths a number of times over the years. His assistant, Karen, was delightful and helped me secure our interview.

Gregg Palmer worked with Jack on a number of early films. They were Universal Studios contract players. Gregg's knowledge of how the studio system worked in its waning days, and how that affected the young actors he and Jack were, was instrumental in creating awareness of that part of Jack's life.

Kathleen Hughes was a Universal contract player at the same time as Jack and Gregg Palmer. She played with both men in *Sally and Saint Anne* (1952), and offered invaluable insight into the life of a studio contract player.

Gloria Pall, a showgirl and actress, shared memories of people she and Jack both knew.

Mamie Van Doren offered thoughts on her remembrance of working alongside Jack in the Universal Talent School.

Earle Robitaille gave insight into being part of the Huntington Beach political scene with Jack.

Laura Wagner supported my "newbie" status in the world of retro TV writers, and gave me much-needed advice.

Walter Hickey was instrumental in putting the pieces of Jack's family history back together. I couldn't have found so much of the information I needed without his help.

Laura LaPlaca, an amazing researcher in Los Angeles, helped me work with the Warner Bros. Archives, referred by Jonathon Auxier, Curator of Warner Bros. Archives.

My business partner, Debbie Barth, has put up with me and this book for quite some time, with grace and patience…*I appreciate you, Debbie.*

I could not have done Jack Kelly's visual history justice without the help of an army of his admirers who opened up vast archives of material, offering whatever I needed to ensure the book was picture perfect. *I owe each of you a great debt of gratitude*: Linda Gallo, Susan Ketcham, Becky Landis, Mike Luscombe, Lisa Oldham, Geri Ann Sefton, and Nell Lynn Young.

Speaking of those Jack Kelly admirers, there are a host of others, and I cannot name them all…more show up each day on a very active website dedicated to Jack. In addition to those just mentioned, some others are:

Colettia Estep, Richard Eng, Nic Fewer, Lydia Guadiana, Chris Hansen, Robert Howe, Marcia Kent, Sharon Klopfenstein, Amanda Marie, Julia Martina, Cheryl Oakley, Patricia Plummer, Melissa Snyder, Liz Terry, Janet Theador, Michelle Wheeler, and Randal Wheeler. *If I did not list your name…my sincerest apologies.*

Susan Ketcham gets an extra thank you for officially supporting me on the website during my recent illness, and for being my professional pre-publication editor. *You're a sweetie, Sue.*

I had many research assists: Marcelo "Bonny" Abeal; Steve Badger; Marc Baron, The Lambs, Inc.; Sue Berry from Shocast Productions, Inc.; Cora Sue Collins; Joe Garagiola; James Garner's daughter, Gigi Garner; Angel Feliz; Caren Ferrera, Sr., Deputy City Clerk for Huntington Beach, CA; Glenn Ford's son, Peter Ford; Susan Fougstedt, Reference Librarian for Pollard Memorial Library in Lowell, MA; Martin Grams with the Mid-Atlantic Nostalgia Convention; Bob Kerivan; Ray Kinstler; Jack Lawson; Lowell Sun Archives; Kirk Moore, son of Dinty Moore who was a lawyer in the Warner Bros. TV legal department in Jack's day; Stephen Moorer with PacRep Theatre in Carmel, CA; Michael Morici of Morici Law Firm; Marvin Paige of Marvin Paige Casting, who helped facilitate communications with Cora Sue Collins; Fred Speaker, Jack Kelly's campaign manager; Richard Turner "The Cheat;" Diane Wagner from Proctor & Gamble Corporate Archives; Tim Woodhead, Marketing Director for Bridgeview Vineyards for Bob Kerivan…if I've forgotten anyone, again, I apologize. It wasn't on purpose.

Last but never ever least, I thank my husband, Tom, who has lived with Jack Kelly almost every day since the day I began this book. I'm grateful to share my life with such a wonderful husband. *I love you, Tom.*

Linda Alexander Prevost
Frederick, MD

Prologue

Jack Kelly had a council meeting that previous Monday evening. As reported by some of the attendees, he seemed different, not his usual jovial, on-target self. He was disheveled and disoriented — out-of-sorts for the perpetually well-dressed Kelly. Always known to read up on everything before every meeting, meticulously doing his research and making sure he was aware of each nuance and point to be covered, this night Jack was not on his game.

"I'm sorry," he repeatedly said to other council members, "I didn't understand what you said. Can you repeat…can you explain yourself?"

At the time, his associates wrote this off. Everybody had bad days.

Nicole's birthday was in two days. Jack was scheduled to do dinner with his beloved daughter and Jo, at Jo's home. He and Nicole had been trying to get together for weeks. One thing or another had gotten in the way, but this time, the date was set. Nicole was going on a trip, and they all wanted to get together for her birthday before she left. Jack looked forward to spending time with his family, especially since he didn't physically live in the same house anymore. He was going to cook for them, and all were looking forward to this treat. The day was a milestone for his daughter, and he would make sure she remembered it forever.

Nicole was also anticipating this special evening. Early that morning, she called her dad to make sure he didn't lose sight of the date on his calendar. She knew he'd never do that intentionally, but he kept a busy schedule. In the event something popped up, she wanted to make sure he wouldn't be overbooked.

"I called him and the line was busy," Nicole remembered. "At first the phone rang, and he didn't answer. I figured he must be doing something. Then I called again and the line was busy. I thought, *Good, he's still home.*"

This was about 10 AM, and Nicole had started calling at 9:30 AM. The line had been busy because Jack was talking with his good friend,

Fred Speaker. Fred had been his Campaign Manager, and was a regular golf buddy. The men had arranged a golf date for the following Saturday morning. Jack, a regular at the local club, Sea Cliff Country Club, was addicted to the game, and everyone in Huntington Beach knew this. Jack Kelly played golf every chance he got.

Nicole waited a few beats after hanging up the phone, and then impatiently dialed the number one more time. "When I called a few minutes later, the phone rang and rang and rang, and I thought, *I must've just missed him*. I figured he was gone for the day."

She knew his regular pattern; the same day-in and day-out. He was thoroughly predictable. Jack would get out of bed, turn on the TV, and leisurely do two crosswords while having his coffee — not one, but two crosswords. Every morning. In pen. Then he'd shower and dress for his day, usually always seeing that a golf game held a prominent spot somewhere in his list of appointments, which he always verified every morning with his secretary, Bette Barilla.

Throughout her day, Nicole couldn't stop thinking about reminding her dad of their date. For some reason, it had become extremely important to get him on the phone ahead of time and verify plans. "I continued to call his cell phone. He did have a car phone, and I called that, too. I called his office, called all over the place. And finally, about 3 o'clock in the afternoon, I got hold of his secretary."

Nicole's voice faltered as emotion caught up with details. "I…I wanted to make sure he didn't have plans because he was supposed to have dinner with us. I figured he went to play golf at someone else's club. That had to be the only reason I couldn't get hold of him." Her voice fell soft, tentative.

His secretary's words had floored her. They were delivered methodically, as if at that moment, she, too, realized something was not right. There had been plans for a golf game later in the afternoon and, "He had a lunch date today with the Fire Chief," Jack's secretary told Nicole. "He scheduled the lunch…and…he didn't show up."

Nicole knew now. She was certain this was more than a busy day gone wild for her dad. In her heart, suddenly Nicole knew something was terribly wrong. She understood that uneasy sense nagging her all day, and why she had been compelled to speak with him, why she had needed his direct reassurance.

She hung up, the receiver clattering loudly into the cradle before she picked it up again to call her mother.

"Go to Daddy's house," she instructed. Her mother was at work, around the corner from where Jack lived. Nicole was at least thirty minutes away and couldn't get there as fast. "You have to go to Daddy's house!" she repeated, her voice rising. "Something's wrong. I can't get hold of him. He didn't show up for an appointment with the Fire Chief."

Hearing the fear in her daughter's tone, Jo immediately rushed out of her office, taking no time to make her way to Jack's place. She explained, "I don't know why I did this, but on the way over, I looked up at the ceiling of my car and said, 'Okay, listen God, no surprises, okay? Not ready.'"

She continued. "I drove in, went to get the key which was in the garage, and saw his car. I thought, *This is not good*. When I went into the house, the TV was on." Another bad sign. "It was a single-story house, and I'm standing in the living room. I had to go down the hall to the bedrooms. I didn't want to go down the hall. I'm calling, 'Jack, Jack?' And nothing."

This is how Jo found Jack, unresponsive, lying in an unusual position on his bed. She had, as she called it, an "out of body experience." Almost as if she were watching a movie, she noted Jack had done his two crossword puzzles. In pen, as usual. He had been watching TV — it still droned on and on in the corner of the room. There was evidence he'd had his regular start-the-day cup of coffee, and his caftan, he always wore a caftan to bed, was on the floor near the shower.

Clearly, Jack had gotten up that morning as he did every morning, preparing for his day as he did, every day. His phone sat on the counter, near the entrance to the bathroom. He'd apparently spoken with Fred Speaker just before…just before his intent to jump in and take his shower had somehow been cut short.

That phone call had obviously been his last. As her daughter had told her, a busy signal from her dad's end had been replaced by a ringing, ringing, ringing sound in Nicole's ear moments later. Surveying the scene now in front of her, Jo knew why. Somewhere between those two attempts to reach Jack, something had gone dreadfully wrong.

A heart attack? Jo wasn't sure. Leaning down over him, she could tell Jack was still breathing. A crucial detail. His breath was shallow but he was breathing, which meant he was still alive.

Trying to process it all, Jo repeatedly spoke to her husband, her voice rising each time in her attempt to get him to gain consciousness. His phone rang, and Jo picked it up out of habit. Nicole. She had gauged how long her mother would take to get there, and timed her call to match.

"Daddy's here but I can't wake him up," Jo told Nicole. She heard her daughter's voice come to her from the other end of the phone, as if relayed through a tunnel. She tried to process what Nicole said but couldn't make sense of her words. Nicole sounded far off.

Nicole spoke again, and again Jo didn't respond directly. Nicole could hear her mother's voice. She was talking, obviously not to her, and the sound was soft, almost a sobbing whisper. Her mother was speaking to her dad.

Jo's tone of voice was absent, teary, almost child-like. "Jack? Jack! Wake up."

Jo was clearly in shock, repeating the same words over and over. Without knowing exactly what was going on in her dad's house, Nicole felt panic rise. "Mother!" she yelled. "Hang — up — the — phone! Hang up and call 911 right now!"

Rather than wait to hear her mother's response, Nicole disconnected from her end and jumped in her car, making the drive to her dad's home in record time. As she arrived, an ambulance was on the scene, preparing to take Jack to the hospital. Her mother had obviously called 911. Jack was still hanging on, still alive, though unresponsive.

Nicole found her mother inside the house. With a blank stare, she calmly told her daughter, "Daddy's fine. They said he's going to be fine. So I thought…I don't know what I thought."

Jo sat in a stupor. She wouldn't go to the hospital in the ambulance with Jack, not because she didn't want to be with him but because she seemed unable to grasp what was happening. She was literally in shock. As soon as the call had come into 911, they knew who they were dealing with…that address belonged to City Councilman Jack Kelly. Once they were there, they tried to get Jo to go with them, but she insisted she wanted to wait for their daughter.

Nicole was forced to take charge. It was as if she talked to a child as she collected her mother, put her in her car, and drove to the hospital, right behind the ambulance. On their way, Jo said Nicole was "panicking and praying."

When they got to the hospital, the doctor took Jo and Nicole into a private room. "He had this X-ray," Jo remembered, "and showed it to us. The doctor said, 'Do you see this white stuff going thru his head?' I said, 'Yeah.' It was blood, he told me. I said, 'Well, fix it.' They gently let me know, 'Mrs. Kelly, it doesn't work that way.'"

Jack's aneurism, that old aneurism which had been discovered in his head about twenty years earlier, and which Jack had ignored, had finally exploded. Blood was running through his system from top down, and there was no fixing it this time. As Jo put it, "He was brain dead, bottom line."

That night, Jo and Nicole stayed with Jack around the clock, neither straying far from his bedside. The press got wind of Jack Kelly's condition, and they were keeping track, waiting for any bit of information on "The Other Maverick."

Nicole prayed. She spoke out loud to her dad throughout the night, tearfully begging him, "Please live, please make it through this, Daddy. I can't live without you." This even though she knew in her heart, he was gone.

The next day, Nicole had an epiphany. She was certain her dad could hear her. She loved him so much that she needed to give him permission to go, for his sake. Jack Kelly would never have wanted to continue this way. Knowing how much her father had loved life, and loved her since the day she was born, she felt she didn't have the right to hold him back. She couldn't force him to hold on if his spirit wanted to let go.

The *National Enquirer*, in specific, learned that well-known actor and California politician, Jack Kelly, was suspended between life and death. Headlines screamed the likes of, "Jack Kelly's family prays around his bedside for his death," and even more cruel, discovered Jack and Jo no longer lived together as husband and wife. Jo was repeatedly dogged in public reports with the tag, "estranged wife." At a time when the one man they both loved deeply and dearly was on life support, the media which had celebrated him when he'd done well and knocked him farther down when he'd made mistakes, now tried to put him — and his family — in a coffin before an official death pronouncement was made.

Medical personnel had already declared Jack brain dead. He couldn't communicate but Nicole, and Jo, knew the special bond he shared with his daughter held strong, and would forever stay that way. With Nicole understanding this, she gave her permission, out loud, for him to let go.

This was the final pronouncement. The time had come.

"It seems reasonable to conclude that fiction is linked substantially to elements of truth or fact. Personal experiences, relative's antics, encounters through travel, observation of a comic or dramatic event, hearsay revelations uttered in strictest confidence…"

JACK KELLY

CHAPTER ONE

The Early Years...
Entertaining Is In the Blood:
The Kellys and The Walshs

Jack Kelly's mother came into the world as Mary Ann Walsh; ultimately, after marriage, she became known as Nan Kelly. In her earliest years, she was one of the top models for noted artist James Montgomery Flagg, an illustrator, cartoonist, and well known painter. Flagg sold his first illustration to the prestigious *St. Nicholas Magazine* when he was only twelve years old. He went on from there, illustrating for, among others, *Life* magazine.

Since Jack's mother was one of his earliest models, and at one point was said to be his top model, assumedly Flagg first crossed paths with a young Mary Ann Walsh, and went on to utilize her beautiful face and form in any one of those book and/or magazines for which he illustrated. Flagg created the famed "I Want YOU" Uncle Sam poster during World War I. Mary Ann may have posed for some of his patriotic works, though unlikely, since by 1915, she was already twenty years old. Timing favors the possibility that she was his model for the book, *The Adventures of Kitty Cobb*. When published in 1912, Mary Ann was seventeen, and the young lady on the cover has a strong resemblance to a young Mary Ann Walsh.

The Adventures of Kitty Cobb *cover art by James Montgomery Flagg.*

Called Ann at that time, sometimes Annie, she was an amateur, and relatively unsuccessful, actress. She was also one of the first models for what is now the John Robert Powers Agency. What has since become a well-known modeling agency was then little more than a man with a plan working in the guise of a company. The namesake, at the time called only John Powers, was in his early days an actor, and apparently not a well-known one. Powers culled from his sphere of acquaintances to ultimately become an agent for the burgeoning film industry and for print ads. He most often placed the fairer sex in spots where beauty was required — for the sake of beauty, to sell a product, or promote an event.

On Wednesday morning, June 23, 1920, Ann Walsh became the bride of John Augustus Kelly, most often known as Jack, in a double-ring nuptial mass ceremony. One article said, "Nan Walsh gave up a promising stage career to marry Irish Jack Kelly." While that may have been true, less than six months prior to the wedding, she was living with her unemployed mother and four brothers, working as a telephone operator. Three brothers also had blue collar jobs, with the youngest, at fourteen, unemployed. Her father had passed away years earlier, and an older sister was out of the house. Ann was already helping to support her family.

The affair was called a "pretty wedding" in the newspapers, and performed at Our Lady of Mt. Carmel Catholic Church by the Rev. Fr. Charles F. Gibney. The location was then New York City, now known as Astoria. The bride wore white taffeta and a picture hat trimmed with Lilies-of-the-Valley, and carried a shower bouquet of bridal roses, also with Lilies-of-the-Valley. She had one attendant, Miss Lillian Reilly of New York City, and was given away by her mother, Mrs. Mary Walsh. After the wedding, a breakfast was served at her mother's home on Flushing Avenue in Long Island. The ceremony was attended primarily by relatives of both parties, and a few friends.

John, Sr. was born and raised in Lowell, Massachusetts. Ann, while raised in New York, had relatives in Lowell. At the time they married, he officially lived in Lowell, she in New York. They set up house in Lowell, where their oldest child, Nancy — born Ann Mary Kelly — started life on March 25, 1921. She was a golden child, especially for her mother. Ultimately, she became a golden meal ticket…the family's major breadwinner.

This wasn't necessarily out of the ordinary for either of these people. They had both grown up in a working-class world, some of it in vaudeville, and being a part of the support system from their earliest years was all they knew. Jack was a "vaudeville performer" who had seen his name on the marquee with a number of lesser-known female leads of the day.

He had bounced between being an actor, a stage manager, and a singer and dancer, basically doing it all. There is evidence his father, John Bernard Kelly, was involved in the entertainment world in Ireland before he ever came to the United States.

Ann had cousins and uncles who had done their time, and then some, on the boards in any number of roles. Her uncle, William Walsh, had a few months earlier formed his own stock company. He and actress, Dora Clement, married and living in Des Moines, Iowa, called their troupe the Clement-Walsh Players. They took their act on the road between Waterloo and Des Moines, years later settling in Los Angeles. William was eventually credited with "discovering" a number of early movie stars, including Victor Jory and Lyle Talbot.

A photograph of Nancy was submitted to a contest, and she won a prize as "a perfect baby." James Montgomery Flagg saw the picture and, as the story goes, he "sent for her. He made her infantile charms famous." Somewhere in there her name became Nancy, and she was soon receiving so many offers her mother had to refuse a good number because "Miss Nancy was just too busy to accept."

Nancy was only two months old when "the big city called" and the young Jack Kelly family made an official move as a unit of three to Astoria, New York — the same area in which the parents married. Their plan was to promote Nancy's growing modeling career. She was already a camera's dream, and would eventually come to be known as "the most photographed child in America due to commercial posing" by *Film Daily*.

Jack had "set himself up in the theater ticket brokerage business" in New York City under the name, The Kelly-Sullivan Agency. By 1925, Nancy's career had barely begun when her mother took her to Paramount Studios in Long Island to personally meet Gloria Swanson, for a role in *The Untamed Lady*. Nancy got that part, and many more were to follow. In the 1920s alone, Nancy Kelly reportedly was in over fifty silent films.

Nan was a stage mother extraordinaire. Since she had had her own stint in front of the lights, she knew the ropes, and occasionally still dabbled in acting and modeling.

By the time her next child was born in 1927, Nan had the entertainment way of life down pat. John Augustus Kelly, Jr., was born in Astoria, Queens, New York, on September 16, 1927. Named after his father, the boy became known as Jack, but was also sometimes called Jackie. His early life was one of relatively comfortable convention, not wealthy but without extreme financial distress. This was likely not because they had any real fortune amassed, but because they were a working family...all of them worked, and age was not a factor.

Nancy was even being dubbed in movie ads as "Little Nancy Kelly," and when those ads were local to her hometown, they included the words, "Lowell's Own Child Actress." That same year, a small newspaper notation showed her picture with the caption, "Eight movies in seven months — that's the acting record of Nancy Kelly, 5-year old cinema queen." Reviews called her "a finished actress."

Family life, from Jack's young point of view, was less about him being a little boy and more about him being able to fit a part — in a commercial ad, or in front of some other type of camera. He was being groomed for the lights in much the same way his older sister had been only a few years earlier. Considered more "temperamental," and a "very boyish little boy," he interjected his own personality into the mix. If Jack didn't want to pose or follow directions...he didn't. His mother claimed in a newspaper article that when this happened, she "never let him be forced."

Whether motherhood got in the way on Nan Kelly's road to stardom, or some other issue stepped in her path, she was working around any disappointment she may have felt by preparing her Golden Children, Nancy and Jack, to make her name for her. She groomed them for stardom. While Nancy dutifully took the bait in role after role, first as a model, then as a radio voice talent and a then a bona fide movie star, Jack, to some degree, only went along only for the ride, at least in the earlier days. He did what he was told, usually, though often in frustration, and even possibly a slight chip on his shoulder.

At all costs, "Jackie" made his best effort to stay out of the way of the extraordinarily strong female presence in his home, and being obedient became his salvation. He was drawn to music, and as a boy, this was called "the real love of his life." His adolescence turned into one of related people living together in the same house, with an attraction to alcohol as a family unit. Despite the other male in the home — his father — family affairs were directed predominantly by his strong-willed mother.

Jack Kelly was a product of his environment. His mother was forceful, one not to be trifled with, so he was a good boy. At first, he was too much of a child to know any different. Jack reportedly made his public debut as a soap ad model at the age of only two weeks, in October 1927. Though the widely-publicized story says he was the first Ivory soap baby model, this trivia is nothing more than part of a created biography, a tidbit which managed to follow him throughout the years. Proctor & Gamble archives personnel have indicated no direct record of Jack Kelly ever modeling for their product as a baby, or at any other time. In addition, the first Ivory Soap baby appeared in the late 1800s. Without question, Jack Kelly was not that child.

Jack likely modeled as an infant for an Ivory soap ad and wasn't credited by name, since there were many infants and babies used. Having such an early credit on his resume gave him notoriety for being in the spotlight almost since birth. He did in fact model as an infant — not only for soap, but for "food, medicine, and clothing advertisements." Newspapers reported that his mother "reluctantly approved his toil as a model." In truth, his mother started him on the road in the first place. Nan Kelly was quite the public relations expert, as well as a grand stage mother.

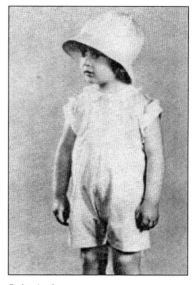

Baby Jack. PHOTO COURTESY LISA OLDHAM PRIVATE KELLECTION

This timing made sense. While Jack was starting out in the limelight, sister Nancy was receding…but only for a short time. She began school, enrolled at the Immaculate Conception School in Astoria on Long Island. Nan continued her work as an agent, grooming yet another child, Jack, while the first, Nancy, was being educated. It wasn't long, though, before Nancy was back. The *Wizard of Oz* was a radio play before it became a movie, and in the 1933-1934 timeframe, Nancy was the radio voice of Dorothy Gale.

An article told of how Nan took care of Nancy in her efforts to make her working world as ideal as possible. She would bring home-cooked soup and vegetables packed in vacuum bottles to the studio so Nancy would "have always the right foods." She also insisted, show or no show, that "the small artist" had a regular nap every afternoon.

In 1933, the stork again visited the Kelly family, and another daughter was born. She was named Carole Lee, ultimately known in entertainment circles first as Karolee Kelly, then as Carol Kelly. Then, though, she was only a baby, and a baby adding to Nan's already busy schedule. Working hard to get Nancy's career off the ground and determined Jack would follow in his big sister's footsteps, motherhood proved to be a demanding job description. Carole was also put to work and before she was six months old, was under contract to model exclusively for "a big concern." Being in front of the cameras was a Kelly family affair.

Nan was admittedly strict. She expected her children to tow the line. "I have few rules," she explained in a 1934 interview, "but the children know I mean those few. They do not have meat. Nancy never tasted it until she

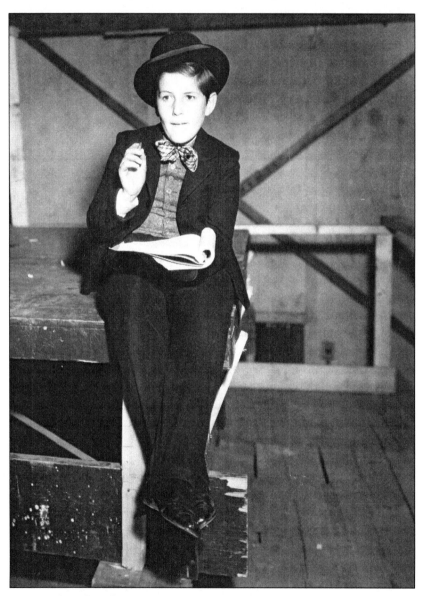

Young Jack studying lines. PHOTO COURTESY JACK KELLY FAMILY PRIVATE COLLECTION

was eleven. They have a quart of milk apiece every day and eat plenty of cheese, eggs, fruit and vegetables. My home remedy for a stomach upset is a tall glass of spinach water. They never take medicine."

In early 1934, the well-formulated plan for child modeling and acting success had to be altered, at least for a while. Nan was pregnant again. On July 24, 1934, William Clement Kelly was born. In early years, he was called Clement, and then Clem, but ultimately he became known as Bill, and some called him a "strikingly beautiful boy." The Kelly family carried good genes on both sides, and each child was blessed with physical attractiveness.

Unfortunately, Bill was sickly and he seemed delicate from the get-go, emotionally as well as physically. He did not measure up to the other three children in his ability to be camera-worthy. When he was two years old, his parents realized he couldn't walk properly. He was diagnosed with polio, and his mother would inten-tionally not mention him when she spoke of her children. This was, after all, Hollywood. Theirs was a show

Young Jack in striped shirt. PHOTO COURTESY JACK KELLY FAMILY PRIVATE COLLECTION

business family, and image was everything. She decided her youngest child wasn't physically able to be a part of their public life, front and center. Bill quickly moved to the background, and he was kept there.

By 1936, the entertainment landscape continued to be an ongoing busi-ness operation for the three oldest Kelly children. They received dancing lessons, and Nan ensured they had proper time in the outdoors to encour-age good health. They "had no special physical training except plenty of play in the open air," she maintained. "And no cosseting. Most children think too much about themselves and their ailments. It's unhealthy and spoils both manners and appearance in the end."

Jack had precious little time to "think too much" about himself. He had moved up in his mother/son duties and accompanied her on trips to theatrical agencies as she would make arrangements and finalize details for Nancy's fast-growing career. While Jack, Sr. built a successful theater ticket agency, Nan had become quite the businessperson herself. She acted as Nancy's personal manager, while fielding any and all modeling or appearance obligations required of Jack and Carol.

Nan took her job seriously. "It is not so much beauty that counts as naturalness and grace in child models," she said. "I have never allowed my children to hear themselves discussed nor to think there is anything extraordinary in their being chosen to pose. I think perhaps they found

The early days: Jack, Carol, Nancy.

their work easier because I always played 'pretend' with them, and we acted everything out." As she continued, her core truth was finally revealed. "I wanted to be an actress myself so their careers have been great fun for me."

On one particular day of trips into the city with his mother, Jack was forced to sit in the anteroom of a New York theater office and, per his mother's strict instructions, "not talk to strangers." As a young, bored Jack acted the part of the dutiful son, sitting all alone awaiting his mother's return, a man entered the room and sat. He tried to engage Jack in friendly conversation and, remembering his mother's instructions to "not talk to strangers," Jack at first remained silent despite the man's avid attempts to get the boy to chat with him.

The man persisted, and Jack wasn't able to remain unengaged for long. Still, he recalled his mother's admonition. He was in a precarious position, and finally decided he could obey his mother while not totally ignore the nice man sitting next to him. As the man continued to speak, Jack looked at him…and made faces. This was the earliest known indication that Jack Kelly was destined to be a funny-man, in one form or another.

As Nan returned to collect her son, she saw him stick out his tongue at a distinguished, well-dressed gentleman. Nan took a good look at the man and suddenly, she recognized him. This individual was none other than Lee Shubert. Everyone who had anything to do with the New York stage knew Lee Shubert. One of the owners of what was becoming a literal theater empire, Shubert was a mover and shaker in the stage world. And he was trying to talk to her son…who was, at her instructions, refusing to talk back.

A young, dressed-up Jack. PHOTO COURTESY JACK KELLY FAMILY PRIVATE COLLECTION

Nan quickly took the situation in hand. "Why, Jack! Be nice to this man. This is Mr. Shubert." She introduced herself and apologized for her son. When Jack got the flick that this man meant a lot to his mother, he became the perfect little boy. As he told Rona Barrett years later in an interview, "Suddenly I became like Little Lord Fauntleroy. So charming and sweet, I thought I'd get sick!"

Jack's mother explained to the theater mogul how she had instructed young Jack not to have anything to do with people he didn't know, and her son was only following her direction. Jack's determination to be the ideal child had much to do with her strict upbringing. She made it clear she taught her children "to think of others rather than themselves and application of that rule is about all they need to establish good manners."

Shubert dismissed her concerns. He smiled, telling her he admired dutiful and animated young children and, in fact, he was looking for "just such a nice boy" for a part in a new play. This production, *Swing Your Lady*, would star none other than Hope Emerson, a rising star in the new medium of Hollywood movies, and quite the player in the theater. Shubert needed a well-behaved "nice boy" in his play…and he offered Jack Kelly the part on the spot, as they all three sat together in that New York casting office. Jack got his first theater role that day.

He had done radio work, as well as print modeling, but this would be his first stage experience. There had been speaking parts on radio in such titles as *March of Time*, *Gangbusters*, and *Famous Fortunes*, as well as innumerable soap operas. Now, with an appearance in *Swing Your Lady*, Jack's stage resume would again be interspersed with more radio. Seemingly even in the earliest days, Jack Kelly played for almost every entertainment medium available.

Famous Fortunes was a radio show dramatizing lives of well-known men. Between the years of 1935-1938, Jack was involved with this production, and through it he discovered a love for dialects and accents. Not only did he learn how to hone in on and master any number of dialects, he was talented at adapting voiceovers to fit all sorts of personalities and types of people.

Everyone listening realized Jack Kelly, standing behind a radio microphone, had a natural ability to take on different accents with great ease. Audiences couldn't see him; they had no idea of his identity or, even more important, his age. This gave Jack a chance to play parts where he was young, and parts where he was old. He was educated. He was from the docks. He was Midwestern, or he was Jewish. Whatever the voice called for, Jack Kelly pulled it off. He would hear a dialect or accent, and then effortlessly adapt.

He took this talent with him into his older years, and enjoyed playing practical jokes on friends and family, as well as using his ability to create a solid basis for a side career as a voiceover artist. His early radio work was where Jack began a life-long love affair with words. He thrilled at being able to change his voice to fit whatever need was in front of him — serious or comical.

Another potential role came to Jack in *School House on the Lot* with George Jessel. The young Jack was fascinated by catwalks and the expansive space a large stage offered. It was a veritable playground for a kid, impossible to ignore. He investigated every inch, hiking up stage ladders, crawling around on catwalks, and finding his way into nooks and hard-to-get-out of corners. After one such adventurous expedition, he fell fast asleep, and missed his cue.

When time for his call, the stage manager was fired up at the boy's seeming disappearance. In response, Jack — true actor he was, even then — leaped off the couch where he had been found, grimacing and groaning as he attempted to explain why he'd not made his stage call. He had broken his ankle, he said, while hurrying to his dressing room. The stage manager didn't buy it, and bellowed, "You're fired!" That role was lost to Jack Kelly before he started.

But he was still able to snag many others, in at least a handful of plays with well-known stage presences — *Stopover* with Sidney Blackmer, *St. Helena* with Maurice Evans, and with the Grand Dame, Ethel Barrymore, he appeared in *Ghost of Yankee Doodle: A Play in Two Acts.* This also starred Marilyn Erskine, Richard Carlson, and Lloyd Gough, and was directed by John Cromwell, father of James Cromwell.

Jack was never to forget that time he worked with Ethel Barrymore. In a 1958 interview with Erskine Johnson, he explained what happened. One scene required him to open Christmas presents while Ethel, upstage, had a big, loud, crucially-important, and emotional, scene. Jack, kid that he was, would have naturally been excited when opening packages — so as an actor, he did what he thought was logical, making a big deal out of rustling and tearing gift paper off the boxes, including loud, ad lib, "oooh!" and "aaah!" sounds of surprise.

This went on for some time. Finally, Ethel stopped in the middle of her lines, turned her back to the audience and walked deliberately to Jack. He remembered, "Ethel leaned over, patted my head and whispered, 'Quiet, you little brat.'" She then walked back into the footlights and picked up her lines as if nothing had happened. "I think that's why she turned me down for a role in her next play," he recalled, laughing.

None of this waylaid Jack's future in entertainment. Roles and opportunities continued to come to him while at the same time, Nancy also moved forward. As the Kelly bunch showed their natural physical beauty in front of the cameras, they proved to be a family not lacking in talent, or for that matter, brains.

"A lot of us appear to be rowing to safety in separate boats."

JACK KELLY

CHAPTER TWO

Hollywood Comes Calling for the Kellys

In 1938, Nancy won an important role for her burgeoning career. She was selected to play Mrs. Jesse James in *Jesse James*, opposite the wildly popular Tyrone Power. She had been discovered by Daryl Zanuck after he viewed her screen test. He immediately signed her to a contract.

Nancy had one slight problem, though. She was under age when offered this opportunity. The Hollywood Board of Education required that for her to accept the part, she had to prove she had a high school diploma, which she did not have. Nancy had been tutored in French, economics and literature while busy with stage work, and attended a Long Island convent school, New York's St. Lawrence Academy, as well as Bentley School. Still, her formal education had been sporadic, and she didn't have a diploma.

Her parents worried over what to do. Nancy could not lose this role. It was decided she would study and cram, in hopes she could pass required exams to receive that diploma in a short period of time. She was given a whole host of testing, from grammar school through high school courses, and then came the time to wait. And wait.

A long week of family jitters passed before her final report arrived. Not only had Nancy passed well enough to get an official high school diploma, she scored three-and-a-half points higher than was required for a third year college rating. Nancy not only completed her schooling in one fell swoop, she won the chance to play opposite Tyrone Power. This went far toward helping her grow a serious "movie star" resume. Nancy Kelly would become a major player in movies of Hollywood's Golden Era.

Whether perceived she had more promise, or simply because she was older and had more opportunities even before Jack had a chance to format stardom, Nancy always took the front seat in mother Nan's efforts to get her children noticed. Karolee had some visibility, though nothing of great note. And baby brother Clem seemed to forever pull up the rear. He was only four, but beautiful. His older siblings had, by his age, been in front of the camera for years; he wasn't given any such attention. His mother didn't even solicit for it. Jack at least got work in plays while in school, and he took on odd jobs to supply his own spending money, all by the wise old age of eleven.

Jack, Sr., Nancy, Nan. PHOTO COURTESY KELLY CARO ROSENBERG PRIVATE COLLECTION

Nancy now had an agent, named Wally Alderton. He went with her on publicity junkets…with Mother in tow, of course. As Nancy got front-runner attention, Jack peeked from behind her petticoats…and the press began to notice. A well-known Massachusetts columnist, Charles Sampas, wrote Nancy was busy "training" her brother, "eleven-year old Jack Kelly," as he made his cinema debut in *Alexander Graham Bell*. Sampas' piece clarified, "Not that he's an amateur, by any means…. He played in four Broadway productions and not a few radio shows…."

The Kellys went to California in 1937, Nan deciding it was time to kick Nancy's career up a notch. She was certain New York no longer held the key to stardom for her, or Jack, for that matter. Hollywood was the place to be, and Jack, Sr. went along with the decision. He didn't want to give up his lucrative and successful business but he gave in, "sold his ticket agency and moved the family to Hollywood."

Whether he was as determined to make movie stars out of his children as was his wife isn't clear. It is known that he'd made enough money to re-chart his career and make sure his children had a chance at grabbing that Golden Ring. One way or the other, Jack, Sr. agreed to the plan.

Nan brought in her share of the household income. In her "stage mother" persona, she saw to it that her children had a place onscreen. Whether she genuinely wanted this for the kids, or wanted it for herself and lived through them…either way, when the kids were working, money went into Nan's pocket. It indeed went into her pocket and not necessarily her husband's. In an article in Spring of 1939, as she gushed about her growing career, young Nancy said, "There's all that lovely money coming in. My half's in the bank; the other half always has gone to Mother and that's only fair, because she has earned it as much as I." Notably, Nancy didn't say the money was going to her parents.

The Kelly family's move to California was without question a strategy to facilitate the growing, and increasingly profitable, careers of their two most Hollywood-savvy children. They lived in a rented house in Beverly Hills, drove a middle-aged car, and had two bicycles and a tricycle in the garage.

They straddled a precarious fence between two worlds. Their family life was a modest one by Hollywood standards, allowed through the combined business efforts of what Jack Sr. did, along with the money the children brought in via their mother. They toyed with the eccentric and wealthy of Tinseltown, giving them all the chance, even in a small way, to be seen as part of the "in" crowd.

Jack's parents were known to party at the Hearst Castle with the likes of Errol Flynn and many other well-known stars of old Hollywood. According to William Randolph Hearst, Jr., "Evenings would begin with cocktails before dinner — whether it was a weekend party or a big birthday gala. Guests usually limited themselves to one drink. Pop did not like hard liquor or heavy drinking. He put the word out that no guests were to bring their own booze to the place. But some did and got drunk."

This fit with asides Jack told later in life about his family's attendance at the Castle. The kids visited more than once, along with their parents. Jack knew enough about the activities of the Hearst family to relate how Castle protocol handled the needs of their guests.

"Daddy told me about going to Hearst Castle," Jack's daughter, Nicole, related. "I remember him telling there was a 'no drinking' rule if you were in the castle, or at dinner. They knew all their guests were [drinkers], so you could drink in your room if you brought your own, but you could not drink around the premises or at the dinner table. Everyone would get loaded, either in someone's room or in their own room, and have these little mini-parties, and then come to dinner totally drunk — but they couldn't drink at the dinner table."

This is a telling tale, showing Jack's understanding, even as a youngster, of how his parents drank, and partied. This recollection rings true with Hearst's son's explanation of how his father handled the constant alcoholic atmosphere at his amazing estate.

No matter that it looked to outsiders as if Nan ran the roost, her vision for the children could never have come to pass without the tacit approval of Jack, Sr. The Kellys were said to stick together "as a family in everything from fights to finances." The life afforded the parents as a result of the children's work, thanks mostly to Nancy, was appealing enough that Jack, Sr. went along with his wife's direction, even if it may have been reluctant on his part.

The relationship between Nan and her husband, Jack, isn't well-documented, but from most accounts, seemed to be passive-aggressive…he was passive, and she was aggressive. She made her desires known, and he usually went along with her, though not always happily. Nan was considered difficult to be around. Jack, Sr. was called "a sweet man," but when there was talk of how he handled her, and life in general, alcohol was usually mentioned. Some say Nan drank, as well, but for the most part, her consumption was considered well-managed.

With their transfer to California, Jack's dad had been forced to rearrange his professional goals. He had been reluctant to make the move, particularly because it required giving up his business and finding a new line of work. Still, Nan was insistent. Once they settled in California, Jack, Sr. went into the coin-machine business. He also engaged in real estate. Jack Kelly, Sr. became what is known today as an entrepreneur, working a variety of efforts to make ends meet.

What was really going on, though? There is evidence that despite their physical move, the family still held a presence in Lowell, Massachusetts, as late as 1939. They lived in Los Angeles but held on to property in Lowell, returning regularly and keeping tabs on the locals and their extended family.

The year of 1939 brought changes to the two oldest Kelly children. An Earl Carroll newspaper column in April stated, "Now that Nancy Kelly's eighteen, there'll be no more teachers on the set. She can work nights, too." Nancy was considered a grown-up, proving that in her career and in her personal life. She had a place cemented as a comely entertainment ingénue, and was enjoying every minute.

While Jack, Sr. held down the home fort full-time in California, Nan and Nancy moved back and forth between New York, Lowell, and the west coast. Nan had well-learned how to get her children seen by those who ran both Hollywood's studio system, and the movers-and-shakers of Broadway. Through her siblings, she also had growing family connections.

Jack was becoming an overall performer — beginning, as had Nancy, on Broadway, and moving on to Hollywood, with stops in between. Firmly ensconced with a home base in California, he was enrolled in St. John's Military Academy. This was not an unusual spot for children of entertainment folks to acquire early education.

Even though Jack was already an industry professional with years of various types of experience to his young name, he didn't yet have a foot-hold in the movies. Mother again worked her magic, and Jack found himself on screen in a few 1939 20th Century-Fox films — including *Young Mr. Lincoln* with Henry Fonda, and *The Story of Alexander Graham Bell*, also with Henry Fonda, as well as Don Ameche and Loretta Young. Both parts were un-credited, yet they gave Jack important screen time alongside notable names.

Jack was six years and a bit younger than Nancy. He was twelve, and she was nearly nineteen. While she was growing her career, she reaped the benefits of being a beautiful starlet. By late 1940, she was seeing Edmund O'Brien, an actor six years older than she; his first film credit had come his way only as recently as 1939. On February 19, 1941, Edmund O'Brien and Nancy Kelly married. Less than one year later, on February 2, 1942, they divorced.

In late 1940, not long before Thanksgiving, Jack's mother had an accident. She tried to stop Clem "from toppling down a flight of stairs," and ended up "black and blue." Jack, Sr., was also a casualty. "He saw Mrs. Kelly lose her balance, leaped to save her, and caught his foot on a sprinkler in the lawn." Fortunately, all ended up okay, and injuries were minor. The baby was unscathed.

The elder Jack Kelly was always behind the scenes, with little heard about him or from him…but he was a player in the building Kelly entertainment empire. Identified as "Nancy [Cinemastar] Kelly's pater," Jack, Sr. was considered "one of the best known Hollywood figures" by Charles Sampas. When people saw only Mother Nan in the forefront taking the children's careers forward, this wasn't the complete picture. Jack, Sr. was involved in grooming his brood for lasting notoriety.

The clan kept in contact with family in Lowell. Now and then, Nancy was seen in Lowell newspapers with her parents, at one time sitting prettily on a sofa belonging to aunts and uncles, drinking a steaming cup of tea; another time, enjoying a happy conversation. At a performance in Boston at a local theater, Nancy and her parents hosted Mary Breen, a cousin, and Margaret Scollin, R.N. Mary was also a nurse. Afterward, they were entertained at Mary's family home at 101 Beech Street. Mary's husband, Joe Breen, was a first cousin to Nancy's mother.

During these years, Jack was only in his mid-teens, but he had a regular gig working as an emcee and comedian in nightclubs, part of an act with a more experienced male performer. Billed as Junior Jack Kelly, he was seen as a lead-in for vaudeville-type floorshows in Chicago, and elsewhere. Slapstick comedy, with a bit of music thrown in, added skills to his live show repertoire. In between acts, he did average, everyday odd jobs.

Jack's official biography of years later said he graduated from University High School in Los Angeles in 1944. Other reports indicate he went to Santa Monica High School. Friends of his in later years recalled when Jack told them he never received a high school diploma. His organized education, he said, went no farther than about the sixth grade. Whether he did, or did not, go to high school, he likely received a high school education in much the same way as Nancy did — on set.

He was on the road a lot, which could have been why his education wasn't officially documented. He had graduated to headline his own emcee act, dropping the "Junior" from in front of his name. One ad announced, "Jack Kelly, who used to be known as 'Junior,' is the comedian emcee heading the new floor show. His droll talks and zany impersonations give zest to the nightly programs." Being in night clubs at such a young age educated him in other ways, too. Jack grew up before his time, and this was part of his routine until he joined the Army.

A few years later, again in February, Nancy was getting remarried, this time to Fred Jackman, Jr., another older man. Jackman was son of a cinematographer/director/special effects expert who had followed in his father's path. Despite the nearly eight-year age difference, Nancy's new husband had barely a few years more experience in the business than she. Nancy probably gravitated to men not in her age bracket because she'd been in the entertainment world for so many years and, though young, was already considered a pro. She'd had little connection to people her age, or even people who'd lived the average daily life of most young women and men with whom she would otherwise have socialized.

Nancy was climbing the Hollywood social, "see-and-be-seen" ladder. That year, her brother was discharged, having spent not quite two years in military service. Jack did basic training at Camp Roberts, California, going to Weather School, and was sent to Alaska as a Weather Observer for the Air Force. He was on the first B-29 to fly over the Arctic Circle and in December 1946, he was honorably discharged, just a few months after his nineteenth birthday.

Jack couldn't seem to settle down to one specific path. He was young, but in his family, children were expected to be focused from nearly the moment they left the cradle. Jack was torn as to what direction he would take, and to mask his indecision, he decided to get some organized schooling. It was a logical thing to do, and he couldn't go wrong by furthering his education.

Jack held a tight rein on his emotions, rarely giving a clue as to what was deep inside. He had always done what he was told to do, when he was told. He learned that lesson at an early age. Young ladies flocked to him, and he had to do little to turn a head. As a new male face in Hollywood, he tested the waters, not taking anything too seriously.

Being a lady-magnet was a heady reality, but there were two women over which he seemed to have no visible heartfelt effect — his mother, and his eldest sister. They were the two women he most wanted to impress, but they seemed to have less and less time for him as he got older. Jack Kelly embraced alcohol early on as a way of life because that's the world in which he had grown up. More telling, alcohol became his way of emboldening himself.

Jack studied law at UCLA, which shows he did have enough formal education prior to this to be accepted for college. He knew his family considered this a respectable alternative to acting, if he ever needed a fall-back. For most of 1947, he focused on his studies. To help his pocketbook, he found odd jobs…including shoe salesman, gas station attendant, life-guard, delivery boy, men's clothing salesman, and — in a way, mirroring his dad's earlier days — he was a legitimate theater manager.

The acting bug never left him. Seeds his parents sewed in him as a young boy had, for better or worse, taken root, and he couldn't deny his attraction to screen and stage. Jack left UCLA to return to radio in Hollywood. He was heard on *Lux Radio Theatre*, *Suspense*, *Tell It Again*, and *Romance of the Ranchos*. As for the lure of live theater, he couldn't ignore that, either. He joined the newly-forming Circle Theatre in Hollywood, building sets, working behind the scenes, and in the process, garnering lead roles in such plays as *Time of Your Life*, *Adding Machine*, and *Love on the Dole*.

Despite his sister's clear success in Tinseltown, Jack wasn't reaching the same heights as easily. Hollywood didn't connect him with his inner performer. He felt his future as an actor was destined to take off in New York, so his next step was to climb in a car for a cross-country road trip. He left Los Angeles with Eric Fleming — who eventually played in *Rawhide*, Carole Mathews — a young actress and occasional girlfriend, and

Jack, second from left at table in front, and cast, in Time of Your Life.

one other woman. All were young and full of themselves. As Mathews said in a later interview, "We were determined to go east because we believed New York was where you break into the business. As it turned out, Hollywood was the place after all."

A good gauge of someone's persona can be found in friendships. For Jack, that trip across country was something akin to a mid-40s version of *Easy Rider*. Eric Fleming was a wild personality who had already lived a tumultuous life. He hadn't been long out of a difficult situation when, as a Navy Seabee, a piece of 200-pound block of steel hit him in the face, requiring extensive plastic surgery. His trip with Jack across country was on the heels of a successful recuperation; one can only guess he was ready for a new and promising life. Jack also seemed ready for something beyond what he'd already experienced.

He did get work in New York City, though not what he had hoped for. His first job in The Big Apple was on live TV on the *Philco Playhouse*. The show was complete with a vaudeville format and Big Band music, with which he was familiar. An easel holding sheets of paper announced the billing, and Jack's big New York break came when he was hired to pull off sheets as they were read by on-air personalities. "My hand," he stated

Jack, far right, in Fighting Man of the Plains *(1949).* PHOTO COURTESY LISA OLDHAM PRIVATE KELLECTION

with humor years later in an interview, "got a big, big debut!"

By the end of 1948, Jack realized he wouldn't make it big in New York City, so he returned to the west coast stage. He snagged a role in *Anna Lucasta* at the Coronet Theatre. His performance was notable and because of his appearance, Jack caught the attention of several Hollywood directors. He had finally matured enough to focus. From there, he made his official adult film debut in 1949's *Fighting Man of the Plains*, starring Randolph Scott. The film's cinematographer was Fred Jackman, Jr., his brother-in-law.

Jack's family continued to visit Lowell on an ongoing basis. Joe Breen on Beach Street was Nan's cousin — his mother and Nancy's grandfather were brother and sister. Mae Carney of Second Avenue was a cousin, about ten years older than Nancy. By 1949, Nancy had inherited a little white cottage near the reservoir in Lowell in which her aunt, Joe's mother, Mrs. Nellie Walsh Breen, had lived. The house was deeded to Nan when Nellie died, and then given to Nancy.

While family ties stayed solid, stardom remained elusive for Jack. For two years, he worked on stage or screen or in radio, whenever and wherever an opportunity came about, even returning to New York for freelance TV bits. His career, such as it was, seemed to have no middle ground. There were high highs — like his adult film debut with Randolph Scott, playing the part of a rancher, though he went un-credited. Interesting to note that Jack's great-uncle's discovery, Victor Jory, had a solid part in this film.

There were also bottom-of-the-barrel lows, such as when he again held cue cards in New York, this time for Fred Waring; he was paid $15 per show. Jack Kelly wasn't a star. At this point, he wasn't even a serious player.

Jack was dating an actress in July 1949 named Lois Andrews. She was George Jessel's ex-wife. Lois' dog, a boxer she called Pug, wasn't much of a protector. When burglars broke in and stole $50,000 worth of jewelry from her home, Pug slept through it all. Jack's car happened to be parked near Pug's kennel at the time of the robbery, and the burglars jimmied their way inside. Pug simply stood by quietly, never making a sound. Five hundred dollars worth of motion picture costumes were taken from Jack's car. It was an expense he could ill afford at the time.

Pug was not sympathetic and neither was Lois. "Maybe Pug likes robbers," Lois told the press, matter-of-factly. "Or maybe it's the publicity he likes." Jack was using his car as a moving closet, and Lois wasn't about to offer him alternatives. This may have been because Lois was married, to actor, Steve Brodie. Still, it was no secret Lois and Jack were an item. By December, columnist Dorothy Kilgallen reported the seemingly ill-fated couple had "put their romance in the deep freeze."

The good news — Jack's name was finally notable enough to make the gossip columns.

He was selected for a small role in a film with high-visibility actors which came out during 1949's holiday season. Robert Mitchum and Janet Leigh starred in RKO'S *Holiday Affair*, a Christmas "wacky comedy romance." Leigh's character was a widow posing as a holiday shopper in a department store; officially she was a "commercial spy." Mitchum played a store clerk who broke her cover but fell for her anyway, and she got him fired. The story was a sweet tale of love. Jack played, of all things, a drunk on a train. Unfortunately, there was no credit attached, and he went completely unnoticed.

Karolee was doing her darnedest to garner attention. In Los Angeles, her own backyard, she was voted "Miss Nonstop of '49." This offered her a grand photo opportunity. She was seen in newspapers wearing a bathing suit which enhanced her considerable physical assets, while she was

Lois Andrews, one of Jack's early girlfriends.

"checked out" by pilot, Henry McCance.

In the early Summer of 1950, Jack jumped into another quick paycheck role, filmed on the Universal back lot. The movie was titled, *Peggy*, and Jack played a football player visible enough to be given a name, Lex, but not prominent enough for credit when the movie was released. The picture starred Diana Lynn, with Charles Coburn as her widowed father and Barbara Lawrence as her sister. The plot centered around a family moving into a new town without a mother, and a neighbor who did her best to guide the girls in the right direction. When the neighbor's son made a move on Peggy, she was forced to figure out how to deflect his advances. She was not in love with him but, instead, she had it bad for a famous football player. During football scenes Jack, aka Lex, had his moments.

Within a short time, Jack again encountered Robert Mitchum on the set, though again, his part was not of serious note. At least this time, his character had a solid name, and Jack had a credited role. He played Dr. Mullenbach in *Where Danger Lives*. Mitchum was Dr. Jeff Cameron, a hospital doctor treating a beautiful woman after a suicide attempt. Faith Domergue was the mysterious woman, and she and Doctor Cameron fell in love. Jack was an attending hospital doctor in an early scene, supporting and directly interacting with Mitchum's character. This was a step up on his resume, though still a far cry from stardom. He received newspaper credit when the movie was rolled out.

About this time Carol made her first notable public splash. Mother
Nan wasn't wasting time in getting her out and about in Hollywood,
and at seventeen, Carol was considered Bob Fellows' "new find for Paramount." Fellows was the "fair-haired boy at Paramount" with two hits
under his belt, *Let's Dance*, and Alan Ladd's *U. S. Mail*. Carol was, however, simply another starlet in a long line of his starlets, not getting

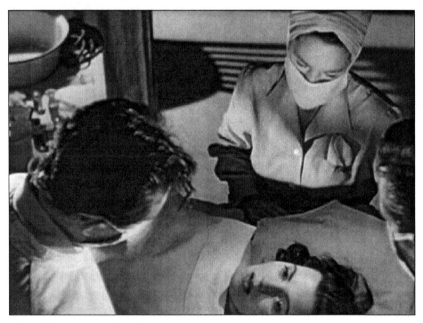

Where Danger Lives *(1950)*.

widespread attention, to her mother's chagrin.

A few months later *The West Point Story* became the next blip on the
screen in Jack's attempt at a film career. Again, this one was a no-name,
no-credit role for him, but a production full of recognizable stars. Officially called a "five-star cast," the names included Jimmy Cagney, Virginia
Mayo, Doris Day, and Gordon MacRae. Jack was moving amongst the
right crowds, but not getting close enough to be noticed. He had to feel
frustrated.

Prior to the New Year, Jack had another chance to put a few pennies
in his pocket when he took a part in one of the last truly old-fashioned
musicals coming out of Hollywood. *Call Me Mister* was nothing more for
him than a quickie, not a big enough role to even give a name — he played
a marching soldier. For Betty Grable and Dan Dailey, however, the film
helped them marshal out the previously wildly-popular genre with class.

The movie was also notable for another reason, and in this, Jack did play an important part. There were no less than six actors in the cast who would in the future receive some measure of notoriety in the entertainment world — Dale Robertson, Danny Thomas, Richard Boone, Jeffrey Hunter, Jerry Paris…and Jack Kelly.

There was a back-story to this one for Jack. He was working as Manager of the Hollywood Little Theater when the play, The *Cherry Orchard*, opened. Various talent agents were invited to scan the troupe's acting pool. The next day, Jack was signed by 20th Century Fox for his small part in *Call Me Mister*. He had made quite the impression on those talent scouts, even thought he hadn't been on stage when they met him. Instead, he had been "behind the scenes."

New Mexico (1951) was next, filmed on location, as well as at the Iverson Ranch in Chatsworth. This was a cowboys-and-Indians plot, set in Abraham Lincoln's time period — just before and after his assassination. Lew Ayres and Marilyn Maxwell headed the cast, with Jack coming up way in the rear as "Private Clifton."

How many times Jack Kelly had stood on the same stage with a celebrated, bona fide movie star and, likely wishing he were him in that spotlight can only be surmised; however, that he stood on a movie set with some of the biggest names of the time…this is fact. Credit upon credit upon credit came to him, some with character names, and some without a single mention. Both roles built Jack Kelly's resume in a fashion many a lesser actor never had a chance to experience.

Jack's next movie was with Cary Grant. *People Will Talk* (1951) had Grant playing a gynecologist dealing with such controversial issues as a suicidal patient with a child out of wedlock, McCarthyism, and unorthodox doctors. Jack's contribution was short-lived as a classroom student. Still, his name is forever linked with a film which has collected a cult following because of how it tackled difficult concerns.

Late January 1951 brought another production and a bit more promise. *Submarine Command* was filmed with full cooperation from the United States Navy, a good thing since a large portion was literally set on a submarine. Also called *The Submarine Story*, it starred William Holden, ten years older than Jack and a solid list of credits to his name. The plot focused on a military man whose career had brought him difficult moments, from World War II to the start of the Korean War. Jack was Lt. Paul Barton, and he received more on-screen time in this movie than he had to date.

Yet another small role came his way in *The Wild Blue Yonder*, filmed circa late October, 1951. A Republic Pictures production starring Wendell

Corey and Vera Ralston, it didn't make a big splash. Corey was a hard-working actor who never went far beyond character-actor status. He was born in Dracut, Massachusetts, not far from Lowell. Ralston was a Czechoslovakian-born figure skater-turned-actress married to Republic studio head, Herbert J. Yates. Phil Harris and Walter Brennan also had prominent supporting roles, with Jack in the much lesser part of Lt. Jessup. Best for Jack he only had a bit part...he had no place in the movie's standing, good or bad, but still brought home the paycheck.

"An unknown author said, 'Originality is the art of concealing your sources.' I'm pretty clumsy at concealing…I've never been accused of originality."

JACK KELLY

CHAPTER THREE

Climbing the Ladder...
The Life of a
Studio Contract Player

Carl Laemmle was the brainchild behind Universal Pictures when he established Independent Moving Pictures Company of America in 1906, buying his first movie theater in Chicago. After a number of iterations to the company's make-up, Laemmle retired in 1936, selling out to Standard Capital Company. In 1946, Universal merged with International Pictures, re-named Universal-International Studios.

Jack signed a contract with Universal-International Studios in late 1951 for "about 150 or 200 bucks a week," keeping him steadily at work. This proved to be a game-changer. The studio put out many movies, and actors of all stripes were needed to fill the sets. Job after job came his way. They weren't the breakthrough roles he desperately wanted, but they constituted steady work for a young man who wasn't even yet twenty-five years old. This was probably the earliest ongoing streak in his career, carrying him from season to season with some sort of movie-acting to his credit.

He was adding his weight to help keep the budget afloat. Nancy, and then Jack, co-supported their family with the money they brought in. While Nancy was the breadwinner, Jack ran a close second.

Bronco Buster, Jack's first official U-I movie, was released in May 1952, and filmed predominantly in four locations — Canada, Wyoming, Arizona, and Oregon. This was another in a line of mediocre, at best, films with Jack's name attached, with second-string actors playing title roles. This one starred John Lund and Scott Brady. One of the most recognizable names in the cast was Chill Wills. Jack played a photographer...an "if you blink you miss it" moment.

He was being noticed, however. All those bit parts in all those movies which had preceded his Universal-International contract got him some much needed, and much wanted attention. A 1952 piece in the *Los Angeles Times* had Hedda Hopper saying Jack Kelly, brother of Nancy Kelly, was "trying to get his foot in the Hollywood door." The family resemblance was unmistakable. Jack's good looks, coupled with his connection to a known Hollywood personality, proved to finally be a winning combination.

Jack in early Universal studio picture. PHOTO COURTESY LINDA GALLO PRIVATE COLLECTION

Jack in sports coat and tie, early Universal studio picture. PHOTO COURTESY LINDA GALLO PRIVATE COLLECTION

Jack didn't want to rely on these ties. He didn't want to get in the door by hanging on his sister's skirt. That would have been okay with his mother since attention was attention, but not good enough for Jack. He was wrapping his mind around the idea of being an entertainer, and wanted to make a name for himself. As a result of the contract signed with Universal, he was eagerly going to classes as part of the fledgling Universal Talent School.

Casual Jack, early Universal studio picture.

This was a major factor in notching up Jack's career. Signing that contract was likely one of the single most important things he did for his early professional life. One article indicated he had been given a "full steam ahead" sticker in his Universal file. In his words, he had come to Hollywood "cold," and desperately wanted to make his way based on skill, not on family ties. "I don't like to be referred to as Nancy's brother," he groaned. "I want to stand on my own name."

Jack's drama coach was Estelle Harman. She had been "plucked" from the UCLA Theater Arts Department to head Universal Studio's Talent School. Jack's schoolmates included Rock Hudson, Tony Curtis, Audie Murphy, Stu Whitman, Dennis Weaver, Hugh O'Brian, Barbara Rush, Lori Nelson, Suzan Ball — Lucille Ball's second cousin, Richard Long, Anita Ekberg, Mamie Van Doren, Buddy Hackett, and Kathleen Hughes — class of all classes, on the studio lot.

Mamie Van Doren said of Jack, "He had a wild sense of humor. He could make me laugh when I was down. A damn good actor, too." Hugh O'Brian noted, "We saw each other on the lot. I thought he was very nice, professional, business-like...a normal man in this crazy business."

Kathleen Hughes said Jack was "one of the nicest, sweetest, dearest people I have ever met." She explained that they went to the studio "six days a week" and "on one day, there would be a movie. We'd watch, and then discuss it. One day, there would be improv...oh, how good Jack was as a game show host, interviewing people. He was a natural." She went on to say that on another day there was a speech class, and on another there was horseback riding. This was in a way like a "regular job." They were all expected in at 9 AM, and stayed a full day.

In an article about Ms. Harman, she said of Jack, "I think Jack Kelly and Dennis Weaver are two of the most underrated actors in the business. One day, these boys will sink their teeth in a dramatic part in the movies and will amaze everybody — but me." She felt his work was seriously underrated. In her mind, he hadn't reached his full potential.

Jack didn't forget his personal life amidst his professional development. He had taken to the camera as if he were born to it since, literally, he was. He accepted female attention as if it were his due because, frankly, he felt it was. Staying away from a collective female presence — in his home life and social life — was not for Jack. He had been raised by women despite his father's presence, and relating to women came naturally.

Staying away from ladies was literally impossible for a man whose physical presence made him a natural magnet for the opposite sex. Women loved Jack Kelly, and Jack Kelly loved women. It wasn't always all sexual. Jack was one of those men who drew women to him as naturally as he drew his next breath. Little effort was required on his part.

In March 1952, the press learned he was "giving a rush" to Adita Gracia, sister of the late movie actress, Maria Montez. The year before, Adita had found Maria dead in her bathtub in a Paris suburb where she lived with her husband, French-born actor, Jean Pierre Aumont. Since then, Jack had become Adita's shoulder of support.

When Jack began courting Dominican-born Adita, she was recovering from this tragedy, and following in her model sister's footsteps. Adita had often taken on the part of a hot-blooded Latin seductress on film and while she didn't ever really make the grade, she played the part off-screen with Jack. They were paramours for awhile, though never amounting to anything serious.

Ada "Adita" Gracia, another pretty lady in Jack's life. PHOTO COURTESY ANGEL FELIZ PRIVATE COLLECTION

By mid-1952, Jack had enough movie titles under his belt — and enough notoriety — to be solidly noticed when his name showed up in the credits. He had a small role, not a nameless part but not a major player, in the movie *Red Ball Express*. He called it a "meaty acting assignment."

This movie told of factual efforts of the United States Army Transportation Corps during World War II. The film became notable by making a point of showing how many Corps drivers were African American. Sidney Poitier took on the role which represented this piece of history. Jeff Chandler starred, and Jack played Pvt. John Heyman.

No Room For The Groom was out in early June 1952. At the time, there was a rash of comedies made about the difficulties of a married man being drafted. The movie starred Tony Curtis, Piper Laurie, and Spring Byington, and viewers gave this one a lukewarm reception. Jack was Will

Stubbins, one of many interruptions in the star couple's married life. A press notation named him part of the "able supporting cast." Another reviewer said, "A handsome young comedian to watch closely is Jack Kelly, a newcomer." Other cast members were Jack's friend, David Janssen — cut in the final version — and Fess Parker, who went un-credited. Interestingly, *Red Ball Express* and *No Room for the Groom* often played on

Jack, sitting on piano, with cast in Sally and Saint Anne. PHOTO COURTESY LISA OLDHAM PRIVATE KELLECTION

a double bill. Moviegoers were treated to back-to-back Jack Kelly, even though they may have not recognized this at the time.

Jack had big plans for himself. He'd only recently become a Universal contract actor but was looking into the future. An early notable gossip column tattled, "Jack Kelly, young U-I comedian, was prancing along under an umbrella in the rain the other day. Just like Gene Kelly in *Singin' in the Rain*. 'If you think I'm not going to Metro next,' he crowed, 'you're crazy!'" "Metro," as in "MGM," was on Jack's scope.

But until such time ever came, Jack was kept busy at Universal. *Sally and Saint Anne* (1952) was next in line, and he took easily to this role, playing a brother of the main character, part of the lively O'Moyne family. Ann Blyth was Sally O'Moyne, his sister, and she was always praying to

Saint Anne. The story was a comedic look at growing up Irish Catholic in the 1940s and 1950s.

This was a subject with which Jack was intimately aware. One article said the movie dealt with "the often ludicrous tribulations of an Irish-American family." A review said Jack, "a promising supporting actor," was one of the "young players who handle important roles with expertness."

Jack, second from left, with cast in Sally and Saint Anne. PHOTO COURTESY LISA OLDHAM PRIVATE KELLECTION

Palmer Lee, whose real name is Gregg Palmer, mentioned this film as a great example of Jack's love of life, and his always up-tempo personality.

Universal International used its stable of up-and-coming players to fill supporting roles. Since there was almost always a fighter in every early Irish movie family, one brother was a boxer, and of all the young men in the U-I stable, Hugh O'Brian, one of Jack's studio classmates, most resembled a prize fighter. He was in topnotch physical condition, and there was apparently no thought given to placing him in any other part.

O'Brian had wanted to play the family magician — the role Jack was given, and he made note of his disappointment in the press. He had once performed a vaudeville magic act, and wanted to reprise his skill. Instead of getting what he wanted, since they were all contract players, O'Brian got what the studio assigned him…as did Jack, and all the others. The movie was considered a "sleeper" and "wholesome entertainment" when released in July to delighted audiences. According to Gregg Palmer, the movie was great fun to make. Frances Bavier, who had her claim to fame in *The Andy Griffith Show* years later, played the mother, and Jack's Universal Talent School friend, Kathleen Hughes, was also part of the cast.

Jack now appeared in America's movie theaters almost monthly, if only

Jack as "Sandy" in The Redhead From Wyoming *(1953).*

in small doses. He was gaining a foothold, though the golden ring of stardom continued to elude his grasp. *Sally and Saint Anne* gave him a solid supporting role, and one into which he could sink his teeth.

In an interview, director Rudy Maté talked about how difficult it was to put out a "large family" picture. "The bigger the cast, the harder it is to make a good take," he said. "A director can go mad. In most of the scenes, everyone in the cast has lines or business or both." He made note of Jack's importance when he said, "If I didn't have good performers it would be impossible to put this story on film. When we get the lines and action timed correctly, [if] one of Jack Kelly's magic tricks go haywire..." and he then explained how the actors, professionals such as young Jack, would get everything back on track.

Western range wars were the topic of the day in Jack's next movie experience. *The Redhead From Wyoming* starred Maureen O'Hara and, in

his first movie role, Broadway actor, Alex Nicol. Universal had this one
on the screens in January 1953. Jack's name was repeatedly mentioned
when media listed the "strong supporting cast."

From Jack's most early years, he was considered a camera's dream. No
matter how it was that someone originally noticed him, through family

Actor Gregg Palmer in The Redhead From Wyoming *(1953).*

connections or his acting credits, he was now being noticed. In an article
talking about what attracted people to actors before they were recognized on the screen, Ben Cook, UP Staff Correspondent stated, "Jack
Kelly was a photographer's model most of his life, before beginning his
acting career." Bottom line, his good genes had always been part of his
step-by-step success.

He was on his way. Universal's public relations department worked
hard to promote young potential-stars, and effects of the extra push paid
off for Jack. He was included amongst a number of debut personalities
featured and interviewed at the premiere of a short film about the Miss
Universe Beauty Pageant. *The World's Most Beautiful Girls* was shown at
the State Theater in Long Beach, California, for the pageant's 1952 season.
The pageant winner would receive in her prize package a contract with
Universal Studios.

Others in attendance for the event, largely for nothing more than promotional purposes, were Alice Kelley, Charles Drake, Hugh O'Brian, and Mary Castle. Also in the bunch was Gregg Palmer, who would soon unintentionally figure into Jack's life in a big way when an unfortunate incident back-tracked Jack in his climb up the Hollywood ladder of success.

Gregg had been right there along with Jack in a number of the Uni-

Jack with moustache, and Jaclynne Greene in The Stand At Apache River *(1953).*

versal movies made in the last few years — *Red Ball Express, Sally and Saint Anne*, and *The Redhead from Wyoming*. As another Universal ingénue, he, like Jack, was being pushed to achieve and succeed.

There was no lack of work that year. Starting with *The Redhead From Wyoming* and ending somewhere around an un-credited part in *The Glass Web*, Jack was seen in no less than six pictures. One relatively small but interesting role was as Hatcher in *The Stand At Apache River*. Jack played a young guest at an inn operated by Jaclynne Greene. He tried to persuade her to leave her husband and run away with him. Starring Stephen McNally and Julie Adams, the backdrop was a "heroic stand against a war-crazed Apache Indian horde." Standard fare, but a good addition to Jack's growing resume.

Jack had landed a top supporting role in *It Happens Every Thursday* (1953), starring Loretta Young. He was to play the part of Chet Dunne. This was his first solid chance to stand out in the crowd, the step-up he needed, and he was thrilled. A celebratory skiing trip the weekend prior to the start of production proved to be a bad decision. A serious accident on the slopes caused Jack's leg to break in two places. Bones had to be put back together with screws; this was a delicate, painful operation, and Jack was laid up for awhile, forced onto the sidelines.

With Jack Kelly not allowed to use his injured leg, the studio made a split decision. Jack lost the part of Chet Dunne at the eleventh hour. What could have been a pivotal point in his career was, instead, a role given to the-also-up-and-coming actor, Gregg Palmer...aka Palmer Lee.

Years later, Gregg Palmer barely remembered the film, and only after a few reminders did he recall some details. Universal didn't create a lot of noise about the change in cast members, and since Gregg and Jack were on a similar career path, the studio quietly put a new actor into the part when Jack was unable to fulfill the obligation. The show went on, without Jack Kelly.

Because of his injury, he was forced out of work for fourteen months and officially put on the studio's "injured" list. This was over a year of professional inactivity, and in Hollywood, a lot could happen in a year. Careers were made and killed in much less time.

It wasn't only that accident which managed to bring Jack down. On Sunday, December 28, 1952, Jack's dad died. He had suffered a heart attack on Christmas, and tenuously held on for a few days. This was a severe blow to Jack. He had all his short life only his father to look up to as a male role model in a family filled with female dominance. Now, not much more than a few months after his twenty-fifth birthday, the task suddenly fell to Jack to be the solid leader of the house.

He wrote to Nancy on Tuesday, January 20, 1953. After a month filled with death, major life-changing decisions, significant personal injury, loss of a loved one, and the drop of income — not only for himself, but also for his family, as well as what could have been his own promising future opportunities...Jack was at an all-time low.

Nancy was in New York and hadn't returned to California for their father's funeral. She felt guilty, and Jack, forever the peacemaker, made every effort to alleviate her guilt. She had paid for almost everything, sending more than enough money to make sure Jack, Sr. was put to rest in grand style. Jack expressed overwhelming gratitude, and did his best to let his older sister know he felt she had done the right thing by staying in New York, and taking care of their family in the best way she knew how. Between them, they would make it all work out.

Jack's letter explained how he'd been laid up more than a month — showing that his accident occurred before Christmas. This would have put the start of filming of *It Happens Every Thursday* in early December, and the accident no more than about three weeks prior to his dad's death. Jack, Sr.'s death appears to have been a surprise. The shock left Nan discouraged, despondent, and in a tenuous mental state.

Jack mentioned, "Carolee doesn't help...she means well but hasn't grown up yet," and he mourned the "non-unity in the family, started by Mom and Dad." He worried about how "Clem raves and rants about the slightest thing." Jack had tried to talk in earnest to his brother, hoping to offer comfort to a troubled kid on the edge of manhood; at eighteen, Clem was not quite an adult but no longer a child.

Bill "Clem" Kelly. PHOTO COURTESY JACK KELLY FAMILY PRIVATE COLLECTION

Clem's physical issues had been a point of concern, not only because of the difficulties they caused him personally, but because of how his mother had treated him as a result. Jack didn't know what to do. He gently suggested to Clem that he see "Father Keane" at the church, "a wonderful young person's counselor." Clem's response wasn't what Jack hoped to hear. "He told me," he wrote to Nancy, in a matter-of-fact fashion, "to roll religion up into a ball and shove it up my ass."

Jack had come home from his hospital stay only three days before writing this letter, and here he was now, unable to move of his own volition. He was considered the man of the family, and felt under extreme pressure to make everything right — with everyone in the household.

Jack was blessed with a healthy sense of humor, even if a bit off-kilter, and after his brother's rugged commentary, his words to Nancy gave insight into how he handled stress. Regarding the ball into which Clem would place religion, Jack mused, in writing, "I hope it's a small ball."

He ended his letter on an up-note, once more relying on humor to assuage concerns his sister might have at being far away in such a time of familial stress. Jack told her not to harp on his bad handwriting. This is something she always did, and since, he told her, it had forever been bad, this would never change. In closing, he let her know what he had been doing in recent years in addition to acting, in his fervent attempts to make a name for himself — and to add to the family finances.

Jack and Nancy all grown up. PHOTO COURTESY LISA OLDHAM PRIVATE KELLECTION

Once again referring to his less-than-legible handwriting, he told Nancy she would just have to live with it. "Perhaps that's why so many manuscripts I send in get rejected," he finished. This revealed how Jack was not only trying to succeed as an actor, but had also been working on a career as a writer. This was something he'd always wanted to do, and he continued to be enamored of writing into his later years.

Jack did eventually recover and get back in the Hollywood game. His

Jack with gun on Mickey Rooney in Drive a Crooked Road *(1954).* PHOTO COURTESY LISA OLDHAM PRIVATE KELLECTION

enforced period of introspection and inaction gave him time to think about how he should play the intricate game of the entertainment world. Once he was on his feet, he picked up small film roles of greater note, and parts in that burgeoning new arena called television.

Something had drastically changed — with him, and with the industry at large. The parts he now found himself in seemed to have more focus and drive. Jack was suddenly approaching acting with intent. He had to...his accident had given him no choice. After all those months on the injured list, Universal dropped Jack's contract. He was a free agent, and had to find work on his own.

Columbia Studios hired him to play Harold Baker, a bank robber in *Drive A Crooked Road* (1954), a film noir starring Mickey Rooney and

Dianne Foster. This wasn't a big screen hit in its time; only years later did the film finally get a large audience share, ultimately called "the single greatest B picture ever made." It did, however, give Jack Kelly visibility and critical public attention for his acting chops — instead of simply a place in the spotlight as Nancy Kelly's brother.

The *Pepsi-Cola Playhouse* had two seasons on TV starting in 1953. Jack was a guest star in November 1954 when he starred in an episode titled, "This Man For Hire," about a woman who had, in her past, written incriminating notes, and she was considering murder to get them back. Television proved to be a boost to Jack's growing resume, and he embraced it as such — nothing more, but certainly nothing less. Since his accident and his father's death, he focused on the new and relatively untried medium of television as a step up the ladder.

Jack's baby sister was seeing her own star rise. With a re-tooled public image of her own, Karolee had also been required to stand in front of an unforgiving camera by her mother almost as long as her older siblings. Despite Jack's concerns a year earlier over how she hadn't yet grown up, she had obviously matured enough to be looked upon as an attractive young ingénue.

Director Bob Pirosh spotted her when she did publicity pictures at the Flamingo Hotel in Las Vegas not long before Christmas of 1954. After watching her work, he asked if she'd like to be in Roz Russell's movie, *The Girl Rush*. "No sooner said than done," was Karolee's response. She played the part of a cocktail waitress with no name. This didn't end up as a Red Carpet event, but at least she got the movie credit.

"A reptile certainly raised old Ned in the Garden of Eden but one heck of a lot of us enjoyed apples since that first forbidden fruit."

JACK KELLY

CHAPTER FOUR

A Wife Enters Stage Left

Jack's life changed forever in the Fall of 1954. While at the time he had no way of knowing how his world would be impacted, he was cast in a movie titled *They Rode West*. This precipitated his first official meeting with a beautiful woman named Donna Lee Hickey. Jack played Lt. Raymond, a cavalry officer, and Donna was Manyi-Ten, a white girl raised by Indians.

Donna found her way into movies via a star-studded path to Tinseltown. She and Jack had yet to make a romantic connection, and she wasn't letting time slip by in her own date book. She was linked to the likes of Frank Sinatra — called "an encounter" — and Merv Griffin, with whom she was said to have had "a relationship." At one point, according to columnist Louella Parsons, Donna was also aligned with Peter Lawford. "They were a dinner twosome Friday night at Romanoff's," Parsons commented in her famous column. Donna moved in well-known circles and was seen by all the most powerful in the industry.

But at this point, neither she nor Jack took any interest in each other. He was pulling in as many roles as he could. In late 1954, he played a credited part in *The Bamboo Prison*. This film ended up not even a blip on the screen but in relation to what was going on in the world — fear of Communism, along with the unpopular Korean War, on the lips of every concerned American — the storyline coincided with volatile headlines. This

They Rode West *(1954) with May Wynn as Manyi-Ten.*

was a Columbia Pictures production starring Robert Francis. Also in the cast were such names as Brian Keith and E. G. Marshall.

Jack was a busy boy. He rolled right into another part, this time *Black Tuesday* (1954), a production styled after the old-school crime drama. Edward G. Robinson starred, playing to type as a vicious gangster. Jack's part as Frank Carson, a cub reporter, was publicly identifiable. He was seen early on when Robinson's character was snatched from the electric chair, moments from his execution. Hostages were taken, including Jack's character, as well as a priest played by Milburn Stone. The movie was released in the United States on New Year's Eve, 1954.

As of that New Year's Eve, Jack was cozying up to actress Mara Corday at a swanky restaurant, New York's Majors Cabin. They were seen swapping serious New Year's cheer…including kisses and "canoodling." Mara had recently become a Universal contract player, and

Jack brought in the New Year 1954 with Mara Corday.

her career was blossoming. She also modeled extensively; the camera loved her exquisite face and form from every angle.

Meanwhile, Donna was making herself known to the public. A third-generation performer, she was the granddaughter of Bertie Black, a vaudeville musical player, and daughter of old-time vaudevillian song-and-dance man Ray Hickey, who had died when Donna was only five. She had a family background similar to Jack's.

Not too many years earlier Donna had worked at a law office, hoping to become a private secretary. She left school to help support her Irish family and worked in sales at a department store — starting at thirteen after lying about her age. She grew up in Forest Hills, New York, and had also worked as a La Guardia Field page girl, and a garment industry model.

But Fate smiled on her and she hit the big-time scene in a big way. She had been winning talent contests right-and-left, and by 1948, was already crowned "Miss American Legion," "Miss Miami Beach," "Miss Fire Fighter," and "Miss See." Hollywood studio talent scouts considered her too young for films. Two years later, she took on the east coast and was chosen "Queen of the New York Press Photographers' Ball of 1950," winning the title on her twenty-first birthday.

Donna caught the eye of Jack Entratter, at the time the manager of the Copacabana nightclub in New York City. Entratter opened doors for Donna. He had started as a doorman, and a bouncer, for the Stork Club before he moved up to the Copacabana. It wasn't long before his smooth way with celebrities, women, and patrons was noticed, and he was sent to Las Vegas, becoming even more powerful and well-known on the west coast…as much for who he knew in shady celebrity/mob circles as for his abilities as an astute businessman.

Donna Lee Hickey as "Miss See."

Now enjoying a widening visibility, Donna found interest from all corners. She had early-on been taught to dance by schoolmate, Frank Arden — a boyfriend to whom she was reportedly engaged in 1949, with an expected November wedding. Those nuptials never took place. Once Jack Entratter became interested in her and what she could bring to his club — lots of men wanted to look at her, and those men brought in lots of money — Donna Lee Hickey took front-and-center in his attentions.

About a year later, Donna stated, "I want to get married. I've got movie offers and stage offers and television offers, but none of them include marriage." She even had preferences — between thirty and thirty-eight, a man earning $50 or $500…she said it didn't matter…but he had to be ambitious, honest, sincere, considerate, and it would help if he were in show business.

"Is that asking too much?" she wanted to know. She said she'd had four proposals in the last year, and twice she came close, which explained the marriage notices the year before. "Both times the guy became bossy. He began to object to my job. He complained about my clothes…. They get crotchety when they begin to think they own you…. I want to be an equal partner, not part of the stock."

As one reporter put it, with Donna's measurements of 34½-22-34½, the one-time high school cheerleader would now "inspire a whole football team," though that was not the type of marriage offer she hoped to entice. Another reporter said she "had a figure like a Freudian dream."

Donna, single and unfettered, garnered a note of introduction from a New York 20th Century-Fox talent scout to see William Gordon of the studio's casting department. Unbelievably, she misplaced the note for a considerable period of time. When she finally re-located it, she scurried off for Hollywood…as the official story goes. However the scenario literally came to pass, based on the power of this introduction, which did occur, in addition to her striking appearance, Gordon gave her a film contract.

Even this wasn't what she really wanted. "My experience at Fox was not a happy one," Donna stated later on. "I had bits in three pictures. And I mean bits. You have to look fast to even see me."

Donna went from there to Las Vegas and was spotted by Max Arnow, Columbia's talent head, who tested her for the lead in *From Here To Eternity* (1953). The disappointment was intense when she lost out to Donna Reed because, as she explained, "I froze." A year later, she captured the starring female role in *Caine Mutiny*, a film that would remain memorable in years to come. She beat out one hundred actresses to play opposite Humphrey Bogart, Jose Ferrer, Van Johnson, Fred MacMurray, and young Robert Francis.

Donna's star was shining brighter than Jack's, and she didn't give him much of a glance when they first met. She reportedly had a role in the 1952 MGM film, *Skirts Ahoy*, though it debuted without her name in the credits. Still, her part in *They Rode West* was prominent, and her name was being widely circulated. Donna Lee Hickey was becoming a known quantity, as much for her appearance as her film presence.

It had taken some time, in addition to *The Caine Mutiny*, but eventually all 5-feet-6-inches and 112 pounds of Donna Lee Hickey were roundly touted far and wide as "exquisite." The Powers That Be changed her screen name to May Wynn — the character she played in that movie — and from there, the only place she could go was up.

Women were jealous; men ogled her every chance they got. Columnist Jimmie Fidler announced she had a figure "better than Marilyn Monroe." Earl Wilson proclaimed, "Copa Gal Donna Lee Hickey passed her MGM screen test sensationally," and Walter Winchell said, "Donna Lee Hickey is No. 27 to leap from the Copa line springboard to Hollywood in the last few years." It wasn't long before she was a regular notation in the gossip columns, with her romances reported as often as her measurements — Ted Briskin, Betty Hutton's ex, and Joe E. Lewis were among her line-up.

By 1955, Jack had snagged an agent. He was finally seen as a "hot new property," even though he'd been around town for years.

Those who put out TV fare were working many angles in efforts of trial-and-error, attempting to make the burgeoning industry indispensable in the eyes of the American people. *Reader's Digest* started in New York in 1922 as a general-interest family magazine. The show was well into its mid-century popularity when TV took the chance, and in January 1955, a weekly TV show called *TV Reader's Digest* began.

Jack was part of the show's two-season history in June for the twenty-third episode, called "My First Bullfight (1955)." As Sidney Franklin, an American artist who created bullfighting posters in Mexico City, one day he drank too much tequila and decided he could battle a bull. Jack was the only non-Hispanic in the cast, with a storyline derived from a short article which had appeared in the magazine.

The press regularly called him "comedian Jack Kelly." He hadn't taken on an overwhelming number of strictly comedic roles in film or on TV, so this must have been a result of his emcee and live entertainment gigs, always presented with a comedic flair. His colorful personality and lively love life, gaining regular interest with the gossip columnists, could have had as much to do with the title. His friend, Gregg Palmer, said he was always laughing, always joking, always happy-go-lucky, and his favorite expression was, "Hoop de doo!"

Cult of the Cobra (1955) was a tale of horror in theaters in May. Jack acted alongside Richard Long, who went on to make a name for himself in TV's *The Big Valley*, and married one of Jack's not-long-ago old flames, Mara Corday. Also in the cast was Marshall Thompson — who starred in *Daktari*; David Janssen; William Reynolds — eventually part of the show, *The F.B.I.*; and Richard Dobson. The men played American G.I.s stationed in Asia witnessing the secret ritual of a group that worshipped women who changed into serpents.

The movie had been filmed the Fall before and all, except for Dobson, worked the morning of October 28th. After a number of line run-throughs, they good-naturedly teased David Janssen. William Reynolds said Jack and Dick Long repeatedly ribbed Janssen, whom they called

Davey, in a "tag team" fashion, giving him a hard time over how he delivered his lines. Jack told him, "Davey, this time, give it a little more Clark Gable." Jack Kelly, ever the comedian.

Double Jeopardy was onscreen in June 1955 in the US, but had already been seen a month earlier in, of all places, Finland. With the strong tagline, "A Deadly Formula for Murder," the film was a Republic release

Jack, second on right, in Cult of the Cobra *(1955) poster.*

often on double-billing with, an unusual pairing, a selection starring The Bowery Boys.

Jack was finding moderate, though not consistent, visibility and success. His name wasn't getting top billing, but he began to have his face show up on promotional pieces. Hollywood was drastically changing, and he was right in the midst of the upheaval. The movie kingdom as known for the last twenty-something years since inception — with studios ruling the roost and stars living or dying based on the strength of their contract, not necessarily individual work — was on its way out the door. New actors had to wend their way through a maze of what was usually confusing and ever-changing scenery…and rules. With TV barely beginning to test its merit, the industry as a whole was evolving. Those with potential to be the next generation of stars weren't sure how to direct careers which could either take them to the top, or drop them hard, never to be heard from again.

Cult of the Cobra *(1955); Top: David Janssen and Jack, Bottom: cast photo.*

Even Jack's sister, Nancy, had something to say about how their working world was in flux. She had been there when the studio system was in full swing and in the serious business of creating the next big name, and she lamented what it had become — and worried over what it would be in the future. "Hollywood, as I knew it, isn't any more," she told a columnist in the Fall of 1955. "It's more business-like. There's more determination in the air. There's a greater beat to the town's pulse." Amidst this, her little brother, Jack, tried to figure out how to dance to that beat.

The Night Holds Terror (1955) has remained memorable since it originally hit the screen, even though the movie didn't light the world on fire when it debuted. The production came about through what was at the time Hollywood's only "man-and-wife moviemakers," Andrew and Virginia Stone. The couple came up with "a sensational suspense drama for a mere (to Hollywood) $67,000." Another article said, "Harry Cohn is so high on this chiller he's putting three times the amount the picture cost into the advertising budget!"

Reviews touted it as a "tight little crime drama that moves rapidly from start to finish," and a "semi-documentary." A headline announced, "Fine Cast of Young Actors" and said the movie was "…a powerfully realistic screen drama that combines solid screen entertainment with an almost overpowering emotional shock."

This was Jack's first real starring role, though in an ensemble cast — this time he was not a background actor — and critics applauded him for giving a stand-out performance as the terrorized husband who made a big mistake by picking up hitchhikers. One commentary applauded, "Jack Kelly is superb as the young father who faces constant death." This role went far to assure those who might look to him for their next dramatic starring role that he was more than just an able comedian.

When the time came to fill the lead role in *The Night Holds Terror*, another Columbia Pictures movie, producer Andrew Stone cast Jack because he seemed self-assured during his audition. "He came in," Stone said, "picked up the script and read it cold without excuses. It impressed me. Most actors want to study the part first, then when they read it for you, it's with all kinds of apologies." A newspaper review said, "Jack Kelly, a newcomer to films, handles the role of the husband with restraint when needed, and the rough stuff when he thinks he can get away with it without endangering his wife and two children." Another review declared, "…his performance should give him a big boost toward star circles." The film was said to hold "realism, excitement, and breathtaking suspense." With a storyline based on the real-life kid-napping of an Antelope Valley, California man, external shots were all done on location, and even actual room interiors were utilized, rather than movie sets.

Jack played a soldier named Kerrigan in the movie, *To Hell and Back*, (1955) the true story of hero-turned-actor, Audie Murphy. Most of the

Jack and Hildy Parks in The Night Holds Terror *(1955).* PHOTO COURTESY LISA OLDHAM PRIVATE KELLECTION

production was shot in Washington State, coming out as a late summer release. Murphy starred as himself, and received full billing in movie ads and media attention. Jack was part of the supporting cast.

This was a time of great turmoil and unrest in the country, and Jack was not immune to the atmosphere seething around him. He was a politically astute young man, with a strong interest in his government, and in civil

Jack in The Night Holds Terror *(1955).* PHOTO COURTESY LISA OLDHAM PRIVATE KELLECTION

rights. When some movie notices for *To Hell and Back* showed prices for theater seats: "ADULTS 80 CENTS — COLORED BALCONY 60 CENTS," Jack's thoughts weren't publicized on how openly such racism was displayed, but his distaste for discrimination was no secret.

Yet there were more personally pressing matters with which he had to deal. On Wednesday, August 25, 1955, Jack's younger sister, Karolee, was

Jack as part of the cast in To Hell and Back *(1955).*

one of three people involved in a murky auto accident when the driver of a vehicle failed to make a turn and ran off the road into a guardrail. Maybe such behavior figured into Jack's earlier concern that his little sister hadn't fully matured. Details surrounding the situation remained confusing throughout the investigation, probably on purpose, and even the police couldn't make out the final truth.

The vehicle which ran into the railing was registered to Robert G. Holmes. Another car was involved, reportedly also registered to Mr. Holmes. The third person in the equation was Jackie Kelk. Kelk was a child actor, as well as an experienced radio actor. His biggest public claim to fame had been as the first actor to bring Jimmy Olsen to life in *The Adventures of Superman* on radio. He had only recently relocated to California from New York.

Either he or Karolee was driving the car that went into the guardrail. Original reports indicated she was behind the wheel. She argued, saying, "Not me! I was driving the other car." Karolee repeatedly stated she had been following in Mr. Holmes' other car, behind the one that wrecked.

Police reports, unable to clearly define facts, finalized the incident, stating, "It is our opinion that Karolee Kelly, 25, an actress, of 10854 Bloomfield Street, or Jackie Kelk, 32, an actor, of Beverly Hills" was responsible. She wasn't able to fully convince officials she didn't some-how play a part, yet was able to throw enough doubt to ensure she wasn't the only suspect. This was another situation Jack had to monitor as the head of the Kelly family. He carried a burden over how his younger sister and brother would responsibly make their way through life.

That Fall, Jack had a setback of his own to handle. This one didn't last long but the impact was regrettable because it could have been avoided. Using a can of starter fuel, presumably on a grill, there was an explosion. Jack suffered second degree burns. He went to the hospital, was patched up, and took a bit of time to recover.

The day after the accident, after the recounting of Jack's unfortunate experience was made public, another newspaper report noted Karolee to be the "third rapidly rising member of the Kelly clan…pretty glamour girl hoping to take her place beside her sister Nancy Kelly and brother Jack in the acting ranks." She was bouncing between success and uncer-tainty, which seemed to be a trait for the Kelly children, except maybe for Nancy. Karolee made her living as a model and, as actress/performer Gloria Pall said about her, "I believe she was a showgirl like me."

In November, Karolee was part of a Western Airlines publicity junket. She and a few other girls were on a plane from Las Vegas to Minneapo-lis to introduce a new flight plan series. A picture taken after the plane landed and the girls stepped onto solid ground, featured Karolee facing the camera, wearing a winter coat, a sleeveless top, a short skirt, and high heels. Clearly, the photo shoot hadn't allowed for cold weather. The pic-ture showed how the strikingly attractive Kelly genes had been passed down to the younger sister.

Finally, things were really starting to look up for most of the family. Nancy was near the top, Jack was halfway up the ladder, and Karolee had her pretty little foot ready to start climbing. Jack saw a glimmer of big things to come. Yet there was one concern which continued to nag at him. Brother Clem didn't fit the Kelly entertainment mold, and contin-ued to be a sad spot for both Jack and Nancy. Neither knew how to help him move forward. Their mother had never tried to include him in the family's efforts, and Clem was a youngster who couldn't figure out how, or where, to join in.

Jack had four major movie studios — Universal, MGM, Fox, and Columbia — bidding at once for him to sign. He also had more intense interest from Warner Bros., but they wanted him primarily for television.

Jack as Dr. Paris Mitchell in Kings Row *(1955) with Robert Horton.* PHOTO COURTESY JACK KELLY FAMILY PRIVATE COLLECTION

Warner Bros. offered Jack $900 a week, with residuals from any future reruns of his shows sweetening the pot. These were unheard-of terms for TV actors at the time. The officially-offered contract also indicated a "call on his services" for future Warner motion pictures.

This was the deal he had been waiting for, despite a heavy leaning toward television and away from the movies, and he could not refuse. Jack Kelly was signed by Warner Bros. in 1955. He began with minor parts, learning the ropes of being a bona fide TV actor with guaranteed work. By the Fall, he was cast as Dr. Paris Mitchell in a weekly TV version of the 1942 film, *Kings Row.* Jack was being groomed to become a television star, and this show was to be his springboard to more grandiose opportunities.

Warner Bros. had high hopes for the series, and for Jack Kelly. The press said the show "had the fine feel of an 'A' production, from stars to props." Jack took the role of an American psychiatrist in 1905, then thought of as a "new science," and he acted "with quiet modesty and restrained authority" according to Jack O'Brian in *Radio-TV Notebook*.

Jack was so sure this would be the ticket for his career that he immediately invested a good amount of his salary in a Hollywood tailor shop. He also bought an acre of land above Sunset Boulevard. When he was asked what he would do with the property, he said he was going to "build his wedding house on the land." He was single, and wouldn't name a prospective bride. This made him all the more intriguing to gossip columnists always looking for new material.

Yet making these purchases proved to not be a good move. Despite the accolades and highest of expectations, *Kings Row* managed to fizzle, folding after only eight episodes. By January 1956, Erskine Johnson reported in his column, "Hollywood Today," that, "Jack Kelly, who had a starring role in the *Kings Row* TV series at Warner Bros., and the studio have called it a day." This indicated the show had ended, but not his contract. Jack remained a Warner Bros. employee.

The abrupt stop of *Kings Row* was seen as a major career setback for him by people throughout the industry, and by Jack himself, who years later stated, "After *Kings Row*, my phone didn't ring for three months." In true Jack Kelly fashion, he added a joke, saying there was good news; his golf score had improved several strokes. "I had nothing else to do," he lamented.

His words weren't completely accurate. He had been occupying his time with distractions. Jack had let no grass grow under his feet insofar as relationships were concerned. He balanced his disappointing career with a hopeful love life. He was seriously dating child-turned-adult actress, Cora Sue Collins, and she figured into that recent land purchase.

As early as September 1955, gossip columns had chatted up their impending nuptials. Tidbits from the likes of Louella Parsons murmured, "Isn't Jack Kelly about to marry Cora Sue Collins McKay?" The date is of note because in August, Cora was still married to her second husband, wealthy Nevada rancher and Reno "gambling king," James McKay. McKay was one-time owner of the famous Cal-Neva Lodge, and columnists enjoyed the speculation over the status of his soon-to-be-ex-wife's relationship with budding new Hollywood sensation, Jack Kelly.

James McKay wasn't Cora's first husband. His name was Ivan Stauffer. Stauffer operated Hollywood's swank Clover Club. They married when she was only seventeen. Collins and Stauffer were not formally divorced until April 1947, when she was twenty. When she and Jack got together, she was already quite an experienced lady of the world.

In October 1955, Walter Winchell called Jack and Cora "gee-whizzy." Jack was fielding rumors he and Cora already secretly tied the knot. This curiosity was bolstered by Jack's remark over buying property to "build his wedding house."

"Oh my word, it isn't true," he responded firmly when questioned. This rumor grew legs in February 1956 when Jack walked into the Wild Goose,

Jack and Cora Sue Collins, would-be Mrs. Jack Kelly; monogrammed handkerchief in Jack's jacket, wrapped hand result of barbecue accident. PHOTO COURTESY LISA OLDHAM PRIVATE KELLECTION

a night club, with Cora Sue on his arm, and he was wearing a gold wedding band on his left ring finger. People immediately noticed and started a buzz. Jack swore it was there because of his last TV show.

His "last TV show" would have been "Kristi (1956)," an episode of *Jane Wyman Presents The Fireside Theatre*. Jack's character was married. He was unable to remove the ring, he claimed; it would not come off. He eventually went to a hospital to have it sawed off…or so his story went. Shaky story at best. Whether or not he and Cora Sue had married is not known for sure but seems unlikely. All references to his marital status prior to his first official wedding indicated him to have been single.

While it surely felt that the building of his career had been a painfully slow process to date, the idea that gossips cared whether he was married, or not, showed Jack Kelly was no longer ignored — by the press or the public. This was a positive sign, and Jack felt good about the attention after waiting so many years.

Singled out in an interview with Jane Wyman titled, "What 'Talent Shortage'?" Jack was, she said, one of the newcomers to TV of whom she was proud. "The claim that TV has depleted the ranks of motion picture actors is all wrong," she said. "And, not only that, but I'd like to point out that some actors may be made great through television — and then turn out some great performances for motion pictures." Jack had been selected to play in a number of *Jane Wyman Presents The Fireside Theatre* episodes, and she personally kept an eye on his progress.

The first role he undertook under the guidance of Ms. Wyman had been in "Kristi"…the supposed reason behind why he wore a wedding band out-on-the-town with Cora Sue. Jack played the part of a married minister who faced intense hostility with his congregation. His next Jane Wyman show, airing the following month, was "A Scent of Roses (1956)." Wyman was indeed watching Jack's work, and she not only publicly supported him, she backed up her praise with her standing and experience, repeatedly giving him a chance to add credits to his resume.

Jack went on to write a TV teleplay for *Jane Wyman Presents the Fireside Theatre* a few months later, in June, which appears to have never been produced. The letter he sent to Nancy after their father died still rang true. Jack continued to enjoy writing. He wanted to float a two-sided career by working on writing in any variety of ventures alongside acting. He didn't want to put all his eggs in one basket.

With a diverse background, doing radio, voiceovers, theater, film, and TV, Jack dearly wanted to add being a published writer to his credentials. He was good with words, written as well as spoken. That being his motivator, he began a novel called *Nothing So Deadly*. In manuscript form, before it was even a book, Doubleday Publishing Company bought the project, but Jack never completed it. An idea on speculation was contracted based on his increasing visibility.

Despite his growing persona, media continued to follow Jack Kelly in great part because he was Nancy Kelly's brother. She had a prominent image which had never really waned, and had been involved with highly-visible solid old-school Hollywood notables. Her relationship with Edmond O'Brien long over, and after a failed marriage to cinematographer Fred Jackman, Nancy was now seen around town with Warren Caro, a Theater Guild executive and Shubert Theater insider.

While on a set, a reporter asked Jack if wedding bells would soon ring again for his older sister. Jack's response was typically and totally noncommittal. "I wouldn't bank on it or against it." Then he went back to work.

Jack was soon up for a new series under the Warner Bros. umbrella after the embarrassment of *Kings Row* had begun to fade. To be titled *Chartered*, the storyline centered on separate plots revolving around private plane charters. Likely this is the same show which ultimately became known on the drawing board as *Flight 313*. Jack was planned to star.

Jack's private life was flying. Cora Sue had jaunted off to New York for the World Series. Jack wanted to go with her but Warner Bros. had him working, and he wasn't able to get time off. Hollywood columnist Harrison Carroll said he had "checked Cora Sue Collins and Jack Kelly. They are still very much in love but haven't set a date yet for the wedding." This announcement was commentary on the obvious…no secret Jack and Cora Sue were a hot-and-heavy item.

Newspaper reports blared, "Don't be surprised if he talks her into marrying him." The story went that Jack wanted to marry Cora Sue in Mexico. He was there playing "Mr. Winthrop" in a movie with Mari Blanchard called *The Basket*. The English title became *Basket of Mexican Tales* and in Spanish, *Canasta de Cuentos Mexicanos*, a collection of short stories. Jack's piece was, "The Canasta." In the United States, there was no fanfare whatsoever. That Jack Kelly was even in the movie is noteworthy only because of his trip over the border.

With or without movie success, that trip had the idea of love surrounding it for the couple. Cora Sue was said to "miss him so much" she cancelled a visit to New York, Miami, and Havana to follow Jack to Mexico, meeting there in early March. The release of this film didn't come about until November. Jack and Cora Sue were still together in May, when they were seen dancing at the Mocambo. By late August, they had officially cancelled marriage plans. No explanation given.

Not too much later, Cora Sue was seen with Dick Cowell, as well as Bob Stanton, a minor actor reportedly soon to marry another woman. Cora would ultimately own a finishing school, marry James McKinley Bryant, then James Morgan Cox, and raise his three kids, as well as her own. Jack Kelly also went on to other conquests.

In the meantime, Jack's sister, Carol — who had changed her stage name, from Karolee back to her original birth name — was romancing and being romanced. She dated Jess Barker, not yet divorced from movie actress, Susan Hayward. This didn't seem a problem, though; they were seen cozying up together at Frascati's in Hollywood.

Spring of 1956 brought Jack immense commercial potential. He had been cast "in a prominent role" as Lieutenant Farnam in *Forbidden Planet*. About this time, he was quoted as saying, "No one thinks of me anymore as Nancy Kelly's brother. But occasionally, I'm asked if I'm related to Grace." This was his way of announcing he continued to fight the same battle. He wanted to be known for his own work, by his own name, and not as anyone's family member — whether real or imagined. The Grace Kelly association wasn't so outrageous. Jack's and Grace's fathers were named John, both called Jack, born in similar times, from working-class Irish families in the east.

"*Forbidden Planet* is Top Film Fare!" the *Big Spring Daily Herald* in Texas announced in their April 8, 1956 edition. "The secret in this movie's success is restraint, plus a fresh and logical development of the tired old formulas." And, "Pardon a lousy pun, but the special effects are out of this world." The tagline said, "Earthmen on a fabulous, peril-filled journey into outer space!"

Certainly not Jack or anyone else had any way of knowing what an effect the movie would have on future science fiction work. *Forbidden Planet* would eventually be recognized by the creator of *Star Trek*, Gene Roddenberry, as an inspiration for his works. With a script written by Cyril Hume, the story was loosely based on The *Tempest* by Shakespeare. Filmed on the same soundstage where The *Wizard of Oz* was filmed seventeen years before, parts of the earlier movie's sets were utilized — Altaira's garden was originally the Munchkin Village.

"Robby the Robot" debuted in this movie, going on to become a well known character, with changes, on the 1965 TV show, *Lost in Space*. The robot proved such a hit, yet few people ever realized there was an actor inside that massive 84-pound, 6' 10" costume. Frankie Darro, a former "tough kid star" from Monogram Pictures who grew up and for the most part left the industry, returned to work, taking on this role, where he was neither seen nor heard…yet his character became famous.

Despite numerous notable points in the making of *Forbidden Planet*,

Jack in Forbidden Planet *(1956) with Leslie Nielsen and Warren Stevens (left to right).*

there was a limited budget, maybe a result of the production being ahead of its time. Casting began at least as early as March 1955, and was in filming by May, entirely on an internal set with a lot of "firsts" and, in the long run, expensive bits of creative process. This venture was well over a year in the making, a long haul for most movies of the period.

Forbidden Planet was destined to have success in the future, much like the storyline itself. By all accounts, it was a fun set. James Best, who later became most known for his raucous role as Sheriff Roscoe P. Coltrane in the 1970s sitcom, *Dukes of Hazzard*, had an un-credited part. He told of a time when there were coffins lined up off-camera for a scene, and he relaxed in one to await his call. Seemed like a logical thing to do. As time wore on, he fell asleep. Jack found him and went into hysterics, awakening him and giving him quite a fright.

James Drury was another player who would make his future mark as a Western star on television but, at the time, was only starting out. Soon after he was signed to a contract with MGM, he was cast as Crewman Strong…no first name. Drury said, tongue-in-cheek, "They didn't have

Jack as Lt. Farnam in Forbidden Planet *(1956).* PHOTO COURTESY SUSAN KETCHAM
PRIVATE COLLECTION

any imagination so they gave me a one-name character. I got killed by the invisible monster. It was important to be strong if you were going to do that."

Jack enjoyed his time on the set. Drury said he "kept everyone in stitches…always had lots of stories and jokes. When Jack came into a room, everybody started to smile. You couldn't help it. It was his personality. You knew, you just knew he was going to do something funny or say something funny and you couldn't wait 'til he pulled it off." Drury compared Jack to his good friend, and ultimately his co-star, Doug McClure. Doug, he said, was "the same way. He had that comic instinct and he kept everyone in stitches. It was a wonderful gift he had."

Jack's good humor was tested when his part was cut short ahead of original intentions — a plot development which came at the hands of the same "invisible monster." According to Jack, his character, Lieutenant Farnam, was originally contracted from beginning to end. Halfway through filming, as a result of the expensive technology, the production ran out of money.

The answer to the budget problem — they had to kill off Lt. Farnam.

The day after the decision was made, Jack walked onto the set and was unceremoniously told, "We've got to put you in the suit." Together, those words, "the suit," was a well-used term understood by everyone in the cast. They all knew what it meant. "The suit" was the costume worn by characters who went into the air, were eaten by the monster…and who died. Actors who played characters put into the suit would no longer be in the cast — or on the payroll.

"*I'm* not getting fitted for the suit," Jack replied. "I'm…I'm in the entire film."

The response, "Not anymore," was final. This is how Jack Kelly learned, from the wardrobe department, that he'd been cut from *Forbidden Planet*. He had thought this would be a big break for him.

"Crisis is a combination of grave danger and enormous opportunity."

JACK KELLY

CHAPTER FIVE

The Plot Thickens…
Real Life Intervenes

After the disappointment of his shortened part in *Forbidden Planet*, Jack snagged new TV appearances. He was seen on *The Ed Sullivan Show* on August 12, 1956, sharing the hour with Teresa Brewer, Dick Shawn, and Mickey Mantle. He then starred in an episode of *Frontier*, titled, "The Return of Jubal Dolan." *Frontier* was an anthology which aired for one season, once a week, between 1955 and 1956. Jack's appearance was shown on August 25, 1956, and he played the title role, working alongside Robert Vaughan and Jean Willes.

Within this time period, Jack again met up with Donna Lee Hickey, now widely known as May Wynn. Their first official meeting occurred while she was making movies at Columbia. Donna said, "I was in Hollywood three years before I had a date with Jack. Of course, I knew him and we'd say, 'Hi' to one another."

Those "three years before" meetings were on movie sets. In *The Violent Men* (1955), starring Glenn Ford, Barbara Stanwyck, and Edward G. Robinson, Jack's credited part was barely noticeable. The movie had been released in the United States in January that year. Filming would've been late the year before, and he and Donna barely had reason to interact. Another set on which they crossed paths was *The White Squaw* (1956). This one was made just before Jack and Donna officially met, and his bit was so insignificant he didn't even get an "un-credited" credit. That he was there at all would have probably been lost to history if the film's female lead hadn't remembered him being on the set.

Jack and Donna were formally introduced by a mutual acquaintance, Patricia Hardy, in mid 1956. She was a friend of Jack's. They'd met when they were in the trenches at Universal. And she and Donna were best

89

friends. Patti, as Donna knew her, thought Jack and Donna would make the perfect pair, and she set them up on a date.

Donna, however, wasn't so sure. She wasn't affected by Jack Kelly, one way or the other. In fact, she claimed she wasn't even attracted to him. "I thought he didn't ring true — he was so nice. He was gallant, kind, almost too considerate. You just didn't find men like that — I thought it was an act." This may somewhat explain why, when Jack went to collect Donna for their first night out, she stood right inside the door, listened to him knock, but didn't answer. On their first official date, Donna Lee Hickey stood up Jack Kelly.

There was more to Donna's reticence than her uncertainty over Jack's overly-gentlemanly manners. Overriding the date arranged with Jack by her trusted best friend was the fact that Donna was involved in a complicated, difficult relationship. Her "other man" was Jack Entratter, a high-powered Las Vegas club businessman. Entratter was well-placed near the top in questionably-legitimate circles, able to have Donna seen by all the right people. He was also able to make her life, and Jack's, miserable.

Problems in her relationship with Entratter had been numerous even before Jack Kelly entered the picture, and Donna wanted to get away from him. He had a ferocious temper, and the means and minions to take care of any issue — by force or otherwise. Not the least of Donna's concerns was that Entratter was married. This all came together, and Donna was genuinely scared. She feared what would happen when Entratter found out she was seeing another man.

When Patti learned Donna had not responded to Jack for their pre-arranged date, she called her friend, and "she got very mad at me," Donna said. Patti let her know what she thought of her cop-out. Despite the impediments, Donna finally agreed she needed a new start, and said she would give Jack Kelly another try. Patti convinced her to call him, apologize, and ask him for a do-over. She did, but from then on, she refused to call him Jack. He became "Kelly" to her. Since Entratter's first name was Jack, this was reason enough.

Jack Kelly put a lot of effort into taking care of his future, trying to solidify a career only beginning to tease him with possibilities. He worked regularly, even if he hadn't yet set the entertainment world on fire. He snagged a small role in *Julie*, a movie starring Doris Day. This was supposed to be a suspense thriller, but one reviewer said it bounced "zanily between the exciting and the ridiculous." As Day's third dramatic role, the plot had her in an uncharacteristic, manic storyline. Louis Jourdan was her lead, cast against type as a villain.

Jack played a pilot; the script called for his character to die before the story ended. Even though the film was ultimately listed among the Golden Raspberry Award's *The 100 Most Enjoyably Bad Movies Ever Made*, at the time there was much appreciation for its cutting-edge innovation. This movie was the first to introduce a "live location technique." Each scene was shot in its actual background, rather than with an artificial backdrop. There were 102 sites used to achieve "the last word in realism," as one article announced. As a member of the cast, Jack was in the thick of the real-time changing face of movie-making.

Even with everything going on separately in their lives, Donna and Jack did eventually come together, and she was happy to realize her initial assessment of him had been accurate. He was that nice.

"It began to dawn on me that this was the real Kelly, and that he was different in the right way, and when I realized that, I acknowledged to myself my feelings for him." On their second date, at the Ambassador Hotel with another couple, she accepted the depth of her feelings. "All of a sudden, we were dancing, and something clicked. I cared for him right then."

They shared interests in cooking and fine food, poker, and nightlife. On the side, Jack got his feet wet in politics, and tried his hand volunteering in local campaign work. He immediately wanted to marry Donna. She wasn't as certain. She was still hotly pursued by Entratter, and he had it in for Jack Kelly, since Jack had become the focus of Donna's affections.

Entratter had no intentions of leaving Donna alone, and did everything in his considerable power to not only ensure she and Jack were separated, but to make life as miserable as possible for both of them. Donna explained, "Kelly was fired off a job. It was a difficult time. When Kelly got fired — I think he was doing a Desilu show — that's what started the whole thing."

"The whole thing" was Jack's determination to make their relationship permanent, according to Donna. He was insistent. He was going to marry her, and had a number of ideas as to how best to accomplish this without Donna's pursuer any the wiser, at least before the fact.

Going to Las Vegas to tie the knot was considered, as were other high-profile locations, but Donna would have none of them. She was certain the end result could be disastrous. In addition to being fired from the Desi Arnaz job, there were other things going on in the attempt to keep them apart. "Something happened Kelly didn't tell me about," Donna remembered. "We both felt a lot of fear." Whatever occurred was serious enough for Jack to shield her from details. He revealed in later years his life had been threatened.

As early as September 12, 1956, columnist Walter Winchell reported "…actress May Wynn is rumored a bride. He is Jack Kelly." The notation, which jumped the gun by a month, was for some reason almost completely ignored by most media outlets. While Donna and Jack were already dating, they had not made arrangements for a wedding.

"We were barred from seeing each other," Donna stressed. "We were watched constantly. We decided we couldn't tell anyone what we were doing. Very few people knew what was going on. We had to sneak out to meet." The next month, the real buzz about the relationship between Jack and Donna started after a sudden trip to Quartzsite, Arizona. The area, near Yuma, had been known for hosting Hollywood types over the years who wanted to marry in a big hurry.

Well after midnight on a Sunday in October, Jack and Donna, along with Jack's sister, Carol, and his agent, Sid Gold, arrived in the small desert town. As they approached the outskirts, the first thing they saw was a sign on the side of the road which said, "Let's be friends. Let's get married." Was it — literally — a sign? Getting married was exactly why they were in the middle of almost nowhere, in the wee hours of the morning. They made the drive for that reason, yet Donna was still skittish.

"What the hell am I doing here?" she asked Jack. She said later, "He was mad, crazy in love with me at that time."

Jack looked at her and cajoled, "Let's get married."

Donna knew they hadn't known each other long enough to make such a momentous decision, but trouble was still after her, and if something wasn't done to stop Jack Entratter…well, there were few options left, and really only one solution. And she had fallen for Kelly. He really was a dear, wonderful man.

"So," she explained, "I decided that's what I was going to do." She gave in. Jack had known she would, and he located the Justice of the Peace. Knocking on his door, Jack woke him and asked him to perform the ceremony then and there.

Since they were both known by different names in varying situations, they brought enough documentation to verify their identities. Donna Lee Hickey, also known as May Wynn, and Jack Kelly, also known as John Kelly, Jr., were married by a Justice of the Peace at 2 AM on Sunday, October 14, 1956, in the dusty, dry Arizona town of Quartzsite. Scarcely two weeks earlier, Donna told Hollywood reporters, "Marriage isn't for me. I'm a career girl. I have no plans for marriage." She really hadn't had plans, that much was true. This had simply happened. Maybe out of necessity. Maybe out of love. There seemed to be components of both in her decision.

The wedding wasn't much — Jack, Donna, the Justice of the Peace, who still had sleep in his eyes, his wife, Carol Kelly, and Sid Gold. After two "I do's" and the signing of the marriage certificate, it was over. The wedding group planned to stay the night in Quartzsite but it was an unheard-of hour, they had no reservations anywhere in town, and there were no rooms to be found on the fly. Instead, the wedding party climbed back into the car — Jack and Donna now as Mr. and Mrs. Kelly — and returned to Los Angeles.

Barely days ago, Donna hadn't had any immediate plans to become a married woman; not this soon, and not this way. She had talked to the press about getting married, and she had always wanted to be a wife, but doing it in this fashion hadn't been her intention. If they hadn't been hounded by her ex-boyfriend, Donna likely would not have married Jack Kelly at that moment, and never in such a rushed manner.

A comment Jack made after they settled into life as husband-and-wife gave insight into their whirlwind courtship, as well as their relationship. "…with Donna and me, it's as if our wildness meets and only we can cure one another. Our impulse, our silly impulse, of one week is always getting trampled by next week's whim."

Jack's impulsive behavior seemed to be his stimulus of choice. He wasn't drinking when he met Donna. At that point, she had no idea he'd had a problem with alcohol in his past. She felt they were good for each other. Donna said, "It was comforting to have somebody I could trust and I could be myself around." She believed he "brought out a very good side" of her, and she did the same for him.

When the Associated Press got wind of their union, Donna, not Jack, boldly if not intentionally grabbed headlines with the simple words, "Actress Weds." Jack was noted as "the actor brother of Nancy Kelly, Broadway and Hollywood star." Erskine Johnson stated, "May Wynn's 'surprise' marriage to Nancy Kelly's brother, Jack, must have been a surprise to May, too," and he went on to discuss her recent commentary about wanting to be a career girl, as opposed to a married woman.

The truth was finally out. Donna's real name was Donna Lee, and Hollywood now called her May Wynn. The next day, the fifteenth of October, she and Jack were back in Hollywood. Donna — who no one, including herself, expected to have gotten married this way — showed up on the set of *Noah's Ark*, the TV show in which she co-starred with Paul Burke and Victor Rodman…and she showed up as Mrs. Jack Kelly.

Not long after they wed, Jack's mother, Nan, who had been living in New York after the death of her husband, returned to California. Donna had never met her in person, but they had spoken on the phone. His

Jack weds Donna Lee Hickey, aka actress May Wynn. PHOTO COURTESY JACK KELLY FAMILY PRIVATE COLLECTION

mother stayed with the newlyweds for a short time until she found her own place, not necessarily a good start to their relationship.

From early on, Jack's mother was, as Donna called her, a "trouble-maker." She never actually tried to cause problems between Donna and Jack; she simply wasn't enjoyable to be around. "It was uncomfortable," Donna explained.

Jack and Donna in relaxed pose. PHOTO COURTESY JACK KELLY FAMILY PRIVATE COLLECTION

"Jack was not happy" about his mother staying with them. Donna spoke of how he felt. "He did not want her to come. He…not that he didn't love her…but he said, 'No, I don't want her around us.'" Donna laughed. "And I understood when she got here. She was really a pain in…the…butt. She was not friendly. She was a problem." There were times when Donna said she "had to tell her, remind her, this is my house. You don't talk to my husband, or me, that way. If you don't like it, leave."

The elder Mrs. Jack Kelly notwithstanding, Jack and Donna got off to a start which didn't befit a couple of up-and-coming Hollywood star types. Jack was not working. For the first three months, including while his mother was with them, he didn't have a job. Donna was employed. They lived in her apartment and, as Jack said later on, "She supported me."

Fortunately, their luck turned around quickly. They set up their first marital home in "a small clapboard house in the Hollywood Hills, in Coldwater Canyon," near Warner Bros. Studio, bought with a $5000 down payment from Jack's earnings. Mother Kelly had found her own place, and the young couple settled in alone. Their world, for a time, became one of marital bliss...and regular entertaining. As one article put it, "Life with

Jack and Donna in their first home. PHOTO COURTESY MAY WYNN PRIVATE COLLECTION

the Kellys is never dull, though sometimes unpredictable." The piece went on to say, "Friends dropping in never know whether they'll be invited to test a new recipe...or be handed a shovel and told to dig."

Jack and Donna loved being in love. He said she was casual, impractical, high-spirited, and a "real softie." In a rather humorous explanation for what appeared to the general public to be an idyllic married life, Donna shared her fanciful recipe for closeness. Private bathrooms, she stated, were crucial to the positive growth of any union between two people.

Months after she and Jack married, she was featured in an article headlined, "Hollywood Beauty Takes Plenty of Time In Complexion Care." Despite their togetherness and intent to never be apart, professionally or logistically, Donna acknowledged she would work solo if a great opportunity came her way. At the time of the interview, she was on the set of her show, NBC's *Noah's Ark*. She was in her dressing room at lunchtime, and more than happy to elaborate on her commentary. "This is the first marriage for both of us and when you have been living alone for so long it requires a lot of adjustment."

The reporter wanted to know what sort of adjustments. "Having your own bathroom is essential to a happy marriage. I am accustomed to begin my day with a shower, and afterwards to take care of my complexion and put on make-up. This takes a great deal of time and I couldn't do this with someone waiting to get in. But I have my best face on early in the morning so I can have no bad habits there." Donna explained that with their own bathrooms, she and Jack were able to take care of morning rituals separate from each other. This was one reason they could stay together, throughout the day, most every day. The separate bathroom rule gave them a chance to start their morning without marital conflict.

Jack's mischievous sense of humor had been cultivated from his earliest childhood days. One example that, as an adult, some things never changed became public as a result of a fad started the year before. Stan Davis was at one time a gag writer for Jimmy Durante and Danny Kaye, among other comedians. His son, in response to cars coming into Hollywood from Texas, carrying signs reading, "Made in Texas by Texans," spoofed the movement with signs of his own. He came up with many humorous sayings, such as "Made in Siberia by Slave Labor," and "Made in Africa by Ants."

Davis, the father, recognized a money-maker in his son's efforts, and started printing these and other quips on signs for cars through his novelty company, Stan Davis Enterprises of West Hollywood. For some time, they were regularly available in auto accessory shops. Stars got into the act, Jack Kelly among them. When they were together on the west coast, he added a sign to Nancy's Swedish car which read, "Made in Sweden by Anita Ekberg's Father."

Jack had a guest part in *The Millionaire* which originally aired in late 1956. The storyline revolved around a country newspaper editor, nearing bankruptcy because of his crusade against corruption. Jack's episode was "Story of Fred Graham." Regular guest-starring roles began to come Jack's way. He had a wife to support, a wife who was giving up her career for him. Now he was working for the both of them.

Jack was a legally married man, but not yet spiritually wed in the eyes of his Church. He had been a practicing Catholic all his life, with his inherent belief system deeply steeped in religious tradition. Despite "I do's" and the parchment document which stated their union to be fact, this meant little to Jack. There was no done deal without a church wedding. A church ceremony didn't matter one way or the other for Donna, but Jack insisted. They repeated their vows in front of family and friends at St. Ambrose Catholic Church in Hollywood, on November 10th. They were now married in every way, not only in the word of their community, but in the eyes of God…and, finally, in the heart of Jack Kelly.

Almost every Sunday found Jack in a pew in his neighborhood sanctuary. "We had to go to church. He made me go to church every Sunday," Donna laughed. In those first years, they attended St. Ambrose. Later on in his marriage to Donna, Jack would locate the nearest Catholic church, wherever they lived, and he would be a regular attendee.

The old nursery rhyme, "First comes love, then comes marriage, then comes Baby in the baby carriage," could have played out in Jack's life almost like a predictable script. On the day after Christmas, 1956, Louella Parsons proclaimed to readers around the country that Jack and Donna Kelly had "dated the stork." This, according to Donna, was not true. She was not pregnant. They were not expecting a baby, no matter what the press speculated over. She said their dogs were their children.

Donna admitted their early days weren't all wine and roses. They weren't always well-off, depending on how much work Jack could attract. "It wasn't easy. The first two years, I couldn't adjust — I didn't like housework, the humdrum, everyday chores that didn't seem to accomplish anything, except for cooking, which I love. I'd rebel, even hysterically at times. We could have been in trouble right then, but Jack, characteristically, would tell me to drop the chores, go out, have fun, do what I wanted, change my perspective — he never pushed me, and respected me and my individual desires."

They spent their share of money, and Jack was upfront about their excess. "We have the most terrible time every month meeting the $100 for the mortgage," he admitted in a joint interview with Donna. He was open as to the reason…they didn't plan. "Just after we had scraped together enough money for that down payment for the house, we got on a Palm Springs kick. Every week we'd have to go down there. Every weekend cost us about $175.00. So, by way of saving something, we bought land there and now we are trying to save the price of putting a house on that land." This was their way of budgeting, which Jack evidenced by finishing, "But that at least keeps us from going there every week."

Jack Kelly internalized everything. He walked away from an argument. On the flip side, his new wife was volatile and immediately reactive. In her own words, she was "a bit bossy." It took them awhile to mesh their personalities with the ways they individually handled life. To the outside world, this was an immediate happy-ever-after. In reality, the relationship was trial and error, as often as much error as there was trial.

Jack and Donna outside first home with Hickey, one of their "children." PHOTO COURTESY LISA OLDHAM PRIVATE KELLECTION

January rolled around. Jack's hopes and earlier plans to be seen as the star of his own TV series, *Flight 313*, deteriorated. Expected to give him visibility and shoot his name out all over the world, instead, nothing happened. Nothing. This show would have been an extraordinary opportunity — he was slated to not only star, but to be the producer.

Newspaper gossip columnist Erskine Johnson announced Jack "clicked on last year's Warner Studio show," and went on to tell of the series. Somewhere between signing the contract and not too long before the premiere, *Flight 313* was pulled, and never aired.

The project's failure may have had something to do with how Jack was so determined he and Donna would do everything together as a couple.

Jack leaves for the studio with a kiss from Donna. PHOTO COURTESY MAY WYNN PRIVATE COLLECTION

If a project, even one already scheduled, didn't have a place for both, there had to at least be a seat for Donna on the sidelines. He wanted her with him all the time. This was at the core of their ongoing effort to find avenues of promotion which featured them as a duo, as Mr. and Mrs., much more than as separate professionals, Jack Kelly and May Wynn.

Why this was important to Jack may have been due in large part to a deep-seated recollection of his parent's relationship. It had only been a few years since his father died, and the memory of how he and his mother interacted was still fresh. Jack Sr. and Nan didn't always seem to work, or play, together, and when they were together, the atmosphere wasn't often a positive one…for them, or for their family.

This practice of keeping his wife close by his side at all times also seemed to have something to do with Donna's past. There was always the chance the enemy he'd made in Jack Entratter could come back to haunt Jack Kelly and his new wife.

There were consequences to this togetherness policy. Jack was still a "second-tier star," while Donna continued to have established visi-

She Devil *(1957) poster.*

bility, even if after their marriage she had decided, for the most part, to give up her solo career. The couple arranged for management that found appearances for them as a couple, as well as jobs they could do in tandem — whether local or on location.

There were a few exceptions, and an early one came in the form of a movie in February 1957 of which little is known. *Thirty 44-40s*, a mystery, was made for Frontier Pictures, but apparently never released. Frontier was struggling. In two years, the company was to stop feature production. Another one of those "almost-happened" points in the life of Jack Kelly.

Jack's next opportunity was a good one. He took the male starring role in *She Devil* (1957). First filmed as an episode of *Science Fiction Theater* titled "Beyond Return," and aired in late 1955, *She Devil* was developed into a full-length B-grade horror film. Jack played a scientist forced to give a dying woman an experimental tuberculosis serum made from fruit flies in an attempt to save her. The "cure," however, created violent tendencies in this beautiful creature, and turned her into the *She Devil.*

Jack's character, Dr. Dan Scott, couldn't help himself, no matter the lady's failings, and he fell in love. He was again paired with Mari Blanchard, who was delightful as the devil lady. The story itself was a re-do, many times over in a variety of formats, of what was originally a science fiction short titled *The Adaptive Ultimate.* That story, written by Stanley G. Weinbaum under the pen name of John Jessel, appeared in the November 1935 issue of *Astounding Magazine.* Jack got his name on the billboards and in the newspapers each time *She Devil* was advertised.

Taming Sutton's Gal *(1957) poster.*

One of Mr. and Mrs. Jack Kelly's early opportunities for professional togetherness came when they appeared on opening night for Frontier Drive-In in San Diego's Del Mar area in April 1957. Included in this promotion were Karen Sharpe, Beverly Tyler, Joanna Barnes, and Chet Marshall. The night's biggest stars were another together couple, Robert Wagner and Natalie Wood.

Jack often took on guest-starring roles, hoping one or the other would lead to his big break and make him a household name. In May, he was seen on The *Ford Television Theatre* in an episode titled, "The Idea Man." The storyline centered on an executive promoted to a top-level job, played by Don DeFore. DeFore's character, after his promotion, didn't get far because he was being exploited by his "bright young assistant," called "an ambitious opportunist," and played by Jack.

He and his wife reportedly did, or were scheduled to do, a film in 1957 titled *Back of Beyond* for Republic Studios. There is no record, certainly not with them co-starring. On the heels of this reported assignment, Jack and Donna — credited as May Wynn — did go into production together on *Taming Sutton's Gal*, acting alongside John Lupton, Gloria Talbott, and Verna Felton. One review called this "an intensely-absorbing etching of the life in the back hill country of California...with a bee-hunting episode, shooting, and plenty of romance."

Jack and Donna socializing with Buddy Hackett at The Harwyn Club, New York City.
PHOTO COURTESY JACK KELLY FAMILY PRIVATE COLLECTION

The tagline said it all, "Seventeen and lonesome." The rest of the synopsis stated, "She'd never been in love before...and no one was going to take this excitement away." The term used for this movie was, "a dramedy." *Taming Sutton's Gal* received little public fanfare, even though Republic Pictures, in its waning days, touted their "Naturama" process, a widescreen technique developed in 1955.

Jack had no idea that around the same time he and Donna were playing a pair of California hillbillies on the big screen, an actor whose name he'd never before heard had filmed a pilot for a new Western TV series called *Maverick*. If *Maverick* proved successful, the show was expected to completely change the way series television was made because of the unique production plan. The pilot sold in eight days, with Kaiser Industries as sole sponsor. The first show aired on September 22, 1957.

In the meantime, Jack was going on with his life, accepting work as it came and learning how to be a married man. Newspaper reports indicated the 5'6" wife of Jack Kelly was "enthusiastic about the companionship of marriage." She was adjusting, and she and her husband combined work and home with growing success.

Donna seemed to be exactly what Jack had needed, not only in his

Jack Kelly and May Wynn in Hong Kong Affair *(1958).* PHOTO COURTESY SUSAN KETCHAM PRIVATE COLLECTION

personal life, but also adding a shot in the arm to his on-and-off again career. His marriage offered him an invisible nudge, and a responsibility to succeed, rather than simply the desire. He and Donna worked regularly, with little time off between assignments. By late the same year, Jack was cast to star in *Hong Kong Affair* (1958). Early on, working titles were *Hong Kong Incident* and *Yuan*.

This would be filmed on location in the title country, and Jack had no intention of going that far without his wife. There was a pointed reason why Jack refused to leave Donna at home without him…she had recently learned she was going to have a baby. He agreed to do the movie, but only if she was allowed to come along.

Once they were in Hong Kong, the couple quickly learned this wouldn't be an easy shoot. "It was a disaster. I could write a whole book about that thing," Donna said. "We were supposed to be there for about six weeks; we were there almost ten months."

Moviemakers discovered the lead female actress, an Oriental woman, couldn't handle the English dialogue. She was unreliable — not showing up on time, or staying the course when she did show up. Whether intentional or not, she seemed to make every effort to sabotage the production's potential. After putting up with it for only a little while, Jack, with Donna's prodding, refused to continue filming unless this troublemaker was taken off the project.

Daily work had become a comedy of errors, though not at all funny, in truth. To fire the lead actress, there would have to be another to take her place. No other Oriental was suitable, or even available. It seemed as if no one could walk right into the part as written. To salvage what had become a dire, expensive and possibly wasted international effort with a lot of money tied up in it, Jack and Donna agreed to re-write the script together. They created a main female char-

Hong Kong Affair *(1958) poster.* PHOTO COURTESY JACK KELLY FAMILY PRIVATE COLLECTION

acter, a Eurasian, which, not surprisingly, was a great fit for Donna.

Richard Loo, an experienced actor, and Lo Lita Shek, a nightclub singer who had never before acted, rounded out the cast. Both did well. The way things turned out, Jack made a good move in insisting Donna accompany him on this trip. She nearly effortlessly stepped right into the lead female character's shoes and with a little make-up to make her look Eurasian, took over the role. Even though Donna and Jack ended up re-writing almost the entire finished project, they received no writing credits.

Sadly, Donna had a miscarriage. Jack's first chance at being a father was snatched away. They tried to create a family via another avenue while they were out of the country. There were a few children Jack and Donna came to know well during their extended stay in Hong Kong, and they wanted to adopt. A young boy, as well as a little girl, became the focus of their attentions. Yet legal concerns proved to be insurmountable, and the Kellys came home without children.

Everything was in the timing. For Jack Kelly, this period in Hong Kong was the lead-in for a new chapter in his life.

Jack, right pinky wedding band, and May Wynn in Hong Kong Affair *(1958).* PHOTO COURTESY SUSAN KETCHAM PRIVATE COLLECTION

"For thirty-one years I've been known as Nancy Kelly's brother. Now, I gotta be James Garner's brother."

JACK KELLY

CHAPTER SIX

The Good Ol' Days… Maverick Is His Name

One commentary said about *Maverick*, "In the days when dozens of staunch TV heroes were chasing lawbreakers in every corner of the old West, this program was indeed a maverick — a Western with a sense of humor." It was considered by some to be "subversive," with a "*dark* sense of humor."

Maverick was originally meant to be the first-ever weekly hour-long filmed dramatic series…but after only the first three episodes, it unexpectedly "developed a comedy streak," seemingly through a will of its own. That wasn't actually the case, though. According to James Garner, the creator, producer, and early-on writer, Roy Huggins, "a Phi Beta Kappa with enviable writing credits and considerable skill as a researcher," was the reason for the change. He skewered visions of a new type of Western before the show ever hit the airwaves.

Huggins developed *Maverick* from a story co-written with Howard Browne in which Huggins tried to see how many TV Western rules he could break. Even more important, he wanted to see how many TV Western rules he would be allowed to break, before getting arguments from anyone in the upper tier. First blush showed his plan was working.

Huggins said *Maverick* came into being "to have fun and to make a point." The show began with multiple writers. A head writer, Marion Hargrove, decided he wanted to liven up his script work, and inserted a simple stage direction, "Maverick looks at him with his beady little eyes." This was the birth of the unique characterization of the title role, the man named Maverick.

All of this went on while Jack was off working in Hong Kong with his new wife. He knew nothing of *Maverick*'s pre-birth and infant growing pains. He still had no idea who Jim Garner was, had never heard of the show, and didn't know Roy Huggins was trying to make a different sort of TV offering. While Jack already had a decent presence in the up-and-coming TV industry, he was at this time focusing on his movie career.

Donna remembered, "It was the next day after we came back from Hong Kong. There was a call from Warner Bros. for Kelly. They were talking about *Maverick*. We'd never heard of it because we weren't here. Kelly went over and they talked about Jim Garner. We'd never heard of Jim Garner, either. The guys at Warner Bros. knew Kelly because he had done *Kings Row*. He had done several things at Warner Bros., and they loved him. And so he tested to do this show with Jim Garner, and that's how *Maverick* got started."

When the role in *Maverick* was offered to Jack, he was surprised. The original pilot, featuring James Garner, was filmed in April. Within about a week, it was sold, and all involved had to get serious. Warner Bros. was said to have "invented the wheel" in regard to the original production of a weekly one-hour series. The process as employed had never before been done.

Roy Huggins explained how things worked. "We shot the shows in six days — we'd start filming on Monday, work through Friday, break for the weekend, then finish on the following Monday. On Tuesday, we'd start filming the next show, and so forth. That meant there were eight calendar days for every show. That was the minimum." Reality quickly became clear to him, and others involved; it "was already taking too long; the show took a minimum of eight days to shoot, but they were being aired every seven days."

Huggins was trying to revolutionize the TV Western. He had some-what flippantly developed what he called his "Guide to Happiness While Writing or Directing a *Maverick*." His rule stated, "In the traditional Western story the situation is always serious but never hopeless. In a *Maverick* story the situation is always hopeless but never serious." This off-kilter attitude figured in not only with the writing, but also with the cast. It wasn't long before actors were tweaking their lines with a bit of wacky humor, and *Maverick* took a distinctive turn away from the average TV fare.

With difficulties in keeping this unique production on track right from the start, it may have seemed in those early days as if things were, indeed, hopeless. Since Huggins had tried to not take the show too much to heart from the get-go, he applied his own rule to his way of doing business, and plod on, hoping against hope things would work out.

There was an even greater problem, though. A lot of other people were now involved in this idea, not the least of which was a financial sponsor, and there were rules to follow other than his own. Scheduling issues forced Executive Producer Bill Orr to employ a duplicate production crew. Despite extensive pre-planning and everything they could think of to make it work, each episode took one week plus one day to film — too much time and work for a lone star and a lone crew to handle. There was always another set of unforeseen circumstances which had the potential to, and often did, delay production even beyond the unique scheduling concern — weather, lack of a particular set, an actor had personal issues, or wasn't feeling well. Whatever could happen to de-rail production often did happen.

The common practice in network-land said pre-empting, any sort of delay for any reason, was unacceptable. It was believed that if the viewer's standard viewing habits were interrupted, those viewers would not come back on a regular basis. This ideology required Powers-That-Be to continue with rigid, pre-arranged production schedules, no matter what was going on otherwise. Roy Huggins said, "The network had ordered twenty-six episodes, so I now had to get a new show ready to air every seven days. We started filming in August 1957; by the first of September, after we'd completed about three shows, we were behind schedule."

When the task of putting on the show exceeded capabilities of cast and crew to air the show in a timely fashion, everyone knew a fix was needed. This was a growing concern which threatened the earliest success of a potentially winning series. There was a cast in place, and the effort to publicly present the show had been put forth. Still, viewers as yet had no major buy-in, and the whole production could fall apart in an instant. To make sure that didn't happen, changes had to be made fast.

Show creators considered adding a father, uncle, cousin, or a good friend to the mix to alleviate scheduling issues…but ultimately, Huggins decided a brother would be the winning concept. This brother would be named Bart, and Huggins intended him to be a permanent character, one that could, when needed, easily and interchangeably alternate with the character named Bret. Jim Garner was contracted to play Bret; he had been signed and already started shooting, but now, he wouldn't have to carry the load alone.

A show with two leads was unheard-of, and ABC-TV and Kaiser Industries, the financial sponsor, weren't in agreement with Huggins and his bunch over how well this would work. There was acceptance for adding a second character, and a brother was the agreed-upon choice, but ABC and Kaiser wanted that brother to be a supporting character, not another star.

Executive Producer Bill Orr went to bat for the theory, insisting, "No, he has to be a co-star. If the audience thinks he's just a secondary actor, those segments would go down the tube, because the audience will figure he's 'not the star.'"

Orr insisted that whoever took the part of Bart must be given equal star billing along with Jim Garner for the sake of the show. He assured the network and the sponsor Garner would appear in as many episodes as possible. ABC finally approved having an addition to the cast, and the

Jack dressed as Bart Maverick. PHOTO COURTESY JACK KELLY FAMILY PRIVATE COLLECTION

Kaiser representatives gave the go-ahead…unfortunately, though, those Kaiser representatives didn't share these impending changes with the big boss, Henry Kaiser, who didn't find out about the upset until the first show with Bart aired. This caused issues down the line.

Some of the actors tested for the role were Richard Jaeckel, Stuart Whitman, Rod Taylor, Don Durant, and Tom Gilson. Not surprisingly, all of these men generally resembled each other. As well, by virtue of physical appearance, any one could have posed as James Garner's brother…an obvious requirement. Each one was a young unknown, and most were acquainted with each other, at least in passing.

Jack Kelly was ultimately the most seriously courted. He also had one of the higher-visibility profiles. Orr remembered him from *Kings Row*. Huggins applauded Jack's acting, and called him in to test for the part of the hastily-created second *Maverick* brother. The characterization of Bart Maverick, laid-back and happy-go-lucky, wasn't far from the truth of the real man who would ultimately portray him. Orr saw beyond physical similarities and focused on how the original characterization embraced the essence of "a roamer, destination anywhere, willing to take chances on life, laughs or love. Independent and rootless, tumbleweed free."

As "laid-back" as Jack could be if left to his own devices, his wife was most often the polar opposite. Donna dug her nails into the meat of what *Maverick* could mean to Jack's life — and to their world as a married couple. She made it known her husband would not take second billing to anyone, least of all to a man they had never heard of, and, at that, a man who didn't have nearly the professional acting resume Jack Kelly claimed.

The call to Jack from Warner Bros. came in October 1957, the day after he and Donna returned from that long, difficult shooting in Hong Kong. A lengthy phone conversation ensued; Jack listened to what was planned, asking detailed questions about what was expected to be his role in the show. He said he would talk it over with his wife, and he'd get back to them soon.

When he sat down with Donna, he explained how the show's creators were still bandying around an idea, even if only in passing, that the show might star Jim Garner, and Jack's character would be secondary to alleviate the over-burdened production schedule. A commercial advertising the show had been created which said, basically, "Maverick, starring James Garner." Jack's name, per the plan, would be in smaller, less prominent type, not bold enough to indicate he had equal footing.

Donna broke in and told him in no uncertain terms, "What?! You tell them you *will* get equal billing. None of this 'James Garner *with* Jack

Kelly' stuff. Everything will be equal between the two of you. Tell them you're not going to do the show. You have to be equal with him or nothing. It's starring James Garner AND Jack Kelly." She skipped a beat only to continue in her next breath, "Who is this Jim Garner, anyway?!"

Regarding Jim Garner, Donna said, "This guy wants this, he wants that…and I said, well, let's see what happens. The people at Warner Bros.

Jack and Donna clowning around. PHOTO COURTESY JACK KELLY FAMILY PRIVATE COLLECTION

loved Kelly but they did not give him any credit." She was concerned about how Jack would be billed, particularly in the advertising. She said if "the first episodes of Maverick listed it starred Jim Garner, with Jack Kelly's name in small print" that wasn't acceptable. She told Jack if this was going to be a sticking point, "Then you quit. You — quit! Because if it doesn't say 'starring James Garner *and* Jack Kelly,' you're out."

Jack, as Bart Maverick, shakes hands with James Garner, as Bret Maverick. PHOTO COURTESY JACK KELLY FAMILY PRIVATE COLLECTION

Donna wasn't the only one asking, "Who is Jim Garner, anyway?" The question also seemed to be on the lips of others in the industry, though in a more positive tone of voice. Even Garner appeared surprised at how quickly he'd been accepted in the role of Bret Maverick. In the Warner Bros. commissary one day early on, he found himself the center of attention right after *Maverick* debuted, with stars of note repeatedly approaching him to say how much they liked the show. "A year ago," he told a reporter, "I couldn't get anyone to talk to me."

There's no doubt Jack appreciated Jim Garner's place in this unique show's path to success, even while his wife was determined Garner would never be his superior in any facet of their alliance. Jack had already had more than one chance to become a rising TV star. *Kings Row* had tanked, and *Flight 313* never got off the ground. Jack was nervous the same thing could happen again.

But once he and Donna hashed out the pros and cons, he was determined to go after what could finally be his big break. His agent, Sid Gold, went to bat with the studio, and details were ironed out to Jack's — and Donna's — satisfaction. Donna was clear she "made a big, big point of it." As she said, "I'd been around Hollywood awhile. I knew how it worked."

Once they met in person, the professional rapport between Jack, and Jim Garner, appeared inexplicably instantaneous and, if nothing else, proved to Jack this show would be a success. Their chemistry was the clincher. "The first time we ever met," he explained in an interview, "we had to make a test together. We weren't even introduced. I asked him why he was standing up so tall, trying to top me, and Jim took it from there." The natural banter between them started right then, sealing the deal for Jack. The two men played off each other as if they were true brothers.

While this hoopla went on behind the scenes, the *Maverick* audience had no idea the show couldn't be successfully produced for any length of time as envisioned. In fact, the public was ignorant of anything related to the growing pains.

Jack sat in his living room in late September watching *Maverick*. He was already involved, even though not yet on screen, and he carefully watched Jim Garner. Knowing he was about to enter the mix, Jack no doubt felt excitement intermingling with trepidation at taking on such a task. He stated in a later interview, "Jim was so darn good I was scared." He wasn't too scared, though, to swallow his hesitation and stand up to the challenge; he plunged in with everything he had.

Jack admitted once he and his agent worked out the details, he wanted the part of Bart Maverick so bad he "could taste it." He had turned down several offers to do a Western series because he felt he wasn't the Western type. For starters, Jack told a reporter, "I hated horses as a kid. I was afraid of them." Growing up in New York City, he wasn't the sort born and bred for Westerns. The joke was that the only range he had known as a boy was the kitchen stove. "When we moved out here to Southern California," he explained, "I used to ride at weekend boys' camps, but I never liked it."

Horse riding hadn't originally been one of Jack Kelly's favorite pastimes. And even before *Maverick* became part of his life, when he had to learn to ride as a young Universal contract player — riding being one of the many skills passed on to neophytes — Jack didn't at first take to it. "The riding class, I thought I could do without that. I missed the first two classes and Bob Palmer, head of talent then, called me into his office and told me, 'Listen, young fella, the measure of your success in this business may well be how you can handle a horse. Now get out of here and get your satchel over to that stable.' I got."

Jack as Bart Maverick on his horse in an action shot. PHOTO COURTESY JACK KELLY
PRIVATE COLLECTION

Those proved to be prophetic words. From his first days on *Maverick*, Jack slowly realized he hadn't given horses a fair shake. Once he did, he was quite fond of the creatures. "I really learned how to handle a horse. In the first place, I lost my fear. I wanted to get out there every day and saddle up as soon as possible." Again speaking of his studio riding lessons, he said, "The wranglers they had at the studio were great guys. They knew horses, of course. And they taught you how to treat a horse. It was their responsibility to see that the horses were not mistreated. They did a good job on the horses and on the students.

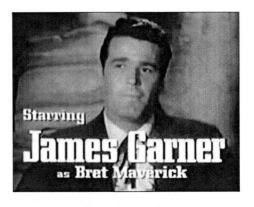

"But *Maverick* really isn't a Western," Jack stressed, going back to the idea of him playing in a Western. "The stories would be just as good if they were Madison Avenue gray-flannel-suiters. Maverick — Bret and Bart — could end up anywhere from New York to San Francisco."

He believed the show was timeless in its application. It had been barely a few months from the moment he had been courted to star in this unique television production, until "Hostage," his fist episode, aired in November 1957. Jack Kelly was introduced to the already-growing *Maverick* audience as Brother Bart.

James Garner and Jack Kelly, starring as the Maverick brothers.

While he and James Garner liked each other and enjoyed spending casual time together, they were never able to become real friends. Their personalities were quite different, and their lifestyles never converged. The progression of their working relationship was a key point in the evolution of Jack Kelly's career during, and after, *Maverick*. The show's pacing was hectic and storylines interchangeable, but the actors were each separate and individual, with their own personal concerns. This meshed into a somewhat odd and uncomfortable dynamic. While they were in tune as the cameras rolled, or when together in an interview, the requirement to get along no-matter-what, for the sake of the show, caused unique disruptions.

Bottom line...they both wanted to be the star; in fact, they both were the star. The show's premise, the never-before-tried practice of having a duo star as one in the title character — while creating separate shows for

Jim Garner and Jack Kelly as Bret and Bart Maverick, playing cards. PHOTO COURTESY JACK KELLY PRIVATE COLLECTION

each actor as that title character — caused distinct fan bases to build for each man in a never-ending contest. Everyone who watched the show seemed to love one Maverick brother over the other.

This was great for the show, but not as much for the actors as individuals. The show's executives played off this once it became obvious, since the relatively good-natured one-upmanship between the two helped boost ratings. Jim Garner may have had a hard time with this in the beginning, even more than Jack, since the show was initially his alone, and would've remained his if mechanics hadn't demanded the addition of a co-star.

That was balanced by the fact that Roy Huggins never completely warmed to Jack Kelly as part of the *Maverick* hierarchy. The character of Bart, or the actor who played him, hadn't been in his original plan, and that made Jack — in the guise of Bart — an interloper of sorts.

Huggins publicly commented on differences between Jack and Garner, and his mentions of Jack were almost always downgrading…intentional or otherwise. "I think Jack also knew that, no matter how much he tried, he was never going to equal Jim Garner — that he was always going to be '*Maverick*'s brother.' Maybe he didn't realize it, but outwardly, he gave the feeling that he did." Whenever Huggins talked to the press about the two actors, his commentary seemed to get around to who was higher on the "star" totem pole — Garner or Jack…and there never seemed to be any question as to which actor was his favorite.

Whether or not Jack did go into the part of Bart Maverick sensing he was a second wheel, Huggins was determined to impress that idea upon him. In a later interview he commented, "I've always thought Jack was very, very good, although I will admit that I was never quite as happy with him as Maverick as I was with Jim Garner. That's because I always judged Jack on the basis of how Jim would play the role — which, I realize, wasn't fair."

Production issues notwithstanding, Jack Kelly was seen by viewers as an equal. After the first four broadcasts, he had received more than 3000 fan letters saying they liked him as Brother Bart as much as they liked Garner's characterization of Bret.

Maverick seemingly overnight became officially known as a multiple-lead series, introducing the concept to the world of TV programming. The whole idea was to not depend on any one star to carry the show. This released pressure on the crew, and the endurance of the actor who would otherwise have had to handle every episode of every season. As a gimmick, this technique managed to singlehandedly dump individualism down the drain.

This wasn't easy on Jack. He not only had to do everything he could to keep his visibility and popularity high on a TV show touted as revolutionary, but he had to constantly ward off any real or imagined rumblings which said he had cut into Garner's turf and, in turn, Garner's potential as a rising new star.

The behind-the-scenes lean toward Garner did slowly wear Jack down. At one point, he was even called on the carpet after Bill Orr wondered, "What can we do to get a better performance out of Kelly?" Huggins has claimed he went along with Orr's concerns at the time, even though he didn't really think there was anything wrong with Jack's performances. This indicates the unrest had nothing to do with Jack's actual acting ability, but everything to do with favoritism from the head office.

For the sake of argument, Huggins allowed for the possibility Jack could become better at his work. He suggested Orr call Jack in and run a previously-televised show in front of him, pointing out where he could improve. This was early-on in Jack's *Maverick* experience, and he joined Bill Orr, Roy Huggins, and Hugh Benson, Orr's executive assistant, in the projection room. As Jack's most recent performance aired with everyone seated together, scene after scene played, and no one said a single word to Jack. Not one criticism was uttered by Orr or Huggins.

Finally, there was a scene where Jack was carrying a tray. He bumped into someone, and dropped the tray. Huggins broke the long silence by joking, "See, Jack — you're clumsy. That's your problem."

Everyone, including Jack, laughed. Orr stopped the film, and turned to the actor. "Well, Jack, go on," he said, "keep doing it. It looks all right to me." Huggins completed the assessment after-the-fact by indicating there was no valid criticism to offer...Jack's performance had been on the mark. What Jack thought of this interlude, there is no record. The way everything turned out, he could've been hurt by the unnecessary episode, and felt vindicated at the same time.

Jack also had a new marriage to encourage and keep alive while figuring out how to manage a growing career apart from, or at least in tandem with, *Maverick*. Jack Kelly was a preoccupied, busy boy.

There was a way to hold his union close as he worked. Bachelor Bart wouldn't wear a wedding ring. Married Man Jack didn't want to take his off, so he and Donna found a compromise. When he was in character, his wedding band became a pinky ring, which looked appropriate for a well-heeled gambler. Invariably his pinky ring was seen in most every show, but since he placed it on his ring finger when he wasn't working, there were times when it was on his right hand — most often, and other times when on his left hand. Either way, Jack knew what that ring meant to him, even if viewers saw it as part of his TV show wardrobe. This practice was also visible in *Hong Kong Affair*, where he played a single man. Some shots, however, show Jack forgot to make the switch, and the production crew apparently didn't notice.

Jack in full Maverick dress; wedding ring on right pinky finger. PHOTO COURTESY SUSAN KETCHAM PRIVATE COLLECTION

By December, Jack's first year on *Maverick*, he was confident enough to realize he was sitting pretty. He was the co-star of a television hit which could seem to do no wrong. The public loved the premise, storylines, interaction and chemistry between him and Garner, and they loved both actors. Fan mail attested to this.

Jack outshone Garner in letters received from the public, as well as

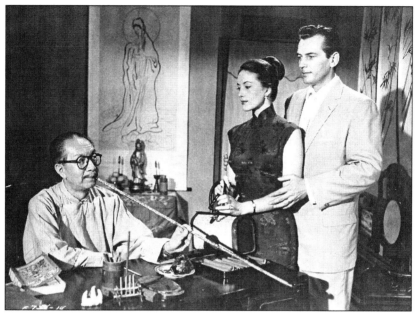

Jack Kelly and May Wynn in scene from Hong Kong Affair; *notice wedding band.*
PHOTO COURTESY SUSAN KETCHAM COLLECTION

ratings, on a consistent basis during the first two seasons. Despite this, Huggins still couldn't stop downplaying Jack's popularity. "The shows with Jack always rated slightly higher than the shows with Jim. The average rating for Jack's shows was something like 8/10th percentage point higher than the average for Jim's shows. That's too small a figure to have any significance whatsoever — but it's strange only because it was consistent."

On a few occasions, *Maverick* out-did ratings for the *Ed Sullivan Show*, scheduled on the same day and the same time slot, on a different network. This was unquestionably a big deal, the ability to bring in more viewers than the venerable Ed Sullivan. Jack later told a reporter, "I remember getting a very large charge out of the fact that one of the shows I did, being considered Maverick's brother instead of Maverick, was the one that won the rating race."

That was the point. Jack's ratings were consistent, consistently high, and the public loved him as one of the *Maverick* brothers. Women, in particular, went crazy over him. With his immediate future secured, he and Donna built that second home on their Palm Springs land.

His life had finally risen above the midpoint line — on an ongoing, contract-secured basis, as well as a personal basis — and he felt good about

Jack and Donna out on the town. PHOTO COURTESY JACK KELLY FAMILY PRIVATE COLLECTION

work and, in those early days, his home life. He and Donna, as the happy couple, did as much as possible together, business-wise and as husband-and-wife. In January, they worked together to write a *Maverick* script.

As Spring rolled around, the name "Jack Kelly" was finally roundly-recognized. When his youngest sister, Carol, decided to marry, this time not only Nancy carried the weight of the Kelly name in press reports. Now,

THE GOOD OL' DAYS… MAVERICK IS HIS NAME

Jack was also seen as a prominent family member. The headline indicated, "Carol Kelly to wed N.Y. actor, Maross." The article went on to discuss details laid out by "Miss Kelly, sister of actress Nancy Kelly and actor Jack Kelly." According to Carol, she and her betrothed had "been going together only three weeks." Must have been a family trait to marry after short-term courtships. That Spring, Jack and Donna made a trip to New York to attend the wedding.

Jack's relationship with his co-star continued to be a point of interest in the press. Reporters weren't sure how well they really got along, and they were determined to discover if their on-screen brotherly repartee was as genuine as it appeared. One press piece stated, "Their horseplay on and off the set is the best running gag in Hollywood these days."

Erskine Johnson had lunch with Jack at the Warner Bros. café one day. A conversation ensued between Jack and Garner as the latter showed up for his lunch time. Johnson was entertained by their exchange, and wrote about it in his column, "Hollywood Today." Their banter went something like this:

"Hi, brother Bret," Jack greeted Garner with a grin. "Did you hear the bad news? John Wayne is going to make a movie on the lot. Next to him, you'll look like Mickey Rooney." John Wayne and James Garner were about the same height — Jack was simply razzing his co-star.

Garner thought a minute, and replied, "I saw your show last night and I'm sure glad they don't give me stories like that."

Jack didn't even blink. "That was the story they decided was too good for you."

Garner snorted and left Jack and Erskine Johnson to finish their lunch…without him.

After hearing this exchange, Johnson decided the "show business-wise Kelly usually" outpointed Garner in the ribbing department. When he said this to Jack, however, Jack simply shrugged. "What a life I've had," he responded. "For thirty-one years I've been known as Nancy Kelly's brother. Now, I gotta be James Garner's brother."

Garner put his own stamp on the dichotomy of the flippant *Maverick* brothers when he told the press, "Well, all I can say is that I'm horribly miscast as Bret and Jack Kelly is a misfit as Bart if they were looking for performers to deliver the melancholy subtleties of psychological drama. We ain't the types."

Despite, and sometimes because of, adlibs and often actor-imbued personality, *Maverick* was delivered in much the same mood in which it was written…with total irreverence, without homage paid to the previously-venerated, and seemingly-untouchable, Western genre. This was intentional, even encouraged, on the part of the creators and writers; the better the impertinence was perceived by the public, the more it was highlighted as new scripts were written and produced. The show's creators saw how the public ate this up and every week eagerly awaited more of the same. *Maverick* was "an adult Western — with humor," according to

Jack and James Garner in front of barber pole in Maverick; *notice Jack's wedding band.* PHOTO COURTESY SUSAN KETCHAM PRIVATE COLLECTION

Roy Huggins. Jack and Jim Garner added their personal stamp and ran with the results.

Not a month later, Jack was receiving even more massive amounts of fan mail, proving what had become more than obvious — viewers liked his rendition of Bart Maverick at least as much as they liked Jim Garner's Bret Maverick, and sometimes more. What was clear to all — the two men were a hit as a pair. That elusive success they hadn't quite achieved separately as acting professionals, they managed to accomplish as a team. The actors made winners out of characters which couldn't have been written specifically for each of them with better accuracy.

Jack revealed to press and public that while there were two brothers, *Maverick* scripts never distinguished between the two. Scripts were written without reference to Bret or Bart; each would simply indicate, 'Maverick.' Whichever actor was available, he got the job. If a script said, "My brother, Bart," an effortless switch was made if needed. Sometimes scripts would use both at the same time if having them together facilitated a storyline, which didn't happen often. This proved the men were on equal footing as the show's star — taking the same material and making that material their own, as the show's needs dictated. They were TV's version of company men.

Talking about the chat going around in fan magazines about which actor was the oldest, Jack responded, "Jim Garner is felt to be the older and have an older-brother protectiveness toward me. Perhaps that is because he was there first and is an inch or two taller than I am. But actually, I'm about a year older than him."

The two actors had become so interchangeable that an overwhelming number of fan letters reflected confusion. "Who is Maverick, anyway — Garner or the new guy?" The studio was forced to send out form responses to explain *the* Maverick was either one — Jack Kelly *or* James Garner — depending on the episode. Neither character was more or less *the* Maverick. This was a feather in Jack's cap, immediately followed up with an announcement from Warner Bros. "Viewer acceptance of Bart Maverick is complete."

Still, a studio effort to play Jack and Garner off each other continued without relief. There was an idea floating around that the two men truly didn't like each other. Jack and Garner did have interpersonal issues, though these concerns, ongoing throughout the years, never really materialized publicly and where the rumor at this time came from was never pinpointed.

When questioned by a newspaper reporter about a potential feud, to his credit Garner squashed it by saying, "Utterly ridiculous." Then he grinned, unable to stop from joking, "I haven't got anything against

Kelly — except that he's so fat." He assured there was no chance of either of them upstaging the other. "They [the studio] don't dare do anything but make us play scenes with both our backs to the wall. If they didn't, we'd be jockeying each other for position all the time."

This was telling commentary. Garner seemed to say while he and Jack had no personal beef with each other, they always had to be on their guard,

Jack as Bart Maverick, the resemblance to Jim Garner is pronounced. PHOTO COURTESY LINDA GALLO PRIVATE COLLECTION

one against the other. Each man was aware how easy he might lose his fan-based footing in the show's hierarchy…and the studio would likely let this happen, for the sake of *Maverick*'s success, if there ever came such a stand-off.

Jack continued to gain headway. He had known success before, and was aware how fleeting it was if not carefully cultivated. He finally understood he had to play the game and follow the rules, no matter how tedious he might find the process. Whereas before he might've not been as willing to fit any mold put in place for him; now he was willing to toe the line to ensure the progression of his career.

Jack had been "almost there" more times than he cared to consider, and despite his still young age, he'd already had more than his share of tumbling-down lows. In the fast-paced world of Hollywood, he had learned the fine line between being a working actor and being a bona fide big-name star was tenuous, at best. As reporter Erskine Johnson stated, Jack was "standing pat with a fistful of high cards…in the Hollywood career game of 'never being there,' 'almost being there,' and 'being there.'"

That term, "being there," indicated the summit, the reality which would tell the world Jack Kelly was at a place where he could map his own career path and have everyone smile, nod, say, "Yes sir," and immediately follow in his wake to do his bidding. As one of two equal-footing stars of *Maverick*, a show which changed forever the flavor of the Western genre, many thought Jack was without question already "there." He knew otherwise. "It is difficult for some people to understand but 'being there' can be as precarious as 'almost being there.'"

He told Erskine Johnson, "I still have problems. I have the problem of sustaining what I have. I feel there is no turning back now and I'm playing it real cool and careful." He was asked at every corner why, in the midst of his *Maverick* popularity, he had turned down several film offers. "Things are different now," he stressed. One part he had refused was "a good villain role. I wouldn't dare accept it now. I must wait for something that is just right for me."

While Jack was under contract to Warner Bros., *Maverick* wasn't the only opportunity the studio presented to him. He was given a chance to be in a variety of TV and movie properties, and there were promotional efforts required of his time. The same held true for Jim Garner. Depending on what each actor had, or didn't have, lined up off the set, the *Maverick* schedule was put in place for the remaining star.

In March 1958, Jack starred in "Explosion," an episode of *Studio 57*, where he played an Englishman whose tour of South America was interrupted by big trouble. *Studio 57* was a series of thirty-minute shows created from a dramatic anthology; it played from 1953 until 1958. Jack's appearance was one of the last four shows — a sideline to his growing success on *Maverick*.

Jack could to a large degree select what he wanted to take on, and he was at liberty to turn down options if they weren't in line with the direction in which he wanted his career to go, though he did so carefully. He had an agent, and with his agent's professional advice, Jack made his choices. If a part came his way, and he had the time to take it on and no *Maverick*-directed reason to do otherwise, he usually accepted. This was all in a day's work. Some of his choices were good, and others proved to be unfortunate.

"It's all tangled up in one word…attitude."

JACK KELLY

CHAPTER SEVEN

Livin' The High Life…
A Straight Flush

Every Friday evening when there wasn't something official on the calendar, Donna and Jack hosted a "lively" poker party for friends at home. Playing cards was one of the pastimes they had enjoyed together since they became a couple, and they took poker seriously — as a weekend diversion.

All sorts of people were invited to join them, and the Kelly's home poker games became the subject of many a reporter's delight. "There were usually two tables going at all times," Donna explained. Jack and Donna always had their eye on promotion, and often blurred the line between professional and personal…counting amongst their friendly acquaintances quite a few members of the press.

With Jack playing poker for a living, of sorts, at least in the persona of his *Maverick* character, he was often asked whether or not he knew the game well. The perception that Jack Kelly could play only in the guise of Bart Maverick was, without question, wrong. He could play…but his wife was probably the better of the two. The Friday night games at their home proved this. Jack told a reporter Donna could easily bluff him, or anyone else, out of a pot of money.

Donna's response? "We like a seven-handed game. Just right for an occasional bluff and some smooth playing."

Jack smiled. While the reporter seemed to want to call her May — as in her stage name — Jack was quick to correct. "Her real name is Donna," he stated determinedly. "I hate the name May. I would have preferred it if they had changed her name to Herman Wouk." Wouk was author of the novel, *The Caine Mutiny*.

Jack was animated during this particular press interplay, and the reporter enjoyed him immensely, saying he was "about as likeable an easterner now playing in Westerns as you're liable to find." He also described Jack as "happy-go-lucky." He got carried away talking about…well, talking about everything, whether "poker, his wife, or why he loved being on *Maverick*."

Jack went on to teach the reporter a new game of chance called 7-28. After listening to a blast of convoluted instructions, the other man said, "For rules, please write to Jack." There is a card game called 7-27; chances

Jack and Donna acting silly. PHOTO COURTESY JACK KELLY FAMILY PRIVATE COLLECTION

are, Jack was having fun with his guest, giving the reporter a good-natured hard time.

The article finished with the writer telling readers if they were in the neighborhood on a Friday night, somewhere near where Jack and Donna lived, they should "give them a call and maybe they'll deal you into their game." But, he warned, "Remember, watch out for Mrs. Kelly — she'll play a pair of deuces to the hilt and force you out even if you have a straight." He should've added it would also be wise to watch out for the joker in the house…Mr. Kelly himself.

That spring, Jack, along with Jim Garner, Clint Walker, Wayde Preston, and Will Hutchins, attended the formal dedication ceremonies of Warner Bros. new $1,000,000 TV Center in Burbank. These were the actors who starred in shows bringing in the big bucks for the studio or, as the article put it, "the Western sagas that are currently wrapping up all that network wampum."

Maverick was direct competition for *The Ed Sullivan Show* on CBS, and Steve Allen's variety show on NBC, often winning out in ratings against both. One night in June, Jack found himself in a paradoxical spot.

Jack, Donna, Patricia Hardy, Richard Egan. PHOTO COURTESY JACK KELLY FAMILY PRIVATE COLLECTION

He and Donna, on a visit to New York City, had a reservation at The Forum, a popular themed restaurant. Waiters dressed as Roman Centurions, wine buckets were in the shape of Roman helmets, and the fare was quite expensive. The place had opened in late 1957, and Jack, a food and wine connoisseur, was wherever he needed be at the right time to check out the newest and the best. His table at The Forum was adjacent to the table of the one and only Steve Allen. Each man was gracious with the other, and the evening was enjoyable on both ends.

Patricia Hardy, who introduced Jack to Donna, finally met her own Prince Charming. Richard Egan was an actor who by the middle-to-late 1950s had started his climb up the Hollywood ladder of success. He had been in a number of feature films, and in the process, met and fell in love with Patti. A devout Roman Catholic, Egan had this in common with Jack.

The four of them — Jack and Donna, and Patti and Richard — became a well-known group on the Hollywood-to-New York celebrity circuit.

When Patti and Egan married in June 1958, Jack was part of the bachelor party. According to columnist Mike Connelly, known as "Mr. Hollywood," "That was quite a party." Connelly hosted the bash. "A bunch of the boys — Rich's brother the Rev. Willis Eagan (a priest), Lou Lurie, Jack Kelly, Bill Steiff of the *San Francisco News*, Guy — The Grover Whalen of San Francisco — Cherney and Rich's agents, Charlie Goldstone and Herb Tobias — were toasting our boy." There weren't only men in on this. "Jane Russell led an army of dolls in the frontal attack on the stag affair, her aides being May Wynn and the bride-to-be herself." This marriage turned out to be an unusually successful Hollywood union, with Egan and Hardy staying together for thirty years, until his death in 1987 of prostate cancer.

Day-to-day, Jack did his part to make *Maverick* move forward on the road to greater success. He and Garner — together and separately — were required to take on a significant number of public appearances, almost anything even remotely related, most often playing on a heavy Western theme.

Soon after Patti and Richard Egan's wedding, Jack and Donna were two of a dozen-plus "top Hollywood stars" to appear at the Elko Stampede in Elko, Nevada. This was a three-day summer rodeo event which included a variety of rodeo-related activities put together to bring great crowds to the area. Along with Jack and Donna, other recognizable names were Michael Ansara, Barbara Eden, and Chill Wills.

Flying home from the successful event, en route to Los Angeles, the plane's hydraulic system failed and landing gear dropped suddenly. The pilot made the emergency call to have the trouble repaired in Reno, the closest airport. With crash and fire trucks standing by, the plane landed at Municipal Airport in Reno. Though this was exciting and a bit frightening, no one on the aircraft was the worse for wear as a result of the potential catastrophe. The plane continued to Los Angeles with the Kellys and the rest of their star friends aboard. Jack was known to make the Sign of the Cross when he flew, and then kiss his thumb, thanking "Big Max" — his name for God. Big Max certainly knew Jack Kelly was grateful after this air trip.

That year was non-stop activity for Jack. In the summer of 1958, he did a brief walk-on for *Sugarfoot*, another Warner Bros. show. The appearance was originally intended as nothing more than a gag, but audiences wanted more, and cameos with stars of other studio shows became an ongoing way to cross-pollinate promotions. Walk-ons by well-known stars came to be, across the board, an expected tool in the TV show publicity arsenal.

Jack had yet to really get to know Donna's family. Late that summer, he finally had a chance to meet them in New York. They spent a week on Long Island, and Jack was introduced to her clan, including nieces and nephews. An article stated, "Donna arrived in New York with a trunkload of 'Cal-ifornia clothes' — meaning bright, light cottons — and spent most of her stay shiver-ing. It had been so long since she'd been home — not since she and Jack were married three years..." earlier, and she had forgotten the damp and chilly east coast weather. They were "lovey-dovey," and the "hard-boiled bachelor reporter said, 'They make me want to get married.'"

Jack and Donna in a loving pose. PHOTO COURTESY JACK KELLY FAMILY PRIVATE COLLECTION

As *Maverick*'s success grew, Jack's paychecks increased considerably. He had become a bona fide TV star, even if he felt the amount of money in those checks didn't match the volume of work he had to do to receive it. His lifestyle as a married man, a married man supporting a wife who gave up a lucrative career of her own, required that he uphold a certain level. "Money still talks," he said sar-castically, "but these days you have to increase the volume."

Jack and Donna's world became more costly as his salary increased. Trips to Las Vegas were a weakness. Donna's earlier problems with Jack Entratter were past history once their marriage entered public awareness, and since Jack had become so visible. The Kellys were known to gamble. A lot. Donna spoke to a reporter and said, "For a long time after we were married we kept away from Vegas. We knew we just had to. Finally we thought we'd go up for one little weekend and take $20 each. We bought 10-cent chips. Sud-denly mine piled up until I had about $75. Jack came over and borrowed some of my chips. We played til I had $10 left and he had nothing. We're such wild gamblers...." They went to see shows when they realized they lost more money than they won. Donna admitted, "...and then we had the sense to go home."

Jack was now a well-recognized face. The female population, in particular, had noticed him and female reporters were not immune to his charm simply because they were on the job when they met him. When he was interviewed by Frances James, a reporter for *Movie Star Parade*'s "TV Close-Ups," she said, "Jack had just rolled out of bed. He washed himself quickly, shaved, threw on a shirt and the things that go with it, and came down by elevator and apologized for being ten minutes late for our interview."

She was in the lobby awaiting him, and his tardiness in no way negated her opinion. She said they walked together into the dining room of New York's elegant Hampshire House. "The waitress hesitated about seating us," she wrote, "because Jack wasn't wearing a tie." The waitress relented, and gave them a corner table where no one could make note of Jack's "faux pas." Ms. James clearly had an opinion about the then-thirty-one year old actor. "Pretty unfair to the other patrons," she remarked, speaking to the special treatment, but then saying, "He's a sigh with or without a tie."

Hong Kong Affair came out in the summer of 1958, most often seen as the second movie on theater bills. The event as a whole ended up being more memorable for the Kelly couple than for the movie-viewing public. The production had been riddled with difficulties, multiple stops and starts, and personal heartache. An effort which should have been simple and short-lived turned into an ordeal costing Jack and Donna more than ten months out of the country, and possibly the loss of a child. Most reviews were not positive, although this wasn't unexpected. Al Ricketts, in his column, "On The Town," doubted the press that boldly avowed, "This Picture, in its entirety, was photographed on location in the British Crown Colony of Hong Kong." He commented, "...After taking a real close look, we seriously doubt this claim."

The production had indeed been filmed entirely in Hong Kong, to which Jack and Donna could attest. Ricketts continued, "Giving them the benefit of the doubt, there's just one fat thought that comes to mind: Why? It closely reminded us of prewar movies about the 'mysterious' Orient; the kind shot on some Hollywood back lot with a bunch of San Francisco chop suey vendors doing their darnedest to look sinister. There was always a lot of that ricky-ticky gong-banging music and scads of process shots showing indifferent pedestrians leaping out of the way as a big black sedan careened through the streets with its horn blowing.... Hero Jack Kelly arrives in the Many Splendored City to find out what happened to his profits from a tea plantation after he was reported missing in action in Korea..."

Press for the film capitalized on his *Maverick* success. Print campaign

Campaign piece for Hong Kong Affair — sample posters, pictures, order options.
PHOTO COURTESY JACK KELLY FAMILY PRIVATE COLLECTION

packets were sent out nationally to theaters, offering suggested wording for newspapers, radio, and television. Angles on each of the stars were a part of the package — predominantly Jack and Donna, but Richard Loo and Lo Lita Shek also had a standard bio. The general poster announced, "BART MAVERICK himself...JACK KELLY...leaps into action in the seething Orient in his first big starring hit!" Other pieces called him "THAT BART MAVERICK guy." His role in *Maverick* allowed *Hong Kong Affair* to get more attention.

Amidst the lukewarm movie hoopla, Jack continued doing his shtick as Bart Maverick, with public appearances as his constant sideline. If he wasn't on the set, he was promoting. In October, he appeared on the *Pat Boone Show* along with co-star, Jim Garner, and other current-day personalities — Edie Adams, Ty Hardin, Will Hutchins of *Sugarfoot*, Peter Brown of *Lawman*, and Wayde Preston of *Colt 45*.

Another promotional duty had him posing for print ads. He was one of a group of Warner Bros. stars seen in advertisements for Acme Boots. With a cigarette hanging from his mouth and a devil-may-care expression — dressed in full *Maverick* Western wear — Jack's picture, in a circle, was included along with the likes of Jim Garner, Will Hutchins, Wayde Preston, and Peter Brown and John Russell, another *Lawman* actor. The

Jack in a pensive pose as Bart Maverick. PHOTO COURTESY SUSAN KETCHAM PRIVATE COLLECTION

accompanying copy read, "From the magic world of the spirited Old West…in the glamorous setting of Hollywood…here is the one gift with the authentic touch…Acme Boots in all their wonderful color and handsome styling!"

The show was riding high, and Warner Bros. made sure *Maverick*, along with other Western follow-up hits, earned revenue from every possible angle. Columnist Erskine Johnson wrote that Jack Kelly, along with James Garner, Ward Bond, and other Universal-related actors were bringing "Hollywood's old star system to TV," and "it is working with the same old audience wallop."

This was a transition phase in Hollywood. Jack and his fellow actors had to be not only good at their profession, but they had to always try to second-guess where the industry was headed next, and how it would get there. The old star system was on last legs and would never again support actors as it did in its heyday. Television was in infancy, still trying to find a rightful place in the hierarchy of entertainment. In the midst of this evolution, actors suffered if they couldn't creatively ride the wave.

Jack was always thinking about this, about how he could jockey into a better professional position. In the summer of 1959, he told a reporter, "To secure a genuine star status, you've got to be able to attract people to a movie theater as well as a TV set." He hadn't wanted to fight the system and potentially harm his options on either end of the industry.

Warner Bros. assured him a few movies with his name on the bill while he was under contract. He had originally planned to become a movie star, and while he was more than happy to take what television had to offer, he still kept his eye on that prize. "I'm dying to get hold of a couple of films. Regardless of how meteoric your rise is on TV, I think you've got to prove you're a star at box offices. Just because I'm Bart Maverick and twenty or thirty million people watch me every week, that doesn't mean I'm a shoo-in in the movies. I'd still have to buck guys like Bill Holden and John Wayne, who are assured people will leave their homes to see them in a theater."

And this was the real problem in Jack's eyes. In his earlier days on *Maverick*, he saw his popularity on TV as a potential game-changer, and felt he had to be extremely careful as to the choices he made. Years ago when he began his career, he had tried everything, almost carelessly going wherever the wind led him, most often to see how far he could move up any one of the potential entertainment ladders. These days, he was stridently cautious.

"Suppose I'm in a picture that flops. I could be finished if I have to carry the burden of the loss. But," he stressed, "suppose I make a picture and someone like Doris Day is in it. If it fails, folks can't blame me alone. And if it does well, maybe someone will see that I contributed a little." Jack pointed out a few examples. "Liberace. He was the biggest thing on television. Then he made that movie, *Sincerely Yours*. It was a big budget thing, had a lot of effort in it and was a failure. Jack Webb also didn't do well in films when he tried to capitalize on *Dragnet*." Jack felt he had to be on his best game.

Henry J. Kaiser, Kaiser Aluminum, was *Maverick*'s sponsor. Having a sponsor often allowed sideline perks for stars of their shows. One opportunity came in the form of vacations. In June 1959, Jack and Donna were personally invited by Kaiser to Hawaii, on the island of Oahu, to stay at the Hawaiian Village Hotel, a lovely place conceived, constructed and first administered by Henry Kaiser.

Afterwards, when they returned home to Los Angeles, Jack and Donna stopped over in San Francisco for a few days. The trip was a welcome respite from a hectic, seemingly non-stop schedule for Jack since he had become a TV star. Their otherwise-relaxing stay in Hawaii was slightly marred when The Hawaiian Village sent Jack a hotel bill for $2000, even though he and Donna had made the trip at Kaiser's invitation. Jack, in a clear-cut move to make a point, sent the bill back, un-paid. The situation was immediately fixed, and Jack was happy.

The late summer brought him his first public golf tournament with his co-star. He and Garner played the First Annual Bellehurst Best Ball of Partners Criss-Cross Invitational Tournament. This was held at Los Coyotes Country Club in Buena Park, California where Garner was a member. It was yet another promotional event for the benefit of the cameras and the news media.

The news media kept up with Jack. His sense of humor always got him mentioned, even for the most innocuous reasons. A conversation he had with columnist Earl Wilson ended up as a notation in Wilson's regular column, listed as one of "Earl's Pearls." Wilson reported, "Jack Kelly of *Maverick* insists he saw this sign on a playground in H'wood: 'Children At Play — So Watch Out!'" Every chance he could grab, Jack managed to get a laugh.

That Fall Jack and Donna were once again invited guests for playtime with Henry Kaiser. They visited his personal home on Lake Tahoe. Jack had never been on water skis, and he wanted to try. Donna wasn't interested, but finally agreed to the outing as long as she could accompany him in a speedboat. Things were going well until Jack suddenly lost his balance, falling off his skis.

Jack decked out as Bart Maverick. PHOTO COURTESY SUSAN KETCHAM PRIVATE COLLECTION

"He dropped the rope and it tangled around his left ankle," Donna related. "The boat dragged him for about ten or fifteen seconds." When he didn't come up immediately, Donna frantically called to the boat driver to ease up.

"I was screaming because they didn't hear me," she remembered. "Stop the boat! Stop the boat!" she said she yelled. "Jack was being dragged behind the boat." Finally she got the driver's attention, and Jack was pulled from the water in a state of shock. "It was a few minutes before his head came up." The fright of the memory was clear in Donna's voice many years later.

"I was dragged under water for a good 200 feet," Jack had said when he related the story. "I kept thinking this was the end of me. I was surprisingly calm, hoping the boat would not swerve." Another few seconds, and the world may have lost *Maverick*'s co-star. Luckily, his wife had decided to go along for the ride. In this instance, the couple's togetherness proved a good thing.

The rope had been the cause of the accident. "The way the cord was entwined on my ankle, a sudden pitch could have possibly cut it off. Donna, God bless her...." The rope cut an inch into Jack's ankle. Immediately after the accident, a doctor was flown to Kaiser's estate from Oakland for emergency treatment, and Jack was taken to a hospital for x-rays to determine the extent of his injury. Initially, Donna told reporters, "He can't get around on the ankle yet, but we don't know if any bones are broken."

At first, Jack's main concern was being mobile without putting pressure on his injury. However, he soon realized the trial wasn't over. When the gash healed, continuing difficulties revealed tiny glass particles in the synthetic rope fibers imbedded and left behind when the site was sewn together. This caused a wound which began to fester. The original incision had to be reopened to remove the particles, bit by tiny bit.

Jack was seen to have a slight limp on occasion in after-the-fact episodes of *Maverick*, as well as in much later TV shows. The injury from the water skiing accident, combined with the snow-skiing accident which had seriously broken his leg only seven years earlier, was the reason behind a barely-imperceptible hitch in his walk which plagued him off-and-on for the rest of his life. He occasionally used a cane in later years.

As *Maverick* continued to hold strong and steady in the ratings, Jack and Donna were living in Studio City. As 1958 moved into 1959, constant studio-arranged promotional efforts, as well as some lost movie opportunities, began to create contention in the *Maverick* ranks. In particular, quiet murmurs of discontent were barely beginning from Jim Garner's camp. He liked his role as Bret Maverick, but he wasn't enjoying the way the studio held tight on his every move as an actor. He wanted to spread his wings, and didn't feel he was being properly remunerated for his seemingly non-stop efforts.

Jack Kelly, all 6' 1" and 160 pounds of him, was in the thick of the

Jack in Maverick *episode, "Brasada Spur" (1959).*

power struggle going on behind the scenes at *Maverick*. He was by contract required to go on city-to-city publicity junkets — selling sponsors' products, appearing on telethons, and doing benefits, often with behind-the-scenes writers to help support these gigs. An article said some weekdays, Jack would fly out of town, "get on the horn for four minutes or so," mingle with fans, sign autographs, lunch with dignitaries…and immediately fly back to Hollywood to be at work the next morning.

He did great work on *Maverick*, and this was likely much of what was at the core of Jack's war within himself. In February 1959, he was singled out for his "best performance to date" in an episode entitled, "Brasada Spur," and he felt rewarded. This show gave off realistic period ambiance through the use of plenty of railroad footage from the Warner

Bros. library. With the show thought to be "so comic lately that you tend to forget it's a Western," this episode was a straight-shooter, with Jack involved in cards with railroad tycoons and romance with a character played by Julie Adams. The episode was directed by actor Paul Henreid, and Jack gave it his all.

In an article that Spring, he explained the differences between not only the characters of Bart and Bret, but between him and Jim Garner. Even though *Maverick*'s writers intentionally wrote scripts to be interchangeable between them, Jack was adamant they were indeed two specifically defined characters — and clearly two different men.

"Basically, both Mavericks are great guys," he said, "and any week the scripts could be switched on us and it'd come out all right. But there's a subtle difference in Jim and me. And it's given us a fabulously partisan audience."

Jack delighted in knowing his rendition of Bret's brother engaged such a loyal and growing crowd of followers. "Some viewers are all out for Jim as Bret, and wish he were doing the lead every Sunday. Others, thank goodness, like Bart." He insisted he and Garner never discussed ratings or rankings between them because "we work too damn hard even to see each other."

Before *Maverick*, Jack had played in many movies, most of his roles forgettable, and in general, he wasn't happy with his film work to date. Though his Warner Bros. contract promised a stab at the big screen, opportunities had been sparse, at best. The TV show had become all-consuming. Most film parts he received were still small, and still less than notable. He even once told friends about his most recent roles, "Go see. You'll vomit."

Once he had won his place on *Maverick*, wholeheartedly investing himself into Bart's persona, he realized being on the small screen required him to work harder, and longer hours, for less money. This awareness came to him slowly, only after he immersed himself in the contractual realities of being a star of a hit TV show.

At first, that didn't sound like the best plan, but Jack was aware "perpetuity might be served. After working at odds and ends most of my life, there's great satisfaction in the knowledge that I may become a success." He felt his previously elusive desire to be a Hollywood star was finally at his fingertips.

Getting that title in hand, and holding on wasn't easy. He worked harder than he'd ever imagined he would, and the studio, not he, or even Garner, for that matter, reaped most of the rewards. While he wasn't anywhere near as publicly vocal about his concerns as Garner had become, they nonetheless wore on him.

Western stars made a lot of noise in general. The studio system was deteriorating rapidly, and the public's insatiable appetite for entertainment was getting harder to manage. No matter the size of the screen on which they watched a show or a movie, the viewing audience had a

Jack as Bart Maverick going for his gun; notice "pinky ring." PHOTO COURTESY SUSAN KETCHAM PRIVATE COLLECTION

never-ending need to be served an ever-changing stable of worthy talent able to carry engaging storylines. The unrest was audible across the board within the ranks of that talent, many of whom felt the burden of carrying a television series far outweighed the paycheck. One article said actors threatened to "unsaddle their talents to become movie stars." Jack was one of a few more notably cautious as to what he said publicly.

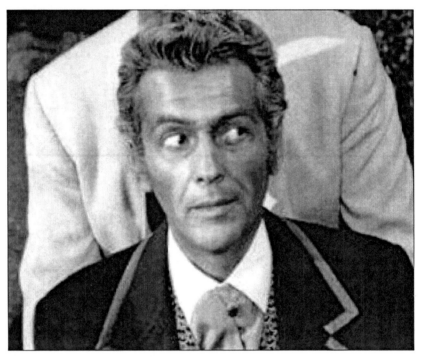

Jack as an old Bart Maverick. PHOTO COURTESY NELL LYNN YOUNG PRIVATE COLLECTION

Hugh O'Brian, Clint Walker, Jim Arness, and of course Jim Garner were complaining with a bit more attitude. They objected to the long hours involved in TV work, and comparatively small salaries received against what they would have made if they were doing movies. They bemoaned the woes of wide-scale public identification with only one character, as opposed to the chance to be seen in a variety of roles if they had more film work.

Jack's response when asked directly by one reporter if he wasn't part of the growing agitation was, "Baloney." The article indicated rightfully how Jack had "collected his lumps in movies for years." The piece said he'd worked some, then sat around between pictures, and then accepted various sized roles here and there to take up the slack.

Now, with *Maverick* as his day-to-day bread-and-butter, Jack appreciated the steady paycheck. He knew a good thing and wasn't ready to complain out loud. Much of his common-sense approach was due to his long history in and around the entertainment world, his familiarity with how the business operated, and that he knew how easily he could fall from the heights. He'd grown up in the business, aware of how success might be snatched away if one piece of the puzzle didn't fit exactly right. This was an understanding the others seemed unable to grasp. Rules may not have always been fair, but there was steady work.

"Those other guys don't really want out," he surmised. "They just want more money. And who can blame them. I'd like more dough myself." Jack played Devil's Advocate to get his point across. He was at the time making $2000 a week, a nice-enough sum, but the other side showed a blatantly obvious point — in movie circles, experienced actors were paid in the neighborhood of $50,000 a picture. A big difference. This was a matter of a comfortable, certain bet as opposed to an unquestionable gamble with a potentially large payoff.

"Personally, I'd like to stay in *Maverick* for another, eighteen or twenty years. We could re-title it *Son of Maverick*," he joked. "I'd be foolish to leave for something of less scope." He was sincere. Leaving such a lucrative role for something that would, at best, be an uncertainty wasn't wise. He already knew the score; he was aware there might not be anything better. "I've turned down two movie offers in the past year because I didn't think they measured up to *Maverick* standards. And I'm one of the lucky ones. My role isn't a type characterization. I could do other things if the series folded."

His words spoke directly to his years of experience. He had already done other things, had played other roles...many of them. "But some of the boys would find it tough sledding. O'Brian and Arness would be in serious trouble. They're so identified with Wyatt Earp and Marshall Matt Dillon no one would believe them in any other role." Whether this was simply Jack's logic or actual fact is up for debate, but he felt certain he personally could go with the flow, as he always had.

"I have never found recognition and admiration hard to live with. It's only the lack of it that bothers me."

JACK KELLY

CHAPTER EIGHT

Work, Work, Work...
Jack and Donna In Love

The *Maverick* brass did everything they could to optimize the visibility of their stars. While Jack and Garner sometimes appeared together, they usually did solo events to maximize the benefit of having two stars who could equally promote the same show. One event Jack and Garner did do together was the "Show of the Year." This was held at the Shrine Auditorium in Los Angeles in February 1959 for the Alex Cooper Memorial at City of Hope. A few months later, *Maverick* won an Emmy for the "hotly-contested best Western series," indicating the show's stars did their job, and then some. Their bosses at Warner Bros. had every intention of cashing in on their popularity.

Jack and Donna regularly interacted with news and gossip column folks, not only during Friday night poker games at home, but when they were out and about on the town, or even on the Warner Bros.' lot. Jack was widely known to be witty and well-spoken, and he always kept the press, as well as the cast, entertained.

Donna often showed up on set, and one story circulated about how Jim Garner learned not to play poker with Jack Kelly's wife — the "Donna Kelly poker thing" again. James Bacon, newspaper columnist, told of how he was eyewitness to, and part of, a poker game which included the *Maverick* brothers. Donna was in on the game, and Garner played only a few hands before he gave up. He confessed, "You gotta be crazy to play poker with Donna Kelly. She clobbers everyone."

Bacon said once the game ended, Jack had also lost big-time, but as usually happened, Donna walked away with the pot.

Jack felt it part and parcel of his job to keep the media up-to-date and happy about continuing to cover him...in a good way. If he didn't do this, someone might get the jump on him and take everything away; he would have none of that. In Spring of 1959, he and Donna were in New York. They had dinner with columnist Earl Wilson at Danny's Hideaway, a popular steak house on 45th Street for well-heeled celebrities to hold court, and for the up-and-coming to be seen.

A conversation ensued over Donna's stage name. She explained this hadn't been her idea. "I was good and mad about it when I heard they were going to change my name to May Wynn because that was the name of the girl I was to play in *Caine Mutiny*. So I was all set for Harry Cohn, whose idea I heard it was." She was called into Cohn's office, and said she was "boiling mad." But he turned the tables on her, asking without preamble, "What's this bit about changing your name to May Wynn? I think it's a horrible name."

Donna admitted her obstinacy to Earl. She told him she had shouted at Cohn, "I love the name!" She suddenly realized she'd effectively been finagled when, smiling, Cohn simply replied, "All right, your name's May Wynn."

Donna finished her story to Earl by saying she'd gone back to Cohn two days later to admit she had made a big mistake, practically begging him to change his mind. She didn't want to be known forever after as May Wynn, but Cohn wasn't moved.

"He told me," she said, "'You were such a smart aleck, your name is staying May Wynn.' And," Donna finished the tale between courses of their delicious promotional meal, with her husband looking on with a smile, "it has been until now."

Her name was officially May Wynn until she married Jack Kelly. Ever since, she had for all practical purposes become Donna Kelly, wife of Jack Kelly, co-star of *Maverick*. This suited Jack fine. He hated the name of May Wynn, anyway.

Donna occasionally seemed interested in testing the waters again in front of the camera, but only in tandem with her husband, or with his pre-approval. Jack still wanted her in his sights as regularly as possible, and anything she did, she did with him first in mind. Thinking about different ways to make this work, Jack told Jack Warner he wanted to do an episode of *Maverick* with his wife. He assured Warner that Donna would happily return to the screen for such an opportunity. He had specific ideas for a script. In particular, he wanted to make sure his character "gets her at the finish."

There was a similar idea with a twist making rounds on set, and it wasn't certain who had been the instigator. Donna was reported to be considered for a guest appearance on *Maverick*, opposite James Garner, not her husband. When asked why she wouldn't work instead with him, Jack replied, "No thanks! I'd kiss her and she would ask, 'THIS is the way you kiss the dames in front of the camera?' and then I would come home to cold cuts."

The comment was made jokingly and since Donna never did a *Maverick* episode, either with her husband or his co-star, the work-up was little more than a way to get added press for the show and the stars. While

Jack and Joyce Meadows in Maverick *in a romantic embrace.* PHOTO COURTESY GERI ANN SEFTON PRIVATE COLLECTION

May Wynn wasn't making much headway in front of the cameras, adding her still-remembered name in between those of *Maverick*'s well-known stars, especially when she was married to one of them, added spice to fan magazines and newspaper columns — always good press.

Still, Jack's reaction to the question about why she wouldn't have worked with him was revealing. There was common knowledge Garner wasn't overly fond of Donna's strong personality, particularly when she visited the set during working hours. And every time Jack was asked about his wife's reaction to his work involving other women, he retorted with a light-hearted, teasing quip which managed to indicate some level of discontent behind closed doors.

Mr. and Mrs. Jack Kelly never missed an opportunity to tell the press how gloriously in love they were, and how they had been in love ever since the first day they met, and how this would be the case forever. In an interview, Jack gushed, "Our love for each other is something very special." The reporter met him for a tête-à-tête on the Warner Bros. lot, and Jack continued, "It was so strange the way it came about, too. It was the most beautiful thing that ever happened to me — or to my wife, either. I can't describe it to you. We were just electrified by each other!"

Jack's words of dedication to Donna grew even more flowery. "Love like ours comes to a couple only once in a great while — I mean the way ours happened. I only hope it can always last…the romantic kind, I mean." How much absolute truth was in these words, and how much was show-generated publicity, or Jack-and-Donna generated publicity, is hard to discern. The question wasn't whether they loved each other. The question leaned more toward how idyllic their relationship continued to be. They were opposites, and keeping an even keel in the Kelly house wasn't always easy; when they gave public accounts of their relationship, this is where their acting began.

As a couple, they seemed determined to be seen as the perfect match, giving off a feeling that Jack and Donna had become an official team for public, as well as private, reasons. Their efforts in the writing and acting arenas showed how their thought processes moved along these lines almost all the time. Jack and Donna Kelly were something of a reality show before the concept had ever been envisioned.

This was evidenced by Jack's rendition to a female reporter about how he and Donna had met and began dating — much of his version in opposition to Donna's commentary about the same events. "You'll die when you hear what happened to May and me when we finally found each other," he began. The words, "finally found each other," are telling, since the truth of the situation did not happen all at once. Also, his use of the name, "May," when he took every chance to make sure his distaste for her stage name was known. This was a story for the press.

"We had been in a play together and I had always liked her, but that was all there was to it. Then about two years later I was talking to a friend and her name came up and I decided to call her just to say 'hello.'"

Jack and Donna at home having a barbecue. PHOTO COURTESY MAY WYNN PRIVATE COLLECTION

As Donna recounted, they did meet on a set early on, but it was a movie set, and Jack re-discovered her after speaking to Patricia Hardy. Jack's version said they made a date and went to a night club for dinner. He didn't mention how she stood him up, why she stood him up, or that the press speculated on how their speed-dating-turned-wedding included the sound of baby rattles.

Instead, Jack glamorized his spin. "We began to talk and romance and dance, and our eyes became magnets. They met, understood and held. I tell you the feeling was indescribable. We couldn't part from each other. Before we knew it, morning had come and our eyes still said the things we couldn't put into words. Two days later I asked her to marry me and she did."

This was a sweet article, if nothing else, and gave off the feel of charm and love-in-the-air. Whether it was Jack talking, or the studio's press department, or simply Jack's love for a good storytelling opportunity, he told the enamored reporter he was sure nothing nearly as magical could ever again happen. They made every effort, he swore, to keep their marriage alive, never being separated by their careers.

"Then Christmas Eve came," he continued. "We went out to dinner and bought some champagne and took it home to celebrate our wonderful life together. Now, you're never going to believe this," he warned the newspaperwoman, "but that same thing happened again." He stopped to laugh. "That's just the way we are. And the stardust has never rubbed off yet!"

But stardust is hard to hold onto. Chances are, not only did that stardust rub off, but its sheen came and went. Jack was painting a picture of what was in his mind the best possible relationship.

While Mr. and Mrs. Kelly did their best to uphold their public image, Jack dealt with his career issues, and this wore on him privately. TV as a medium was in the throes of violent growing pains. Westerns had made their mark from television's beginnings and the stars, actors who forged ahead with this revamped genre, began to demand a standard which had never before been in place.

These pioneers made it known in a big way they felt abused. As a group, they were often called the "Warner's Mutiny," touted in papers as "a big uprising on the TV range." From Wayde Preston of *Colt .45* to Peter Brown of *Lawman*, and many in between, including James Garner… all had at least a few words to say about how badly they were treated — seriously overworked and drastically underpaid. Preston went so far as to walk off the lot and go into a new business. Brown jockeyed for a new, bigger and better contract.

All while Jack Kelly kept his powder dry in most press reports. Saying little aloud, he did make it known in personal circles he wasn't happy. His co-star, on the other hand, talked to most anyone who'd listen, and made no apologies. "I feel like a slab of meat hanging there," Jim Garner boldly told columnist Bob Thomas. "Every once in awhile they cut off a piece."

The dissatisfaction in TV's Western world seemed a symptom of a larger, growing alarm within the entertainment industry as a whole. The battle loomed between TV as everyday fare versus going out to the movies as a singular event. Each vied for much the same audience. Did viewers more often want to watch *Maverick* and other programs in the comfort of their living rooms, or did they want the more glamorous opportunity to dress up, leave home, and go out for the evening to the big-screen movie theater?

Watching TV morphed into a day-to-day occurrence, especially as more homes acquired television sets as an expected part of regular family life. This previous luxury was becoming readily available to the average person; as long as they invested in a TV set, they had all sorts of entertainment available to them. Movies required more effort, more time, and, in the long run, more money.

But the movies had always seemed magical, holding sway over the consumer in a way the regularity of TV couldn't seem to achieve. Going to a movie, leaving the home, was an event which offered a chance to see a favored star bigger than life on a bigger-than-life screen. Movies were also going through a transformation, as much because of TV as because of the evolution of technology.

The war between the two mediums didn't spare any actor, from movies or TV. Movies had reigned since they started, and movie actors, for the most part, felt it beneath them to cross paths with those who'd decided to ply their trade on the smaller screen. The size of the screen was not only symbolic. The battle was waged between being seen in grand size, and being seen on a minimized scale...often how the movie industry tried to portray the battle, making for antagonistic exchanges.

Jack was in a unique position. He had throughout his career spanned both mediums, going back and forth. He'd done movies since he was little, and he had done TV practically since it became an option for an actor. One of those vocally hostile arguments between big-screen stars and TV stars went public, involving Jack, and Robert Ryan. Jack wasn't often one to air his agitation for large numbers to hear. Many were surprised when he went head-to-head with Ryan in the media.

Robert Ryan's career officially began in a Bob Hope film titled *The Ghost Breakers* (1940). He had a small part which went un-credited. He had since taken roles on TV; it wasn't as if he didn't know the score. His words clearly indicated he felt his nearly twenty-year history, much on the big screen, gave him a perspective that less experienced actors — purportedly actors such as Jack Kelly — would do well to emulate. The real issues seemed rooted in the idea that Ryan believed younger actors were in such a rush to make money, "they have an appalling indifference to their acting craft and just don't want to work."

This opinion didn't sit well with Jack, and he made his irritation known...in print. He had "some news for Mr. Ryan," and told Erskine Johnson that Ryan "seems to be unaware of the speed with which a filmed TV show can make, or break, a young actor." Jack warmed to his topic as he continued, "And if he doesn't believe young actors are working in

Hollywood today he should spend a week on any telefilm set. He would discover we never stop working."

This was a time of pain-filled growth for the industry, and there was considerable conversation — heated and otherwise — as to which format would win the top spot in the hearts and minds of consumers in years to come. Everyone had something to say. This interplay was of equal importance to the old-school actor and to the new, up-and-coming actor; success meant sustenance and livelihood. Jack's career spanned both sides, and his response to Robert Ryan seemed the culmination of a lot of thought borne of the upheaval going on in his world.

"A hit show can make an unknown star in seven weeks but if the show bombs, an actor can be looking for a job the eighth week. I know. I bombed-out in *Kings Row* before *Maverick*." Jack wanted Ryan to be aware of the real issue. He said twenty-six telefilms in one season equaled twenty-six movies...over a period of seven years. "Young actors in TV today can be burned out before they can get started." After working in that many shows in one season, Jack believed actors had the right to "attempt to progress — to improve their position for future financial security."

Jack Kelly's bottom line? He didn't mince words; this time he did not in any way soften the blow of his commentary. "If Ryan had appeared in twenty-six movies in his first year in Hollywood he would have been screaming for more money, too." Jack finished his tirade against Robert Ryan with words which mirrored his growing frustration. "He (Ryan) was lucky — he wasn't caught in the middle of the TV rat race."

Jack indeed felt as if he had been caught in the middle of the TV rat race. Movies and TV had violently collided, and he was smack in the center of the explosion. "I have the problem of sustaining what I have," he avowed. "I don't want a lot of money. I want to touch all the bases. Maybe I'm lucky to have such problems," he finished, letting his natural sense of humor take over in place of his earlier protest.

Jack was often this side of being totally discouraged. While he had TV to thank for finally finding a wide-scale sense of notoriety, he also had TV to blame for some of his career concerns. He had lost out on large, potentially-winning movie deals because he was caught up in *Maverick* obligations and not allowed to deviate from that path, thanks to his lucrative but binding contract. He had turned down well-paying and highly-visible promotional opportunities because of how much he would have had to share with Warner Bros. The contract which gave him the freedom to finally become well-known for plying his craft in some ways also shackled him.

When he wasn't working or promoting, which was rarely, he was on the golf course. Some of Jack's time on the course was for promotional, official appearances. As good an actor as he was, he was as good, if not better, a golfer. Jack got almost as much attention for his crack golfing skills as for his part on *Maverick*, and goings-on in front of, and behind, the camera. One article said, "Jack Kelly is a skilled golfer and plays in many tournaments with the top stars, such as open golf champion Arnold Palmer, and Ken Venturi." Jack stated how his game had improved by three or four strokes thanks to "private lessons" from Art Stuart, a Los Angeles golf pro who had guest-starred on several episodes of *Maverick*. Stuart would give Jack instruction between takes in a remote corner of the set.

August that year turned out not to be a good one for Jim Garner. He suffered from an ulcer and was unable to keep up his demanding schedule. Jack had extra episodic work shifted his way because of this. Warner Bros. "quietly made some fast switches in shooting schedules, giving more work" to Jack "to make Jim's load lighter" until he felt better.

Maverick had offered Jack a steady foothold in an industry in which he had been "almost there" more times than even he could count. This was without question the reason his name was now a household commodity. He was on top of the world while, at the same time,

A well-dressed Jack on the golf course. PHOTO COURTESY JACK KELLY FAMILY COLLECTION

feeling as if he were a caged creature. James Garner had made clear he wasn't happy with contract negotiations and Jack, while not as vocal, still made his concerns known.

A newspaper article in November 1959 said even though Jack wasn't "militant" about his agitation, he did have complaints. "We have no opportunity to parlay what popularity we have achieved through the series," Jack stated. "The studio wants half the money we would get for rodeos, etc, so why try?"

"Sadly, too many encounters result in the off-key dissonance of wondering what the hell we're talking about."

JACK KELLY

CHAPTER NINE

Cowboys and Range Wars...
Do What You Gotta Do

Garner's rumblings became more strident. He didn't seem concerned the studio would take his words the wrong way — quite possibly he didn't care. Now, with no holds barred from Garner's camp, Jack was left to diplomatically handle as best he could the growing unrest which became increasingly outspoken. He carried on with a happy face, at least publicly, though that wasn't always easy. He loved doing *Maverick*, but wasn't feeling positive about how he, and Garner, were treated...they seemed to be considered more as chattel and less like the backbone of the creative storylines in which they acted.

"I'm nuts about this show," he stressed. "I hope it runs twenty-five years." He was seen as one of "the few TV Western stars" who didn't want to get out of his series; at least, as far as the press knew. Privately, Jack wasn't as happy as one would believe but he did what he had to do to keep the paychecks coming. He plodded along, always turning in a solid performance. His fan mail remained consistent and strong; the public continued to want more Jack Kelly.

Away from the set, he worked all sorts of angles, hoping at least one would stick and secure his future, and his legacy, *Maverick* or no *Maverick*. One project took into consideration Jack's extensive cooking talents. He and Donna loved to spend time together in the kitchen, one forever trying to out-cook the other. Jack did give Donna her due. "My wife is a marvelous cook on Italian dishes and that's one of our favorite pastimes — scheming up new dishes in our dream kitchen." That kitchen was in the process of an extensive renovation. He revised his statement with confidence, "When we get through remodeling, it will be a dream kitchen."

The Kellys, into the culinary arts in a big way, were writing a cookbook together, an "anecdote-type volume of recipes." When Jack's *Maverick* sponsor found out about their joint expertise in the kitchen and their hoped-for book, a lot of thought went into figuring out how to capitalize on it to benefit the show…as well as the couple.

In his usual easy-going way, Jack spoke nonchalantly of the network's efforts to worm into his cookbook, not showing his opinion one way or the other. "There are all sorts of ways it could be promoted." He meant

A smiling Jack as Bart Maverick. PHOTO COURTESY SUSAN KETCHAM PRIVATE COLLECTION

the cookbook had many angles, and he knew having his *Maverick* sponsor behind him wouldn't hurt. On the other hand, studio involvement could minimize him as an individual, as well as him and Donna as a professional couple. The way Jack's contract was written, almost anything he did while a part of the show was subject to carrying a *Maverick* connection as well as the Warner Bros. seal.

Jack and Donna discuss kitchen renovations. PHOTO COURTESY JACK KELLY FAMILY PRIVATE COLLECTION

Like most conversations at this point, Jack's speech always returned to references to the show. "I wish we were having that kind of luck with our scripts," he said when talking about the success of the recipes he and Donna concocted. "Maybe our scripts just aren't worth what we think, and maybe it's because *Maverick* has such a good stable of writers — guys like Marion Hargrove." He finished with a sarcastic jab at how skewered the show's process had become. "I guess you can see influence doesn't count around here anymore."

There were always indications of how closely aligned the actor was with his character. Whether this was coincidental, or happened because of how writers had come to know the man behind the fictional *Maverick* brother, Bart often spoke in much the same fashion as Jack would speak in any given situation.

One reporter said, "Jack Kelly speared a virulent cliché in Sunday's *Maverick*." He explained, outlining the show's storyline, "The sheriff, urging him [Bart] to remain in town after he'd killed or captured the villains, said, 'We could use some new blood around here.'" The response

Jack and Jim Garner looking out for each other as Bart and Bret Maverick. PHOTO COURTESY SUSAN KETCHAM PRIVATE COLLECTION

from Bart didn't skip a beat, with words Jack probably would have used if having the same conversation. "I'm not bleeding."

Jack wasn't bleeding, but he often seemed to feel bruised. Yet despite difficulties brewing with the *Maverick* brothers and their "parents," Warner Bros., Jack and Garner had good times together onscreen and in light-hearted off-camera moments. Their chemistry effortlessly clicked when cameras rolled, and when the cameras were off, they were still likely to have fun...as long as they were in a professional environment. As best as Jack knew, he and Jim Garner respected and enjoyed each other's company as fellow actors. Their relationship seemed somewhat like two brothers who were totally different men, personality-wise, but who still could think well of the other.

Jack was specific about this in one interview with Vernon Scott. "There isn't any feud between us," he avowed. "Never has been. I've griped a few times because I wanted some of the stories that were assigned to him. But Jim personally had nothing to do with it. We're not close buddies but we play golf together and get along just fine."

He tried to explain in more detail how this complicated dynamic worked. "It's been like that [since the beginning]. We work together like a right and left hand. All Jim and I have to do in a scene is turn and look at one another and we know just what to do to make it funnier."

On set, the men were known for devilish behavior, and they often pulled tricks on others when the opportunity was too good to resist. One day they decided to give the cast of *Bronco* a playful hard time. Another of the Warner Bros. stable of Western offerings, *Bronco* starred Ty Hardin, as well as a long line of guests in any given episode. The *Bronco* stage was nearly aligned with theirs, and offered the perfect chance for practical jokes. Interviewed together, Jack and Garner seemed to have a great time telling how a particular lark came about.

On the Warner Bros. back lot, the boys decided to bust in on a scene of more than fifty Indian extras on horses. Jack and Garner told how they managed to inspire "a stampede of mounted Indians, an acute attack of nerves on the part of a director, and several hundred feet of film to be annexed to the junk heap." They went on to explain, making a case for their side of the story, relating the tale "without a bit of remorse."

"We were shooting our show in the back lot," Garner started out.

"And the *Bronco* series was shooting right next to us," Jack interjected.

"Well," Jim went on, throwing a frown Jack's way, "they had hundreds of extras over there — you know, Indians and cowboys jazz."

"So those extras kept slopping over onto our set."

"Anyway," Garner seemed not to appreciate Jack's additions, "we decided to get even." He explained they weren't angry with Ty Hardin, "just the extras."

"Jim and I waited until we heard Andre De Toth begin a take," Jack explained, ignoring Garner's side glances. "Then we climbed over some

Jack and Donna share a hug as she visits the Maverick set during a break. PHOTO
COURTESY LISA OLDHAM PRIVATE KELLECTION

rocks and jumped into the scene shooting the place up real good with our six-guns."

Andre DeToth directed this episode of *Bronco*. "De Toth lost his head," Garner recalled. "We picked the wrong scene, I guess. There were thirty-five Indians charging around on horseback, and De Toth channeled them off toward us." He hesitated. "Must have been fifty horses ready to mow

Jack and Jim Garner ready for the golf course. PHOTO COURTESY GERI ANN SEFTON PRIVATE COLLECTION

us down...no, maybe it was fifty-five."

"Oh, come on," Jack broke in again. "You don't stop to count horses at a time like that. You just run like hell. Which is what we did." The exchange was a good indicator of how easily the two men could interact.

There was considerable physical activity for both men as a star of such a show as *Maverick*. After visiting the set, watching her husband go through his work for the day, Donna said, "No wonder he comes home tired and bruised." This worried her. "He could have a double, but he won't. He believes in this part so. It's the same way with Jim Garner. The Mavericks are real to both of them."

Jack and Garner knew what buttons to push to make the other jump, and they both had a healthy sense of humor when it came to razzing one another. They even finished each other's sentences. They shared leading women, also, but only onscreen. Anyone who didn't know them well, and who had only watched them interact in a working environment, would be surprised to know the camaraderie between Jack and Garner existed, for the most part, only at work. After hours, they were cordial but rarely shared anything even remotely resembling a real friendship. Garner was invited to parties at Jack's house but always manufactured a reason he couldn't attend. He showed up once, stayed but a few minutes, and left with little fanfare. Those close to Jack believe Jack's drinking habits didn't appeal to Garner.

But when *Maverick* was on the air and Garner and Jack were in their roles as brothers, they watched each other's back. They did what they had to do for the show, and if they were together, there was usually an interview involved. When a "Best-of-Movieland" survey came out, promotion between them worked well. Over 22,000 teenagers — not adults, but teenagers — deemed Jack Kelly and James Garner, "Top Western Types."

Despite the positive and glowing appreciation, it became harder not to end up in the press as the result of some sort of ongoing unhappiness on the *Maverick* set. Jim Garner's issues with the Warner Bros. brass were clear in a UPI article titled, "TV Cowboy Turns in His Saddle." Plain and simple, Garner gave up — he was leaving because Warner Bros. "quit paying" him. "And that is a breach of contract," Garner stated.

He made $1500 a week and the studio had first rights to his talent in all show business angles. This was the same contractual deal for Jack, though he was paid less. The situation seemed to have started for Garner, or at least come to a head, in March 1960. Because of a TV writers' strike, the studio claimed no scripts were available. They said they didn't have to pay the actors. No writers writing, no scripts to produce. No scripts, no show. The lack of scripts to turn into *Maverick* shows — insofar as Warner Bros. was concerned — meant Garner, and Jack, weren't under contract for the show, but were under contract for other bits of business each man regularly did as a Warner Bros. contract actor.

The studio may have played both men against each other. A Las Vegas hotel appearance deal was dangled in front of them, with Garner offered more money than Jack. An idea for a "big" movie was bandied about…a Western, of course, titled *Cantaro*, shot in Texas, "with Texas money." Neither opportunity — Vegas or the movie — got off the ground.

In turn, the studio took Garner, and Jack, off salary until they could resume filming new episodes. When the lack of scripts had become an issue for the studio's interpretation of his contract, Garner saw a clear-cut problem with this. No longer was he arbitrarily complaining out loud. His interpretation of the issues was different, and he hired an attorney who was paid to agree with him. Garner said his contract stated he was to be paid for

Jack takes a bath for Warner Bros. PHOTO COURTESY SUSAN KETCHAM PRIVATE COLLECTION

fifty-two weeks a year, under any conditions. If the studio "ran out of scripts," this meant nothing to him. He should still be paid — end of discussion.

Their shooting schedules were from July to March 1st. Garner had been on the show for three years. "We made seventy-nine one-hour shows, and I appeared in more than fifty of them," he avowed. What was he going to do about his displeasure? He sued. He took Warner Bros. to court for breach of contract since they suspended him during the January-June writers' strike. Jack Warner admitted he "personally decided to suspend" Garner. The studio justified their move by invoking the force majeure clause. The clause read that if forces beyond the studio's control made it impossible to create the expected product, they weren't liable. The studio was not required to continue paying salaries.

Nonetheless, the studio claimed first rights to Jack's, and James Garner's, talent in all fields of show business — no exceptions. Each man had made personal appearances for Warner Bros. TV, and done Warner Bros. movies, and each had been a part of other Warner Bros. TV shows in addition to *Maverick*.

In May, Garner did an interview, one of many during that period. He brought other actors into his public argument, saying not only he was displeased with how Warner Bros. did business across the board. "I think it's significant that Jack Kelly and Clint Walker both told the studio their contracts were over after I made the first move. There wasn't much publicity about Clint's move. He got back on salary with back pay one day after service notice. Jack got a new deal; I managed to get him a $50,000 yearly increase in salary."

That Garner wanted to be released from his contract was no secret around town. "Contracts are completely one-sided affairs," he was quoted as saying, sounding bitter. "If you click, the studio owns you." What he actually did for Jack's contract was in question, but the two actors did go to bat for each other during this trying period.

Jack at one point was listed as "suspended" along with Garner. He was also initially sued by Warner Bros., with the studio alleging he "became antagonistic against his employers in a show of sympathy with" Garner. Jack countered that his contract was dissolved when the studio stopped payment of his $1,000 weekly salary during the strike. Garner was paid $750 a week more than Jack, another consideration which seemed unfair. Jack was carrying the same load — and he was the subject of as much positive public reaction to the show.

The salary differences didn't end up meaning much in the grand scheme. Jack dropped his lawsuit, and ultimately played the studio's game after they agreed to give him a raise. His comment was pure Jack Kelly. "The only thing I wish is that the studio had given me the raise eight years ago when I really needed it."

Jack's return to *Maverick* was officially announced by Warner Bros. Jack Warner put out a statement saying he had "reached an amicable agreement under which Kelly returns immediately to the studio." Despite this,

Jack and Jim Garner, as Bret and Bart Maverick, watching each others' backs.

Jack did a bit of uncharacteristic public griping at a weekend party soon afterward at the Sportsmen's Lodge, at an event actually sponsored by the studio.

He caused "raised eyebrows and low mutters" when he came out with a "startling diatribe against the outfit." He had apparently recently been in what was called a "session" with his "ex-brother," Garner, and was letting off steam…not the best place to do this but the stress got to him, and he blew his stack. Even though this was the wrong place and the wrong time, Warner Bros. looked the other way, and the new norm continued on.

Most everyone knew Jack Kelly returned to the show because he wasn't willing to gamble with certain success. He didn't believe there was any benefit to maybe, or maybe not, ending up in a different winner's circle than the one in which he was already in. He had made a success out of a character which had become part of the fabric of American television. Would his fame and success grow beyond what he had now if he were to change the playing field?

There was no way of knowing, and betting on an unsure thing wasn't Jack Kelly's style. Instead, he put the best face on the situation and told the press, "I got what I wanted." Warner Bros. had signed him to a new contract for seven-years, covering his work on *Maverick* in addition to as many as four movies — and all the publicity the studio could muster.

As part of the deal, a number of ancillary business opportunities were thrown Jack's way, likely incentives for him to hold down the fort and not make any more waves. For example, he was offered a considerable amount of money and a partnership if he let his name be used on a string of bowling alleys…though Jack had never been much of a bowler. Still, this was padding for the deal, and Jack went with the flow.

He was enamored with restaurants, every facet of restaurants. He was considered an excellent cook. He loved food, and knew the best places to go. He even flirted regularly with the idea of opening his own place. His promotional schedule took advantage of this love. In 1960, Jack Kelly was seen in the press congratulating a young lady, Miss Fern Cortez, for being chosen "most photogenic waitress" by the National Restaurant Association. There may have been issues on the TV set but when it came to keeping himself in front of the cameras, Jack knew what angles to pursue.

That year, an announcement was made that the Kellys would form a production company to review scripts and new projects. They called it Majak, combining Donna's stage name — May — with Jack's first name. Majak Productions was expected to film independent feature properties. The first would be made in conjunction with producer/financier, John Bash. Bash made his way up the ropes in Hollywood. In the late 1950s, he had produced maybe a half-a-dozen forgettable films, and was now ready to back projects fitting his criteria. He and Majak intended to negotiate for the rights to Roy Chanslor's novel, *The Trouble With Paradise*, and film in England. This would be a starring vehicle for Jack.

Because he was still under contract, Jack had to be on loan-out to his own company from Warner Bros. to accommodate this plan. Since the movie never came to pass, Warner Bros. apparently didn't make the time available to their still-solid *Maverick* star. There were times Jack felt they were playing games with him — one moment giving him the world, the next moment taking it away.

FERN CORTEZ is congratulated on being chosen "most photogenic waitress" of National Restaurant Assn. by Jack Kelly, left, and Lawrence L. Frank, co-founders of Lawry's where Miss Cortez is employed.

Jack, Fern Cortez "Miss Photogenic Waitress," and Lawrence L. Frank. PHOTO COURTESY JACK KELLY FAMILY PRIVATE COLLECTION

In mid-Summer, July 1960, the Democratic National Convention opened in Los Angeles. In the week prior to the convention, two individuals stepped forward to challenge the nomination of John F. Kennedy. Lyndon B. Johnson was the powerful Senate Majority Leader from Texas, and Adlai Stevenson II had already tried for the top spot in the country two times before. Both announced they would throw their hats into the ring.

Jack Kelly had been politically astute from a young age, and he was concerned about what went on in his world. He was incensed over the growing racial divide, among other crucial issues. He had definite viewpoints, and as the convention revved up, he compared notes for each potential candidate. Kennedy appeared to be the one to beat, but Jack went to work to nominate Adlai Stevenson. Before too much time passed, Stevenson's star had waned.

Once Stevenson officially threw in the towel, Jack changed gears. Rather than walk away from the effort, he became part of the Kennedy camp. Jack Kelly, good Irish Catholic that he was, became more than simply a Kennedy follower. Not only did he campaign for him; he was connected from the sidelines with many of the same people who personally surrounded the candidate.

Kennedy had a host of intimate Hollywood supporters, and Jack was now among them. Jack was a friend to Sammy Davis, Jr., and Peter Lawford, directly related to the Kennedys through marriage. These were people in Kennedy's inner circle. Donna had dated Lawford, before she and Jack became an item.

All this happened as *Maverick* continued amidst new growth pains. Garner's lawsuit went all the way to court, and in December 1960, the case was decided in his favor. Jim Garner won his teeter-totter bet. During the course of overall testimony, it was discovered that during the strike, Warner Bros. obtained under the table somewhere in the neighborhood of one hundred scripts. This didn't shed positive light on the studio, and went far to support Garner's claims.

At one point, the studio reportedly had over a dozen writers working under the pseudonym of "W. Hermanos," Spanish for "brothers." This was not a new tactic. It was an industry pseudonym for scripts written by stock, unidentified writers, a tactic used over the years — in movies even before TV — and most notably during the Red Scare.

Jack felt the strain. The contract dispute had been a genuine issue — not only with Garner, but with him. He also had made personal appearances, done movies, and guest-starred in other TV shows, and all in some way connected to *Maverick*.

While Jack handled things in a much less obvious fashion, occasionally he let his feelings show, more often as time went on. At one point, he told the press the show was "sinking like a setting sun." He was frustrated to the boiling point but the difference was — Jack Kelly had a less defined boiling point. He had worked hard to ensure he didn't often air his dirty laundry in public, instead employing back-door efforts to make his feelings known while still holding his place on the show.

In this situation, the writing on the wall was in front of all of them, and had been from the start. Warner Bros. would, in the long run, come out on top. How Garner and Jack handled this would tell where they ended once the dust settled.

Jack wasn't thrilled knowing he could've won a lawsuit if he had held on during his strike, but he was philosophical. Tables could have as easily turned against Garner — and against him. He didn't like to throw a sure bet to the wind. He was back on salary, and that was a good thing. "I have

Jack getting out of his car. PHOTO COURTESY JACK KELLY FAMILY PRIVATE COLLECTION

a contract with the studio, and if they continue to produce *Maverick*, I guess I'll continue to be part of the show."

Jack didn't sound completely satisfied, but more as if he had resigned himself to how things turned out. Again, that Kelly off-beat sense of humor got him through. "Maybe I should quit and let Garner be my agent in the future." He didn't quit, though the press stated at one point again after the initial hoopla, both actors were "talking about court action" against Warner Bros. At issue was the salary they did not receive during the layoff. Jack didn't take on that lawsuit, either. He plodded ahead, carrying the show on his back no matter what the brass threw his way. He still thought he'd come out on top if he played the game well.

The perks of becoming the sole star of *Maverick* were well-earned; that became Jack's take on recent troubles. He may have had many regular perks, including the use of the sponsor's private estate and all the trimmings, but he'd paid for the privilege. Though contract issues primarily centered on what had been required of Jack and Garner as the stars, in addition to show work — and how little each man was credited for extra effort — not much really changed once Garner was gone. Jack was still required to constantly be on the road for press junkets, "going from city to city selling sponsors' products." He did interviews, TV spots, print media, and other fanfare dreamed up by Warner Bros. None of this was new. The difference now was that he was the only one making the effort. This created even more work for him.

He wasn't ungrateful; he was frustrated and at a loss as to how to balance his feelings about the overall experience. This had something to do with his being the one major star on the fence in the midst of the Western wars. Jack was thankful for what had come his way, and he was loyal about showing his appreciation for those who had done well by him. Still, he harbored normal human emotions when he felt as if he was being used.

"Prior to *Maverick* I was a fairly, and only fairly, successful actor," he admitted. "I didn't pay any attention to ratings or business ends of shows. I drove up to work in a flashy wagon, went through my lines and forgot about it all on the way home. Like the guys who hang out at Schwab's drugstore, I thought I had an acting career."

He was the first to say he used to have a "lack of direction," something his *Maverick* character wore like a badge but which he, the actor behind the character, knew to be a deterrent if he wanted to stay employed. He found direction and drive as *Maverick* had turned into a smash hit. That delicious and meaty taste of success was exactly what he needed, and he "picked up the scent of a career like a hound dog."

Jack's contract made him feel a bit like a hound dog during these promotional trips, all required during what would otherwise be well-earned weekends "off." The constant travel took a toll. At times he visibly suffered consequences of being on the road too much, in a variety of climates. He would catch bad colds which he couldn't shake for weeks. He went from Hawaii to Chicago, then to Phoenix, back to New York, to Philadelphia, and on and on, and often didn't know in which town he'd wake the next morning.

One local California promotional event proved to be unintentionally entertaining for Jack. He was part of a skit during the taping of a March of Dimes special, taking on the role of an irritated Western director. While he did his shtick, the 1960 March of Dimes poster child, four-year old Linda Breese, rode a tricycle through the scene. Linda, who had Spina Bifida, became the annual featured child after going through breakthrough operations and exercises to strengthen her damaged-but-working leg muscles. Because of the success of the procedures, she could ride a bike, despite her handicap.

Jack spoke his lines as the director, screaming, "Cut!," as he was scripted to do. Little Linda suddenly stopped her bike-riding, fixed scared, hurt eyes on him, and petulantly stated, "You yelled at me." The child refused to do the scene again, despite cajoling, until Jack promised he would not holler. This made the taping logistically difficult but Jack took it in stride, mouthing the word which was ultimately dubbed into the sound track after the fact.

Being a promotional tool, in addition to being an actor, was physically tiring, as well as emotionally draining, especially since Jack spent the week in all-day filming, and memorized his lines at night. When the next weekend came around, he was on the road yet again. This turned into another learning experience for him, requiring him to figure out how to balance all aspects of his career — the TV side and getting the shows in the can, as well as the promotional side which required him to be away from home more often than he cared to be.

This was another reason he wanted Donna with him wherever he went. If she wasn't on the road right next to him, it meant she was at home and he was not — a less-than-perfect recipe for marital bliss, in his book. He knew what he had to do to keep his career moving forward, and he felt as if he knew what he had to do to keep his marriage on an even keel. The mix was a challenge.

"A career," he lamented, "demands formulation and propulsion." He was doing a lot of formulating and working regularly at propulsion. In the process, he and Donna made plans for a summer tour while he wasn't filming *Maverick*; if he played his cards right, he would work it in without Warner Bros. getting involved. He and his wife also took piano lessons together, for work and play, when they had rare free time.

Jack was making a tidy sum of money as star of a top-running weekly TV Western, but he still deeply wanted to do movies. He continued to hold out for big-screen visibility. In addition to the artistic draw he felt pulling him in that direction, he was certain films would allow him more stationary time, giving him the chance to be in one place for longer periods, even if shooting away from home base.

Jack had the opportunity in late 1960 to escape the stress of the set for about two months. A potentially explosive movie finally came his way, a Warner Bros. production, co-written by *Maverick's* own Roy Huggins.

Warner Bros. encouraged him to do the film, but he had to work during what would have otherwise been his vacation. Jack Warner, the boss himself, initially brought the offer to Jack via a phone call.

"Kelly, baby," Warner asked, "how'd you like to work for *me*?"

Jack didn't know what was up. "I thought I'd almost choke to death when he called," Jack remembered in an interview with Rona Barrett. "I figured, with the boss calling me, he finally realized I was the only one with the formula for mass stardom. After all, Jim Garner was giving him plenty of problems."

At Warner's request, Jack visited the boss at his office. "He offered me the sun, the moon, the stars and the earth. I figured for sure that Gable and Taylor would soon have nothing on me and the Empire State Building would soon be my dressing room."

Jack had specific ideas as to how much he had done for Warner Bros., in general, and *Maverick*, in particular. He was sure he had much more to offer the studio and the buying public eager to eat up every bit of entertainment he could throw their way. "There was only one thing I wanted — stardom in any form." Warner really heaped praise on thick and reeled him in. Jack continued, "When the boss said, 'Baby! Baby! You've got it,' I figured I did."

What "Kelly, baby" got from their meeting was a set chair without the *Maverick* name on it. There was nothing visibly *Maverick* related. Warner offered him a starring role in a feature movie titled, *A Fever in the Blood*. Jack was a worker, and he was still a contract player. He gave Jack Warner all he was worth, and then some. He had asked for this for some time.

He got word about that time he would be on tap for even more, nonstop work after the movie wrapped and was on the market. The studio told him in no uncertain terms he'd have to cancel an already-planned vacation to New York at the end of August 1961, the year the movie was released. He would immediately begin the first of eighteen new *Maverick* episodes after completing the movie.

A Fever in the Blood told of activities inside a state political campaign for governor, a murder, and a sensationalized trial. The story revolved around politics of the day, a topic in which Jack Kelly was well-versed. He played the devious prosecutor looking to win a seat in the upcoming election. He said it was a "difficult part, particularly after being the happy *Maverick* hero for so long. But an actor can't always play the same role."

A series of wardrobe and scene change photos showed Jack's usual good humor as he goofed around during what otherwise would have been a tedious task.

Besides Efrem Zimbalist, Jr., Angie Dickinson and Don Ameche were in the cast. William Pearson, the author, had resigned from a successful Colorado law practice to write the story. Jack's work was memorable, and future references would call this one of his best performances. Being in another film with Don Ameche was a positive experience for him. It had been many years since he had been with Ameche in *The Story of Alexander Graham Bell* (1939).

Jack as Dan Callahan in the "duck blind," wardrobe test for A Fever In The Blood *(1961).* PHOTO COURTESY BECKY LANDIS PRIVATE COLLECTION

In real-time, the movie didn't do well at the box office. The production was little more than a way for the studio to give a few up-and-coming actors, namely Jack and Efrem Zimbalist, Jr., a chance at big-screen exposure since they had made a name for themselves on TV. The studio system had all but died; a factor which played heavily into how the movie was made and promoted — less fanfare than would've been given a major

Left: Jack goofing around as Dan Callahan, wardrobe test for A Fever In The Blood *(1961). Right: Jack as Dan Callahan in picnic scene, wardrobe test.* PHOTO COURTESY BECKY LANDIS PRIVATE COLLECTION

studio release in years past. Something was lost in the translation between the big screen and small screen actors, and the movie didn't achieve what it set out to achieve. Financial returns were disappointing.

But Jack and Donna were busy. He was finally climbing to the top of the heap, even if the heap wasn't exactly as he had originally envisioned. In the midst of *Maverick's* legal craziness and finagling, he and Donna had purchased a new home in the "most expensive section" of Sunset Boulevard in the Brentwood area of Los Angeles.

Their home had three bedrooms, three baths, and a maid's quarters. Jack said they had plans to add a fifty-foot playroom. "I'm a hopeful do-it-yourself addict," he declared. They moved in over the weekend of August 12-14, 1960, roundabout the same time he had started work on *A Fever In The Blood*. As a special gift from Kaiser, *Maverick*'s sponsor, the Kelly home was given a "hefty aluminum siding job." Jack also received a brand new Willys Jeep from them. He was being courted, treated like a top-of-the-line star of a show, which, in actuality, he had already starred in for three years.

Jack as Dan Callahan in convention hall scene, wardrobe test for A Fever In The Blood *(1961).* PHOTO COURTESY BECKY LANDIS PRIVATE COLLECTION

Jack was "pushing out walls and installing a swimming pool." As they got situated, "surrounded by packing boxes," Donna did all the cooking and housework since "no maid would submit to the clutter everywhere." They were "eating off a two-foot coffee table while seated on old camel cushions," their only chairs. This was considered roughing it — Kelly style.

Jack and Efrem Zimbalist, Jr., in A Fever In The Blood. PHOTO COURTESY SUSAN KETCHAM PRIVATE COLLECTION

Eventually they did get a housekeeper. Johnnie B. Williams was loved by both, and became a member of the household as much, if not more than, an employee. When the phone rang, she would happily answer, "Johnnie B. Maverick here!" As Donna put it, everyone knew Johnnie B.

Donna said Jack's brother, Bill, would occasionally stay with them. He'd help around the house, especially when they were out of town, and she called him a "sweet, sweet man." She mentioned a time when she and Jack had come home from a trip to find Bill and Johnnie B. sitting at the table, playing cards.

"I thought you both were supposed to be working!" she playfully scolded.

"Oh, we will," they answered, "just as soon as we finish this game."

Jim Garner and Jack Kelly on cover of promotional Maverick *record album with "Kaiser Willys Motors" logo.* PHOTO COURTESY BECKY LANDIS PRIVATE COLLECTION

"You can't make pebbles arguing with a stone wall."

JACK KELLY

CHAPTER TEN

Ridin' Solo…
With a Heavy Saddle

Despite Jim Garner's departure, the *Maverick* set continued to be unsettled. Every soul involved with the show seemed at least a little bit unhappy. There was no rest yet at hand for Jack Kelly. Jim Garner had made it more than clear he was finished. Nothing left but formal details. The 1960 season had Jack opening the show solo. Officially, Garner was "still on the hold-out list" until everything was legally ironed out between him and Warner Bros.

This put the weight of everything *Maverick* squarely on Jack's shoulders, including fielding questions from press and public. Being the star gave him seniority, as well as the glory of success or the heat of failure — depending on how the show was perceived by the public without Garner in the cast. No matter what else the brass would decide to do, or what direction they might take, Jack had been there almost from the beginning, and now he was the veteran. He would carry the show, even if another actor was brought in to fill the spot vacated by Jim Garner.

There would be no breaks now, but Jack knew what he had to do to hold on. He told a reporter how he felt about the others who had recently gone into a snit over upsets at Warner Bros. He had thoughts on how they each handled the changing climate.

"Clint Walker can really live in the wilds," Jack explained. "He likes it. The last time he walked out on the studio, he took his family with him and they were really free people, not dependent on the comforts like most of the rest of us are for happiness…Ef Zimbalist is talented in a dozen ways, but me, I'm just an actor." This commentary gave insight into the direction in which Jack had taken his career to this point. "It's all I've ever wanted to be — a good actor, preferably in light comedy."

The interesting part about his musings was how he thought of himself. He felt he was a comedic actor, as he had been billed in the early days when he was trying to get his name circulated. Even then he had been considered a comedian as much, if not more, than an actor. "I'm the kind of goof who cried at *Father Knows Best*, and all the time behind everything else I'm thinking about how I can be a better light comedian."

He was taking over the lead now, and he saw no end in sight. "I don't mind going for a year, and maybe two or three, without time off," he

Jack as Bart Maverick, gun at the ready. PHOTO COURTESY SUSAN KETCHAM PRIVATE COLLECTION

said when he was asked about how Garner's departure would affect the show's filming, and his lifestyle. "Actors rarely get a wished-for vacation anyway. If they're not under contract to a studio, they start looking for their next role as soon as they finish one. If they are under contract, then the most time off they get in one chunk is perhaps a week, or two weeks at the most." It didn't matter that Jack Kelly had lived this hectic lifestyle almost since the show started. The departure of James Garner was a headline, and discussions began anew. For a time, *Maverick*'s popularity was revived.

Jack had his eyes set not on time off, but on continuing to work. He felt as if he'd blown some of his earlier years, and was determined to catch up. "The kind of a vacation that would mean something to me is to be able to go away for a month or more, forget Hollywood completely, and travel to those parts of the world I have not seen. Until that opportunity comes along I'll be content to work fifty-two weeks a year, especially if I have a chance to do an occasional picture like *A Fever In The Blood* along with the *Maverick* shows."

Jack continued to want to expand his working experience. Audiences had become attuned to him in the part of Bart Maverick — the laconic, life-is-easy and always happy tumbleweed, and it was hard for him to be seen as a tough guy, or any character with an edge. *A Fever In The Blood* had debuted while Jack actively played Bart. This had put him in two totally different personas at the same time — one on small screen, and one on the large screen. Bart had become not only Jack's professional saving grace, but in some ways, his shadow, his ball and chain, holding him down from successfully doing other types of work.

Maverick was in flux. The press soon announced that Garner wasn't the only one who'd no longer hang his hat on the show's doorstep. By October 1960, Roy Huggins decided to leave...not only *Maverick*, but Warner Bros. The show hadn't evolved as Huggins had wanted, he had grown tired of the speed of the studio's production schedule, and he felt less-than-appreciated for his place in *Maverick*'s creation, as well as other shows he'd done for Warner Bros. In those days, he wasn't even originally credited for the creation of *Maverick*.

Jack's reaction? His words were safe when he commented about Huggins, "He has a zest for new horizons." Huggins, maybe trying to be diplomatic, claimed he had proven his point with *Maverick*, and he was ready to move on.

Jack hoped writing quality might improve. The show started out well-crafted, but over the years, storylines had been diluted, and Huggins lost his chance to make a difference. While expectations early-on believed the level of budget would be maintained after everything evened out, this looked to be less and less likely. The "custom in Hollywood" then was to trim budgets on running hit shows, shows which had already hit their stride and continued to hold strong. Since the high mark for *Maverick* had, by all intents and purposes, been made in the eyes of the brass, quality was at best now simply being maintained. They believed there was no reason to throw added money in that direction.

"In this race, they didn't put spikes in my shoes," Jack told a reporter in response to rising concerns on the *Maverick* set. He felt he hadn't ever been given equity in how scripts were doled out between him and Garner, and he was looking to finally see an exploitable script come his way. He felt he had earned that much. Yet there was nothing easy in figuring out how much stronger Jack's position might become with the next season, Garner or no Garner. The boss contingency, changing though it was, wasn't talking.

"I would work on *Maverick* for the next twenty-five years if equity was involved. I like the show and I like my work. I liked *Maverick* even before it was a smash. And I'm proud to say I thought it would be a hit." When the show started, there were only maybe a handful of people who would have agreed. One believer was Henry J. Kaiser, who continued to hold fast in his faithfulness, a good thing because he remained the primary financial backer. Kaiser personally beat down opposition, and though he had been vocally unhappy when the show originally added a second brother to the mix, he discovered having Jack Kelly's name on the title page proved to have been a good move.

Jack's name on most every marquee now received attention in ways not previously offered before Garner's departure, and he made sure he worked the added leverage. He was no longer going to let his career work him. "I have management and press now. We have direction." He'd sought counsel and carefully created a smart professional group to direct him. "I can't put a time on it, but there will be a day when we will be boss." Notice he said, "we," and not, "I will be boss."

Jack courted the press even more than before. He saw it as more crucial now to keep his name in the headlines, and he granted interviews at every turn. In one such chat, he reminisced about what life was like when he first signed his Universal contract. "They had regular classes for young actors in almost anything you can name — including riding and Balinese dancing where you'd have to strike a lot of kookie poses. This was the greatest thing that ever happened to me as far as training was concerned.

You learned poise. You learned how to cock your head or lift an eyebrow to get an idea across. I do that a lot today in *Maverick*, if you'll notice."

Many viewers had noticed. Once *Maverick* got through the initial changeover, with James Garner gone for good, Jack was the main star, despite a soon ongoing revolving door of assorted relatives, each of whom were supposedly on the same playing field. The brass used the identical technique they had used when they added Jack to the mix with Garner, trying to make *Maverick* continue as a double-billed starring show. Second time around, the winning chemistry never materialized. *Maverick* remained, from then on, a vehicle which starred Jack Kelly. Any other actor for any other season was listed alongside him.

BIG EFFORT FOR LITTLE ONES. M. C. Dennis James (left) holds Anne Marie Fellin, 6, while Jack Kelly, of TV "Maverick" fame, holds Toby Kleiner, 6½, at the Cerebral Palsy Telethon, 202 W. 58th St. In center is singer Jane Pickens, veteran on annual benefit television show. Both children are Cerebral Palsy victims. When the 18-hour telethon ended at 5:30 p.m., yesterday, $502,-425 had been pledged to the cause battling the dread disease.

Not long after Garner left, his attorneys sent Warner Bros. "a nasty note about using Jim's name on Jack Kelly's *Maverick* TV show." Garner's name was tied up with various cast lists in any number of announcements. This was because of reruns, which Warner Bros. had full rights to air. The studio used reruns while reorganizing and continued using them after Garner was no longer part of the cast. Another problem arose because fans thought he was back on the show when they saw his name still attached — or

WOR-TV Cerebral Palsy Telethon, 1961. Left to right: Dennis James, Anne Marie Fellin, Jane Pickens, Jack Kelly, Toby Kleiner.
PHOTO COURTESY JACK KELLY FAMILY PRIVATE COLLECTION

again attached, depending on how it was read. The confusion surrounding *Maverick* never seemed to go away.

Jack made as many public appearances as he could fit into his tight schedule. He started out 1961 by being a part of WOR-TV's "Celebrity Parade" Telethon for cerebral palsy. Alongside TV emcee Dennis James and singer Jane Pickens, Jack smiled broadly as he held a poster child for the cause, six-and-a-half year old Toby Kleiner. In May, he played nice-nice with a group of Los Angeles-area Boy Scouts when he appeared for a photo opportunity about "Scoutcraft Fair." He and three young Scouts from Troop 139 sponsored by St. David's Episcopal Church of North Hollywood, stood in front of the camera, with Jack giving the pledge. These were pleasant, innocuous opportunities to do something for kids, while keeping his name current.

Jack was a good writer, and his wife seemed able to match him word for word. He was quick to point out to anyone who'd listen, "I'm a lucky guy. Here I thought I was getting a nice wife, with a pretty face, and she turns out to be a writer, too." In mid-1961, Donna wrote her first screenplay, and Jack lobbied Warner Bros. to buy it. This wouldn't be just any screenplay, of course. Titled *All For Love*, it would star none other than Jack. When asked by gossip columnist Sheilah Graham why Donna hadn't written in a part for herself, Donna demurred in a lady-like manner. She reaffirmed that she had given up her acting career for her marriage. With this script, her husband would "prove he's a sexy lover, not a fighter." Unfortunately for her writing career, and Jack's end of the promotion efforts, while the studio bought the script, they never picked up the option to produce.

True to his status as a town insider, Jack was seen on shows which peered into lives of screen stars, large and small. *Here's Hollywood* was a one-on-one, casual look at the "real" life of the stars, something of a precursor to what has become standard fare on television. This was then an innovative idea. By the Summer of 1961, the show had been on the air for a year, and Jack had his turn. His lovely wife was at his side as he mugged for the camera in their home.

Jack never missed a chance to make sure everyone knew he and Donna were still the ideal couple. They enjoyed press junkets, taking every opportunity to go some place new, or revisit a spot they'd already explored. On one such trip, this time to a place near Palm Desert, not too far from home, Jack met Tom Chevoor, a man who remained one of his best friends for the rest of his life. Tom was Manager of Desi Arnaz Indian Wells Resort, and Jack was there playing in yet another celebrity golf tournament.

"Jack was a natural at golf, and played a good game. He didn't look at it as a career or anything. He was just a good golfer," Tom remembered. He and Jack hit it off.

Another activity which kept Jack and Donna together was revealed when the press was told they both liked to paint. The intended public image was that of a couple who weren't truly happy unless they were side-by-side. They continued to work on their cookbook, trying to find the right combination of good food and good stories. The text had changed angles, and now they called it *Love 'N The Oven*. The couple playing together....

And *Maverick* plodded on anemically.

Everyone in the business knew Jack Kelly would do what he had to do, when he had to do it, to work with the media, and media-related shows. He

Jack on drums with friend, Tom Chevoor, behind microphone. PHOTO COURTESY JACK KELLY FAMILY PRIVATE COLLECTION

was not in any way camera-shy. He did a segment for a show which aired in September 1961 called *Meet the Star* with host, Bill Bradley. Jack hammed it up. The feature aired prior to a rerun of *Maverick* in which, of course, he headlined. There were fewer *Maverick* episodes filmed at this point, yet reruns were put to good use and worked overtime to fill in the blanks.

Jack and Donna lived well. They conducted their life at a certain elevated material level, afforded them as a result of the considerable salary and contract benefits Jack received because of his changed status on the show. While the money was good, contract issues continued to be a point of strain on his creative and personal platforms since no matter what he did professionally, by contract he remained under the thumb of Warner Bros. His hands were, in many ways, tied because of his contract, no matter how lucrative it might become.

Jack Kelly was now more than ever a kept actor, and he made no bones about his position. Speaking out in an article in December 1961, Jack talked about how money didn't go as far when there was more of it. The piece was titled, "Jack Kelly Too Rich," and he sounded frustrated with how things evened out...or didn't even out...in the long run.

Jack had seen his salary increase more than four hundred percent over the previous four years. He told the reporter his income, along with his health, had vastly improved since he had become well-known. "I'm disgustingly healthy. It's hard for me to even catch the flu anymore!"

So what was his problem?

As had, for the most part, always been Jack's way, he was playing things by the book. He'd become what he had wanted to become — a sought-after actor with a solid bank account, a good health record, and a lovely wife — but somehow, something stilled nagged at him. While the discourse was worded to sounded as if the issues were in how he handled his finances, the bottom line for Jack was not so much money but a sense of being caught in a rut.

"Before *Maverick*, I felt financially secure," he explained. "I was appearing in several motion pictures a year and somehow managed to save a little money because the income tax bite wasn't too high and I could live modestly yet indulge in extravagances without going into a hole." Well and good but — he continued, "Would you believe me if I tell you that now I find myself less able to save money than when I was averaging about $300 a week?"

The more money made, the more money spent. This was partly Jack's issue but there were other concerns. He went on to explain how since he had become well-known, there were costs associated with notoriety. Before he saw his check, ten percent went to his theatrical agent, five percent to his business manager, five percent to his publicist, five percent to miscellaneous deductions, and thirty percent to withholding tax...which doubled when tax time rolled around each year. Everything added up — nearly sixty percent of his check was gone without him seeing a penny.

"I don't want to mislead you," he hastened to add. "The tax bracket I now find myself in would make that except that my business manager has me making investments which give a shorter tax rate, but they're still risks — mostly real estate." His point? The money was being put away to insure his future would offer him more money and more security. After all, he was the boss of his money. He had hired the business manager. Still, because they were investments, they weren't always sure things and the money may, or may not, be there in days to come.

Since Jack Kelly had reached a level where he had expendable income to plan for his future, his day-to-day life was what caused him concern. "If there's an appreciable amount of money to be spent for necessities, like furniture, I have to sit down for hours with my business manager and figure out if I'll be able to pay it!" But business-related expenses, what about them? He explained, "This tax structure is such that I can give a $4500 party for business reasons without too much worry."

For Jack, in some ways the problem had become a big case of, "Watch what you ask for, you may get it." His career had given him what he'd only dreamed of but a few years before, and he was not complaining. He was trying to wrap his mind around how to handle the conundrum, and where he might find balance. He'd never been poor, not even as a child. He now knew what it meant to be rich by most people's standards, and with such a privilege came real adjustments.

Not the least of which was the pressure this status brought to his marriage. Jack and Donna had been husband and wife for three years. They were seen as one of the most solid, successful unions in the TV world but behind the scenes, things weren't always steady. Jack was a drinker; Donna was not. An occasional glass of this-or-that was her limit. Jack could put away the alcohol. When they got to this point, she was combative; he was retreating.

Bart Maverick was a ladies' man...literally part of Jack's job. And in his personal life, prior to marriage, he had not lived like a priest...his relationships with the opposite sex had been healthy and numerous. He was known to have a bit of a jealous streak, and had joked on more than one occasion Donna felt he often enjoyed his job too much. However, Jack was not known to be a womanizer, and everyone was aware he was deeply and sincerely in love with Donna. Their issues were most often driven by personality clashes.

Jack spoke to a reporter about how he balanced being a man attracted to, and attractive to, the opposite sex, while having a wife he loved waiting for him at home. He gave what he considered Donna's take on what at times became an issue. "She has a funny way of registering displeasure if she thinks a love scene is just a bit too realistic," he said, referring to his work. "After the show she'll say, 'Just for THAT, you can take me out to dinner.' But she never says just what THAT is."

Jack's coping method often involved alcohol, along with a tactic he employed when he didn't want to deal with difficult issues — he went inside himself and refused to interact. Donna, in turn, handled Jack with a forceful hand. One tactic didn't always take kindly to the other.

Nonetheless, Jack and Donna kept up appearances, and when questioned about their wedding anniversary, Donna told columnist Harrison Carroll she and Jack happily celebrated each year on two different days, October 14th and November 10th. They enjoyed honoring their first, hastily said, "I do," in Quartzsite, Arizona, and then their official church ceremony in Los Angeles.

Jack and Donna in a happy pose. PHOTO COURTESY JACK KELLY FAMILY PRIVATE COLLECTION

Organized around Jack's *Maverick* schedule, he and Donna planned any number of activities they hoped would secure their place in Hollywood infamy. With possibly too many irons in the fire, Mr. and Mrs. Kelly may have sabotaged their own success. One effort ran non-stop into the next. One new idea became another, and much was lost in the mix.

With Jack's political and social sense inherently important to him, he was naturally drawn to the upheavals of the day. He had no concern for race or color, was in fact color blind, a trait which wasn't necessarily considered fashionable. His friends ran the gamut.

One friend of both Donna and Jack, separately and together, was Sammy Davis, Jr. Sammy married Swedish-born May Britt at his Hollywood home above Sunset Strip on November 13, 1960. He was thirty-four and she was twenty-six. He was Black, converted to Judaism, and she was born a white Protestant. Though she had early-on stated she would retain her Christian beliefs, she went ahead with religious instruction and was accepted into the Jewish faith. Their wedding was performed by Rabbi William M. Kramer of Hollywood's Temple Israel. Frank Sinatra was Best Man, and Mrs. George Rhodes, wife of Davis' musical manager, was May's Matron of Honor.

May nearly missed her wedding. Due to a severe case of the flu, complete with a 103-degree fever, she was forced to bed only hours before the ceremony. She rallied enough to exchange vows with Sammy, but immediately afterward returned to bed. With a full house and a planned reception at the Beverly Hills Hotel, Sammy went solo. There was a 200-person guest list, including Jack and Donna, as well as Peter Lawford and his wife, sister of President-elect Kennedy, Mrs. Dean Martin, Peter Brown, Janet Leigh, Leo Durocher, Shirley MacLaine, Milton Berle, and Edward G. Robinson, Jr. An eclectic group. Davis was known for mixing crowds full of movers and shakers.

"After 'they went thata way sheriff,' the most used expression in early Western lore must have been the Sheriff's line, 'I want you out of town by sunset, mister.'"

JACK KELLY

CHAPTER ELEVEN

The End of the Road...
Should We Shoot The Horse?

Jim Garner's last official *Maverick* episode had aired in November 1960. He'd successfully broken his contract and as a result, the Powers That Be felt they had to create another character to take the co-star spot. Jack had made it clear he wasn't interested in pulling the full load, even if such a concept was considered.

Columnist Bob Thomas stated, "Jack Kelly is not mulling revolt but feels he is working 'in an area of servitude.'" Jack was a workhorse, and while his status as *Maverick*'s star had been secured, something in how he was treated still made him feel as if he wasn't really appreciated.

Still, he was sitting high in the saddle, and despite concerns, he held on. He played Brother Bart with conviction, as a gentleman gambler and a horseman — two points which hadn't changed since the beginning of the show. "In the situations in *Maverick*," he stated, "I could look awfully silly if I didn't know how to handle a horse. I could look foolish if I didn't know what I was doing." The last thing Jack wanted to do at this point was look foolish. He was leading the troupe, and he had every reason to want to do it right.

He didn't want to give his bosses any need to reconsider his place in the show, and he was careful as to how he handled himself. "I've got too much at stake. A broken arm or leg and my career might be wrecked." Jack had had enough physical concerns in his career to make this a lesson learned the hard way. He wasn't about to indulge in any mad gallops down the side of a mountain or any other such stunts, literally or theoretically. Even when he wasn't thoroughly happy with how the process worked, he knew it was best to go with the brass, rather than against them.

So Jack went along with the program when another family member was brought onto the scene to fill the void left by Garner's exit. Sean

Connery had originally been offered the role, but turned it down. Roger Moore, a relatively unknown British actor, also had concerns.

"I was very reluctant," Moore explained. "My contract with Warner Bros., I thought, was for movies with a possible option for TV. That was re-written and included TV as a mandatory part of the deal. I'd done long running TV series — *Ivanhoe* (1958) and *The Alaskans* (1959) — and

Jack as Bart Maverick having a chat with his horse. PHOTO COURTESY JACK KELLY FAMILY PRIVATE COLLECTION

there was a stigma attached back then. If you did TV you were a 'TV actor,' and couldn't cross to film. I'd managed to return to movies after *Ivanhoe*, not without a bit of a struggle I might add, and wasn't keen to go backwards again by doing yet more TV work." It was what it was, though, and, "In the end," he said, "I had no option but to take the job — if I wanted to remain employed. The carrot of further films was also dangled."

Roger Moore became part of the family, introduced onscreen as Cousin Beau, a Maverick from the other side of the pond. A quirky twist in all this showed up a handful of years later when Connery was offered, and accepted, the what-would-become-iconic role of James Bond...a role Roger Moore took on years down the road. Whereas the two men didn't share a role in *Maverick*, they both had a run as the one and only James Bond, and made the character their own.

Yet Moore was never able to make Beau Maverick his own. The episode in which he was introduced to the viewing public was predictably titled, "Bundle From Britain" in September 1960. That was the only predictable outcome.

This was an episode originally meant for Jack, under a different title. Everything was going as planned, and Jack was prepared to go to work. The complicated plot had him involved with a group of Irish patriots about to purchase a cache of stolen guns to help with a planned invasion of, of all places, Canada. The guns would be held for ransom in exchange for the freedom of the "Ould Sod."

Not long before they got down to the business of getting this story in the can, Jack had another accident. He fell and broke bones in his hand. This would without question slow production, and as had been proven early on, slowing production was not an option. Since Moore was new to the cast, it was decided this script would be given to him, and used as his premiere. The only major alteration, not including the title — true to the basic *Maverick* way of doing business — turned out to be a few tweaks to accommodate Moore's accent.

The press jumped all over early photos of Jack wearing a cast on his arm. Stories said he "got a couple of weeks off from filming." The reason behind this accident, however, has continued to be a point of speculation. Many reports indicate he had fallen "off the back porch of his home and broke a couple bones in his right hand." He was given time off from shooting because "the cast he had to wear on the hand was not photogenic."

Another story told of a party he and Donna hosted in their new home. Jack explained to Hollywood insider, Army Archerd, that he was helping her pick up after the bash. Archerd had, in fact, been at this party, along with other movers-and-shakers. Jack was carrying plates and trash to the kitchen when he tripped. He knew he was going down, and braced the fall with his right side.

Seemingly both stories were true, with the porch incident part of the party's clean-up afterward. Likely, the version told to Archerd was the spruced-up public account. During those days, Jack and Donna entertained many in the Tinseltown community. Jack drank his share each and every time, and an accident in this scenario was the result.

During an interview not much later with the show's newest co-star, Jack was in the wings, waiting to throw his usual good-natured barbs. He could never resist. As Moore talked to the reporter in the Warner Bros. commissary about his new role, Jack dryly interrupted. "He's the first Alaskan refuge we've had on the show." Jack referred to Moore's most recent part

Roger Moore in The Alaskans *(1959).*

prior to *Maverick*, as Silky Harris in Warner Bros.' defunct, *The Alaskans*. The show had been filmed in 90-degree weather, using fake snow, and on a Hollywood studio lot… nowhere near Alaska.

Jack continued lazily, "They really threw us a loser on this one." Moore responded by tossing an ice cube at Jack, dredged from his glass of tea.

In fact, Jack heartily supported Roger Moore as an equal part of the cast. The press was now calling Jack, *Maverick*'s "top gun," and he didn't appreciate the title. "It's something I can do without." He didn't want the pressure, and didn't want Moore to feel in any way as if he were pulling up the rear.

Jack had learned the hard way what it meant to play second fiddle. No matter that he and Garner had always been co-stars and shared equally high ratings, for at least the first two years of *Maverick*, Jack had never publicly been regarded as an equal. Behind the scenes, it seemed to remain unbalanced. *Maverick* was seen as Garner's show with the top brass.

"I know from personal experience that it's terribly discouraging..." he told a reporter about this artificially-created power struggle. "I banged my head against a wall for two years before the thing finally equalized itself."

He acknowledged, at least publicly, how he didn't feel as if it was any one particular person's fault. "It's just a peculiarity of the audience that it picks out one guy in shows like this and makes him No. 1." Jack didn't

Jack as Bart Maverick with Roger Moore as Beau Maverick, looking like happy family members.

want the same thing to happen to Roger Moore. For that matter, he didn't want it to happen to him yet again. "After all, we're both in the same show getting the same exposure. And I know how hard Roger is going to have to work. When this 'top gun' business comes up about two people who are working together...well, you know what can happen."

Moore recognized this from the beginning. Garner may have been physically gone from the production but his ghost haunted every corner of the set, and he, and Jack, continued to deal with the aftermath.

"Jim Garner was certainly considered the star of the show." There was no getting around this. "I knew I'd been brought in to replace him despite the producers saying otherwise." He and Jack got along well but their ability to mesh wasn't enough. "Jack was supportive, but I think we knew without Jim the show's popularity wouldn't ride as high."

A show with a previously-solid presence, *Maverick* was mightily struggling with identity issues. This had been a never-ending problem for Jack, but for Roger Moore, possibilities ended before they ever started. When Moore left the show prior to the 1961 season, never having gained a concrete foothold, it once again became obvious Jack would be in the middle of the upheaval which had become a regular part of *Maverick*'s production woes. Moore had stayed only one season, for any variety of reasons given to the public. The last script with him in it had him heading east, never to be heard from again.

Moore stated, "I argued and argued against doing the series. In the first place, I didn't like the idea of being a replacement for anybody. Secondly, I thought it would be risky for an Englishman to do a Western."

Why did he take on the role if he was convinced he wouldn't fit in? "I was one of many contract players back then, and we were all told to toe the line or we'd be replaced." He had signed on the dotted line. "I must say they were very convincing," he admitted. "They told me I wouldn't be a replacement, and *Maverick* wasn't really a Western. I was completely sold — for all of five minutes." By then, they had him under contract, a contract which he ultimately didn't fulfill. Moore had stories about how he and the directors gently butted heads.

"The scripts were okay," he said, "and some were quite funny in fact. They were very American of course, and I — as a Brit — was expected to deliver lines which I didn't believe any Englishman would. I argued with one director about saying 'I've been away...' or some such line. He wanted me to re-dub the line to say, 'I've bin away....'"

This didn't sound right to Moore. "I said, 'It is BEEN not BIN.' He said no one spoke that way. So I asked if he'd ever had Boston Baked

Bins before? They said I sounded too English. But was I not supposed to be playing an English cousin?"

Even though he had been assured he wasn't added "in place of" Jim Garner, Moore knew otherwise. "I think it's always a mistake to try and replace an actor in a well-known, long running TV series. That was brought home to me when the costumes I was given were all

Jack and Roger Moore in Maverick. PHOTO COURTESY SUSAN KETCHAM PRIVATE COLLECTION

embroidered with 'J Garner' — they'd just altered them slightly for my measurements."

There was one director, Les Martinson, and he and Jack liked to, as Moore put it, "wind up." He said Martinson and Jack wanted "to clown all the time." All of them generally enjoyed their time on set. "I got on very well with Jack," he commented, "and only have happy memories." They did socialize. "We played poker a lot — at Jack's house. We were all still Warner contract stars, and we had a few drinks," but Jack was always professional on set. Roger Moore said he never came to work drunk, or with any indication of having been drinking.

Drinking wasn't the exception in the industry, it was the norm, and not only for Jack Kelly. Another actor of the day said, "When I got to Hollywood, everybody drank. It was in the movies — you saw Bogart or Gary Cooper or John Wayne or any of those people, and they always had a drink in their hand in publicity pictures. It wasn't a drink of wine, it wasn't a drink of beer…it was a drink of whiskey. I did my best to emulate those guys. I was a heavy, heavy, drinker for many years…probably a fifth-a-day man. By the time I quit, I was drinking three quarts of whiskey a day, every day, seven days a week."

During this period, Garner's leaving didn't stop working conditions from being a continuing concern. Moore remembered, "We all decided, at one point, to take issue with unfair working hours. We went to the Screen Actors Guild, of which Ronald Reagan was president, to complain that we often started very early and worked right through, regardless of time, until late evening. The studio often took advantage. We obviously ruffled a few feathers as Warner Bros. brought in a time clock and insisted all actors clock in and out. We were furious. I refused to clock in, bought my own make up and ensured I was always in the wings ready to go when I was called. I'd hear the whispers around the set, 'He never clocked in today, he wasn't in make-up either.' But there I was ready to go."

Jack dealt with this in his manner of characteristic understated humor, nonetheless getting his point across. Moore explained, "A few days later, Jack suggested we have a game of soccer. We didn't have a ball, so Jack tossed the clock in and we used that!"

When Jack was asked by reporters why Moore had left, he simplified what was a much more complicated issue, while solidly backing Moore's explanation. "Roger was unhappy with the material," he stated. "He was English, and he was in a Western. And he didn't feel this was a sound combination — even with the drawing room comedy approach."

Jack also had a strong opinion on reviewers, and how they could, and did, affect the outcome of a show or a movie, and whether or not they were always on the mark. He applied his thoughts on where the show was at this point, and Moore's part in it. "Criticism can be most constructive if placed in the hands of the right critic," he stated. "But I've seen so many who write for themselves and not the reading public…. There are times when I'd give my marked poker deck to review their reviews."

Though Jack was sad to see Roger leave the cast, he couldn't help but be happy as the one left standing, the one who had survived each upheaval. "It's interesting to note that changing the actors hasn't lost us an appreciable amount of audience," he observed. "I would imagine there would be interest in the show no matter who is in it." The series did hold onto an audience and Jack's commentary gave evidence of the strength of the basic story idea which, no matter the changes in cast, had not altered since Day One.

The revolving door had become tedious, and Jack wasn't interested in having another relative introduced into the mix. He felt it would confuse viewers and "water down the show's potential." As had been evidenced, the show's potential was already diluted.

On the other hand, he still didn't want to do the show alone. "It's too much work. It affects every phase of my life, home and theatrical." The studio had made the effort worth his while to continue, renewing his contract with a sizeable salary increase. Quite possibly they realized their mistakes with Jim Garner, and Jack was reaping a few rewards. While he felt these financial perks should've been doled out years earlier, he was happy they were coming his way now.

The expected happened. To fulfill script obligations, yet a new brother — no other type of relative this time would do — was written into the storyline. The whole process had become a losing battle… nothing seemed to work anymore. The brass was trying not to have to shoot the already-injured horse. Despite Jack's misgivings about throwing in another family member, Robert Colbert was introduced as Brother Brent.

Colbert did a total of three shows for *Maverick*; one of them early on in a guest starring appearance as a bad guy, before being considered as a relative. He had a part in *A Fever In The Blood* with Jack, and for the most part was hired based on a similar physical appearance to Jim Garner. Jack had been hired partly because he and Garner had enough of a resemblance to make the idea they were brothers believable. With Garner having such an impression on the series long before Colbert showed up, trying to make Colbert fit into Garner's mold seemed almost an insult — not only to Garner's loyal fans, but most definitely to Colbert. Producers even had him wear a costume identical to one Garner wore early-on as Bret.

Colbert bristled, reportedly saying, "Put me in a dress and call me Brenda, but don't do this to me!" He seemed to feel like a second fiddle from the start. After only two episodes, his character disappeared and was never heard from again.

To be fair, producer's hands were tied when they originally added Brent. When Roger Moore's contract finished, there were still episodes left to be taped in Season Four. A solution was found, in part, with the new role filled by Colbert. Through all of these maneuverings, Jack stood firm, always patiently — at least in front of the cameras — waiting for his next relative to show up. Many press reports stated, only half-jokingly, it was a wonder somebody didn't think about giving him a sister.

Robert Colbert.

Colbert's unhappiness was no secret. His reason for giving up a lucrative and visible role when he left the show was at best nebulous, at least the reason he gave publicly. "I got a little lazy being a contract player," he lamented. "In many cases, a contract situation can cut interest and enthusiasm if the actor is not careful."

Jack gave another spin on Colbert's departure. "We originally planned on the two brothers again this year. But because of our earlier time — 6:30-7:30 Sunday nights instead of 7:30-8:30 — we'll probably be pre-empted from the air a number of times for sports specials and spectaculars. So Warner Bros., ABC, and the sponsors decided to go with only one of us. And it fell into my domain."

Maverick's next schedule rolled out with Jack Kelly as its only star. An Ohio newspaper put it this way, "The thirteen new *Maverick* shows for next season will have Jack Kelly as sole star, without any brothers, nephews, cousins, or even shirt-tail relations to spell him as in previous seasons."

The inevitable had finally happened. In front of the camera, things went on as if this were nothing more than another set of circumstances in Bart Maverick's life. Behind the scenes, the final unraveling had begun. Acting-wise, Jack was fine with the schedule and material, but continuing degeneration with the revolving cast door, and dropping viewer response, indicated no one knew anymore what to expect. The show had lost charm, and to a large degree, integrity. The whimsical, sometimes satirical *Maverick* was at one time ranked among TV's most popular series. With erosion in casting, scripts, time slots and disagreements amongst the TV front office brass, Jack knew there was only an uphill battle in front of him, at best. Problems seemed more than the show, quality or no quality, could continue to handle.

But he was nothing if not determined. When asked why he stayed, he replied simply, "Security." Jack needed to work, and whether or not *Maverick* was up to par wasn't the issue. He had a job to do, and it was his nature to do nothing less than his best with what was offered him. "I'm happy knowing I can provide for my family in the future." Speaking of "family" gave insight into what drove him. He was not only responsible for himself and his wife, but continued to contribute to the upkeep and lifestyle of his mother, and his brother, Bill, who stayed close to her side.

Jack was, however, worried that his name was still attached to an obviously faltering show. "I feel certain we're doomed to oblivion and it's not our fault," Jack said, unusually discouraged as he spoke to the press. "This show will go down in history as a milestone in TV production, sating the public appetite and adding up to everything symbolic that television means. The worst episode now is better than any we've made in the last five years." His voice was heavy with frustration. "But nobody knows we're on the air."

Nobody knew *Maverick* was on the air because reruns were shown each time behind-the-scenes maneuvers had to be figured out. Of all the *Maverick* shows still shown every week, some were new, but as many were reruns co-starring Garner, by now long gone. Jack felt reruns, changes in air time and cancellations in place of other shows bewildered the public. Many viewers weren't aware *Maverick* was still in production. In fact, some dared to ask what he was working on. Jack continued under contract to Warner Bros., and they knew he would stay with the show if it went on another season — but another season was seriously in question.

Even so, Jack defiantly held onto a fondness for the role which made him a star. He no longer worried, as in earlier times, about how movie audiences would identify him only as Bart. "It doesn't have the stereotyping characteristics that some other Westerns have," he explained. "I like doing this show. The stories are usually whimsical. The spirit infiltrates into the whole company and turns into a lot of camaraderie. It helps to make the work easier." Jack was back to his usual bright-side sentiment despite the changes and uncertainties in his life, and his career, in little more than a handful of years.

If the show continued, Jack had definite thoughts on changes to be made. "I don't want to work *Maverick* this way," he said, going on to explain. "I don't want them to use it as a filler like it is now. If it's renewed, I want *Maverick* to have a renaissance. It's embarrassing the way it is now."

He made suggestions, offered ideas, and his voice finally earned attention. When he had started, his commentary on *Maverick* script issues was barely recognized. His bosses felt he simply didn't understand such things. He was "just" an actor, and he was made to feel as if he shouldn't bother with the business side of the business.

Only after he became the lead, and writers had to ensure *Maverick's* voice fit him and him alone, did he get a serious audience with the Front Office. Jack felt as if he'd been shooed away one too many times, and figuratively raised his voice. He was tired of being ignored. Jack gave producers an earful as he tore a script apart from beginning to end, giving logical, well-thought-out, and smartly creative reasons for changes. He was angry, but he wasn't unreasonable. The writers and producers realized maybe Jack Kelly had been underestimated. His suggested script changes were implemented.

Jack felt as if he'd been forced to be blunt. "When I find out that it was my story that got the highest rating of the series, I think I have a right to make a stand."

And he made a stand, more and more. He was the only one still standing despite the never-ending stream of actors trying to take on the second *Maverick* role. The "two brothers" concept was the show's original cornerstone of success, but at this point, had turned into what well could be its ultimate undoing. Jack was now *the* face of *Maverick*, but since he no longer had a solid co-star to play off his character — as had been the case before — the show was slowly, painfully losing that winning edge. There was little Jack could do, no matter how well he acted.

This may have had something to do with a notation which appeared in Sheilah Graham's column in December, 1961. She reported that "Jack Kelly is waiting to hear what plans his Warner bosses have for him after he finishes his current thirteen *Maverick* segments." She went on to say, "He can't keep on doing them as the sole star. And he would just as soon star in some feature movies."

All this was true, and that a gossip columnist knew as much was testimony to how obviously troubled the show had become. There were concerns publicly floating around between Jack and his "Warner bosses." Yet barely a week later, Jack and Donna were seen cozying up to none other than Jack Warner at the premiere of *A Majority of One* (1961), starring Rosalind Russell, Alec Guinness, and Jack's friend, Ray Danton. This

Jack Warner with Mr. and Mrs. Jack Kelly at movie premiere while behind the scenes, Jack's contract was up for discussion. PHOTO COURTESY JACK KELLY FAMILY PRIVATE COLLECTION

was, of course, a Warner Bros. production...and Jack's appearance at the premiere was, of course, a promotional gig.

In an ad out not long before the show folded for good, Jack was seen on a billboard proclaiming, "Blonde or brunette? Inside straight or flush? These are Bart Maverick's problems." As if those were the only problems Bart Maverick, or Jack, faced. He still believed in *Maverick*. He had in many ways put everything he was into this one project; not always on purpose, and not always of his own doing, but Maverick had become his personal and professional shining star. If decisions were up to him alone, he would've been happy to run with the show without end. He stated with conviction, "I would do it for the rest of my life."

That wasn't going to happen, though, and Jack could see reality right around the corner. He was smart to keep his eye out, continually introducing other projects into his resume. As *Maverick*'s final demise became more of a certainty, Jack found himself staring down the barrel at another potentially exciting opportunity. He was in talks to star in a Warner Bros. movie, *The Devil In Bucks County*, with Simone Signoret. The film would be produced by James Woolf. In late 1960, James Poe had prepared a screenplay from the 1959 Edmund Schiddel original novel of the same name, and everything was on target to make the film.

The Devil In Bucks County was all the rage on current reading lists, a bestseller about "a sixteen-year-old girl from one of the fine families" who got mixed up with the town's aging delinquent. With a complex and complicated, rather dark, plot, filming would take place in Bucks County, New York. The project was a long time in development. While the screenplay was in process, Jack's name was seriously bandied about for the lead, but his wasn't the only hat in the ring. One notation stated, "Jack Kelly is another *Maverick* who would like to be free from the series for a while [sic] — long enough to co-star...in *Devil in Bucks County*...."

Signoret petitioned for Henry Fonda, but Glenn Ford looked more likely. In September, Hedda Hopper wrote that the producer supported Ford to star. His problem — he was working on *The Four Horsemen*, which wouldn't be finished filming before Christmas.

This made it necessary to look for another star, and Jack was still being considered. Ford's inability to make the schedule indicated that the movie was to have gone into production before the last few months of the year. A notation in Hedda Hopper's "Hollywood Today" for January 13, 1961, said, "Jack Kelly, so good in *Maverick* on TV, gets his wish; he'll go into *Devil In Bucks' County* with Simone Signoret under the direction of Peter Glenville." He responded, "I won't believe it until Jack Warner hands me the script."

There was a lot of behind-the-curtain finagling going on. *Maverick* was on a limited taping schedule, which meant if Jack were selected for the movie, he would have no filming conflict. Yet as the production continued on a shaky path toward a start, for whatever reason, Jack lost his chance. In February, Earl Holliman was said to have the part. A month later, reports announced Robert Taylor "wanted the role," and planned to film during his "TVacation" from his series, *The Detectives*. That didn't happen. The starring role of this movie was like a game of dodge ball, going from one actor to another, and then to another, and then back to an earlier possibility...now, Henry Fonda had the nod.

Ultimately, Horst Buchholz was cast and by March, preparations were underway, but with nothing solid to show for the effort. Warner Bros. offered producer James Woolf a million dollar contract for five years. He wasn't interested, saying, "I already have a million dollars." Instead, he wanted to be free to come and go as he pleased, promising to stay in one place for six months "while 'Devil' is shooting."

While this project waffled, Jack and Donna stole away for a long week-end to their "small but comfortable" home in Palm Springs, only to find a disaster had occurred in their absence. Vandals broke in and looted the place. Among items Jack reported as stolen were "one poker table, cards and poker chips."

An article about this same time mentioned how Donna was "still a bride to her doting husband. From all appearances it would appear as if they were still honeymooning." She avowed, "Jack wouldn't have it any other way. And whatever Jack wants he gets." If Donna had made this comment all on her own, she probably would not have called him "Jack." She never did.

Her husband and Warner Bros. had some issues of their own to iron out, away from the public eye. Late in that month, within "Short Cut," a column written by Dave Kaufman in *Variety*, Kaufman said, "Jack (*Maverick*) Kelly has to be notified by Warners by March 25 whether it's picking up his option." Jack sustained another injury in late March when he was thrown from his horse and received a cut over his eye which required attention but, real trooper that he was, he completed taping for the season on schedule.

There is no certainty as to what finally happened on the disorganized set of *Devil In Bucks' County* when all was said and done. Maybe producers couldn't decide on the right direction for the leading man. Most of the actors considered were a good deal older than Jack, though Horst Buchholz was a few years younger. Sheilah Graham reported in May 1961 Signoret was "disappointed over the abandonment" of the movie. The entire project had gone south. James Woolf claimed it was "too hard to cut." Possibly the subject matter was before its time; the public wasn't ready for such realism. Whatever the downfall, Sheilah Graham reported, "The project is abandoned by Warner Bros."

Another possibility for Jack was being ironed out. Universal-International wanted to borrow him from Warner Bros. to appear in *The Spiral Road* (1962). The press reported this development, but said Warner Bros. was "balky" at letting Jack go to the other studio for a sizeable role in this movie. He lost the chance.

Jack Kelly was set on transitioning into movies but until a solid option came about, he faithfully continued with *Maverick*. He was still contracted, had in fact been "re-opted" a month ahead of schedule for another year, and Warner Bros. was required to pay him fifty-two weeks of the year — a sweet deal, considering how most contracts were signed for forty weeks, with a twelve-week lay-off. Jack would be paid whether he worked or was on lay-off. And if the show went off the air, he would definitely be on lay-off.

He was still required to do promotion, yet he had leeway in what he was forced to do. For example, Kaiser asked Jack to perform an announcement gig in Las Vegas. He agreed...but only if they paid his regular fee — not simply made him do the work as part of his contract. They gave him what he wanted, and he did as they asked. He had mastered the art of negotiation.

Jack received a top-of-the-line salary, and his visibility remained high. He was a well-motivated hard worker, not one to rock the boat. If he didn't feel cornered, he was much happier with the status quo. When he felt he was in a solid place, there was little reason to take chances and potentially endanger his security. After all, Jack Warner had promised him two top feature films in the upcoming year.

Jack had so much work coming his way that anything he might have wanted to do away from the *Maverick* set was usually nixed before ever gaining steam. A chance to go to England to do "two BBC spex in London" landed in the trashcan because of his shooting schedule.

Later in life, talking of this pivotal time, Jack said wistfully, "I'd drive to Warner Bros., whistling." He commuted to work each day in his brand new Jeep, a vehicle supplied free-and-clear by the show's sponsor. "I was so happy," he continued, "and I thought *Maverick* was going to go on forever." A lot of his commentary was Jack giving well-rehearsed press-speak. He was always aware the show in those latter days was teetering on the edge of the abyss.

Still, and maybe because of this, Jack was treated better by Warner Bros. than he had ever been, and that Spring, he and Donna took their first vacation in two years. They chose to go fishing in Northern California. Something in his relationship with Warner Bros., though, felt like the calm before the storm. He couldn't put his finger on the problem but he knew something was brewing. Things were, on the surface, going swimmingly. While the show had only recently been considered on the skids, with literal talk that it was over, "a new batch" of episodes was being filmed, and Jack was in them all.

An unusual project showed up in early 1962. He was given the lead, as a contractual obligation, in a production originally titled, *Freedom and You*, produced by the United States Defense Department Armed Forces Information Services, and filmed by Warner Bros. Jack L. Warner was a retired reserve Air Force colonel, and he personally supervised filming. The producer was William L. Hendricks, a Marine reserve

Jack in a happy scene from Maverick. PHOTO COURTESY SUSAN KETCHAM PRIVATE COLLECTION

lieutenant colonel. Originally a "dramatic short film," this work was made to teach "troops the dangers of Communist ideology," and "show the contrast between the concept of American freedom and life in Communist states."

Despite the odd content — odd in an uncomfortable way due to the mix between Hollywood and the United States government — the cast

Jack in Freedom and You *(1962) which came to be widely known as* Red Nightmare *or* The Commies Are Coming.

was a veritable "Who's Who" of Warner Bros. actors. These were solid performers and visible faces — Jack Webb narrated, and Robert Conrad, Peter Brown, Peter Breck, and even a young Chad Everett, who went un-credited, were among the many cast members. Jeanne Cooper, who became well known as a soap opera star, played Jack's wife. Patricia Woodell, who played Jack's oldest daughter, Linda, soon signed to a Warner Bros. contract.

By January 1963, *Freedom and You* was seen on AFRTS — Air Force Radio and Television. Eventually, it was re-titled *Red Nightmare*, then *The Commies Are Coming*, and packaged for entertainment purposes. As of 1971, there were only 900 prints still in circulation.

His professional life was hopping more than it had ever been. Offers were flying his way but, as had always been the problem for him with *Maverick* — and even more, now that he carried the show — his part as Bart Maverick came first, and everything else was second…and only if the studio gave him time off. In July 1961, Jack was offered a fantastic opportunity to co-star in *PT Boat 109* (1963), based on John F. Kennedy's wartime adventures. Jack was reported to have his fingers crossed that his *Maverick* chores didn't conflict. They did, and he lost the chance. The movie was made with Cliff Robertson playing Kennedy, and Ty Hardin and Robert Culp in co-starring roles.

His nonstop schedule never stopped Jack from voicing his political and social opinions. He took every chance he got to speak out when he thought something needed attention. That July, he did just this when he discussed with the press the shaky state of international affairs, and how the public could be better protected from potential danger. He suggested that he was writing to President Kennedy to ask that bomb shelters be FHA-financed and income tax deductible. The news piece ended by saying, "Kelly is dead serious."

Jack was beginning to wonder if those "two top feature films" he had been promised by Jack Warner would ever come to pass. Not a word had been mentioned, even though *Maverick* was clearly not doing well. Jack was worried, and he optioned a play called *Westward No* for Broadway, in the event Warner Bros. didn't cough up any movies after he finished his series tapings for the season.

Even though things weren't always rosy with *Maverick*, Jack had received a wonderful new contract, and his future looked financially secure. He and Donna spent "fifty grand to tidy up their Hollywood hacienda." This was a large sum, yet they had to spend it because "the ground was slipping away from beneath them." Engineered retaining walls, city permits, and better-secured foundations were a required investment. Their home had been sinking.

News as to how things were going on the *Maverick* set was all over the map. A report came out stating that "Bill Orr's so hot over Jack Kelly's soloing of the new *Maverick* skein, there may be more than just the thirteen new ones promised," but this seemed nothing more than hopeful wishing, and promotional wording. In mid-December, Jack was said to be "waiting to hear what plans his Warner bosses have for him after he finishes his current thirteen *Maverick* segments." Feelings on how things were not progressing as promised just a few short months earlier were evident. "Jack can't keep on doing them as the sole star." This was what had threatened to kill the series in infancy, one actor being forced to carry the entire hectic production. The scheduling didn't work then, and wasn't working now.

By the Spring of 1962, despite all the effort Jack had put into making *Maverick* work without James Garner, and anything Bill Orr may, or may not have wanted, Erskine Johnson's one-line commentary was, "Jack

Jack as Bart Maverick, looking perplexed.

(*Maverick*) Kelly and Warner Bros. calling it a day." The whimsical, sometimes satirical *Maverick* had once been ranked among TV's most popular series. Not anymore. Not only the show was finished, but so was Jack's contract. The option on his contract was not renewed.

To his credit, Jack Kelly had taken the full ride, more than could be said for anyone else involved with the show, including James Garner. While Jack had his concerns, and had taken serious career hits — more than Garner, if truth be told — he had not aired his laundry, dirty or otherwise. In the end, Jack had come out on top in the *Maverick* heap with few ticks against his name or his image.

Still, everything runs its course, and *Maverick* was over.

"Even reptiles molt to accommodate growth."

JACK KELLY

CHAPTER TWELVE

Well, Howdy, Ma'am…
Ridin' Another Trail

In talking about Jack and his first wife, Donna, Jo, his second wife, said, "He was very much in love with Donna, and I think he was totally shocked when she divorced him. It happened about the same time *Maverick* was cancelled. And he did not…this is my opinion…he did not handle it well. It freaked him out because he was Catholic. He thought he'd be married forever, and she divorced him, and *Maverick* was cancelled, and I think it totally tore him up. Totally."

The end of Jack's marriage to Donna didn't coincide exactly with the end of *Maverick*. There were a few years between those two major life points. The demise of the show changed not only how Jack perceived his professional life, but also his personal life. For awhile, day-to-day seemed to continue much as it had before *Maverick* — only now, without a steady paycheck and regular work routine. These points had an effect on his marriage, though at first, the change was harder to notice.

Jack still received attention on the small screen and, occasionally, on the big screen. None other than the legendary Hollywood gossip columnist Hedda Hopper called him "an excellent camera subject." Someone who looked like Jack Kelly, with a wife as beautiful and well-known as May Wynn, and who was the brother of well-known stage and screen actress, Nancy Kelly, well, the likes of Jack Kelly could not go without attention for very long.

He saw this time as a potential for career transition and rebirth, and he hired an even better team to surround and promote him — he kept the same agent, and added another manager and publicist. Considered "handsome, virile, and talented," Jack wanted to shoot for second or third movie leads to get such parts on his resume; he felt this would be a better move than trying to always be the headliner.

"I just want to be in a good movie in a good part — not as the star. I feel that I have time enough to make that." His reasoning was solid — especially since the movie box office record of many TV stars had proven disastrous — and he was considered refreshingly modest for an actor. The general thinking in Hollywood indicated the public wouldn't go to the movies and pay to see someone they could see for free on television.

Jack, called "a better than average movie actor before he turned to TV," agreed. "I say let the Elizabeth Taylors and the John Waynes carry the pictures at the box office," he avowed, "but don't give the second or third leads to unknowns who don't mean a nickel at the box office. TV stars do have a name."

He was making a point — adding a now-bankable name like his to the cast of a movie could easily bring in secondary support which would help push a movie over the top…selling that many more tickets. He had a solid fan base and his fans would go see a movie, any movie, with his name on the marquee; of this he was convinced. The responsibility was his, though, to prove this. Now that *Maverick* was no more, he was careful in renegotiating his image.

Despite the face they put on for the media and the public, both together and separately, Mr. and Mrs. Jack Kelly's home life hadn't always been as rosy as they wanted people to believe. As *Maverick* made its way into the sunset, Jack was seen in what was a re-run of the Valentine's Day 1956 airing of "Kristi," an episode of *Jane Wyman Presents The Fireside Theatre*. The episode had him playing a businessman whose marital problems threatened his career. While Jack and Donna took great pains to not make personal issues public, this storyline could have mirrored what went on behind closed doors in their household. The original air date, on Valentine's Day, was sadly poetic.

The weight of his star power, mostly as a result of his success with *Maverick*, slowly began to wane. After *Maverick*'s last episode had aired in Spring of 1962, technically Jack still had nearly six years left on his Warner Bros. contract. While the contract mainly covered his work on the show, he had been bound to the studio for other ventures until they decided otherwise. The slow death of the show had been painful in a variety of ways.

Jack had seen the writing on the wall as it was being written, and upped his efforts even more to pick up guest spots, and find his seemingly ever-elusive "just right" movie role. He actively looked for good, solid film parts on which he could put his own unique stamp.

He hadn't wanted the show to end, and had stated loud-and-clear he would've done the series until the day he died. Jack knew *Maverick* had been exactly what his career needed at the time it arrived in his life, despite ensuing problems. The show had evolved into a trendsetter, in not only Western fare, but TV shows, in general. The gimmick had been intended to create ratings durability. It had done that, and much more, changing the face of how episodic TV would travel through future generations.

At the same time, that format managed to downplay any individuality which may have otherwise stood out. In the long run, this had power to do damage to the career of one, or more, of the multiple lead actors by limiting their access to variety in their career choices. The whole experience had been like playing on a teeter-totter. *Maverick* had made Jack Kelly an undeniable part of television history. He understood and appreciated this, knowing he had a place in the hierarchy of the Hollywood TV elite.

What he didn't appreciate, however, was how Warner Bros. suddenly dropped the option on his contract, coldly putting him out to pasture when the show stopped production. He had years left in their agreement but as *Maverick* bit the dust and faded into the sunset, Warner Bros. gave him his walking papers. Another show had been considered for Jack, one titled *The Deathmakers*, but details were never ironed out. "It was the biggest blow to my ego," Jack said. "It was like having Atlas' back broken."

He told the press he believed *Maverick* had been dropped because ABC "didn't own a very big piece of the show." He went on to explain, "I understand that the networks are more interested in promoting shows that they own a pretty good piece of. We just sort of slid out of position. Then there was some disenchantment that I'm not particularly in tune to between ABC-TV and Warner Bros. For years, Warner Bros. supplied most of the ABC material, and in the last year this little marriage kind of hit the rocks."

He was forced to reevaluate everything professional, and that fed into his personal life. One newspaper reported Jack was "permanently pink-slipped." He finished up some loose ends, and then suddenly had to review his options, once more reinventing himself. The press and promotional machines in Hollywood could be cruel, and quickly forget a headlining, star personality, almost faster than the ink could dry on the cancelled contract.

Jack was considered for a recurring role in a CBS show originally titled, *The Nurses* (1962). A few months later, "feelers were out" for him to take on a regular role in this series. Executive Producer Herb Brodkin had signed Ed Binns, and Jack was asked to join the cast. For whatever reason, he never did. The series ran for three seasons under the name, *The Doctors and the Nurses* with an extensive recurring cast list. This gave little chance for any of the actors to stand out, a problem with which Jack was already quite familiar.

There was a lot going on; Jack needed to figure out how best to direct his career — where exactly he should go next. He was offered "several series," but none appealed to him for any number of reasons. One option which may have come his way was another buddy sort of TV Western, titled *The Virginian*. James Drury, Jack's fellow actor in *Forbidden Planet* years earlier, ultimately took the title role. *The Virginian*, who never went by any other name, was a ranch foreman who worked side-by-side with Trampas, a ranch hand.

James Drury as The Virginian *(1962).*

According to Drury, "Jack may have tested for a role in *The Virginian*. I think he did a screen test to play Trampas, which he certainly could've played very well. Doug McClure was ideal. They said about seventy-five actors tested for the part of *The Virginian*. I think about an equal number tested for Trampas. It turned out that Doug and I were the ones that were chosen." Whether Jack got anywhere in the line-up and was decided against, or chose not to take an offer…this is unknown. He likely would not have accepted a part which was not a lead after what he gone through to get equal billing for his role in *Maverick*.

Another possibility which "didn't happen" turned out to be a Broadway show he co-wrote with Donna. They were always writing together, and this was one more item added to a list of opportunities which didn't materialize.

What did come about — Jack sat down with his agent, business manager, and press agent to carefully plan out where to go next…a meeting where Jack decided he had to do Broadway. A trip at this point to New York was meant as a "way station" on his ongoing career path, not a forever move. He would use Broadway as a circumspect tool to pad his way back to Hollywood, presumably in greater glory than when he left.

Jack could have stuck it out in Tinseltown, doing a rash of second-bill films, TV guest shots, commercials, and voiceovers — all offered to him, and all easy catches. Yet while he wasn't discounting such work, he believed taking his talents to Broadway had great potential to better

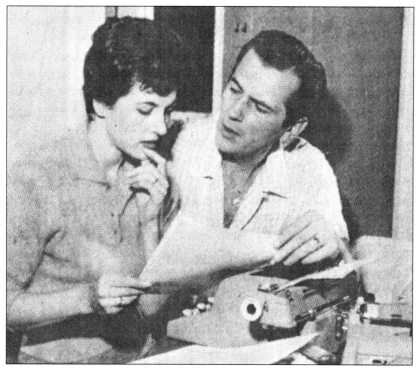

Jack and Donna writing together. PHOTO COURTESY JACK KELLY FAMILY PRIVATE COLLECTION

propel him forward. Staying in Hollywood, taking only what was offered simply because it was work, not being aggressive in reaching for starring roles — this would keep the paycheck coming in but wouldn't help in the long run. He wasn't interested anymore in skating along to see what happened next. He wanted to hold out for enduring stardom.

While he formulated his next move, Jack never stopped working. He did take on some of those incoming offers, mostly for TV guest roles to capitalize on his still-hot name. This was also part of his plan, hedging his bets to see what would stick. He said, "I stayed in town for awhile" hoping things would change, "but the offers I got were for exploitation pictures and second-rate television shows. I'd had enough of that." He had a long history with "B" grade movies; none of them had been his ticket to higher places.

Jack wanted something different, something startlingly different, and he wasn't willing to settle for second best. "I didn't want to become the King of the Bs, like Marshall Thompson. As for guest shots, well, there's fair money in that. But I wanted to work into better things. I was getting beat out for the movie parts I really wanted — the top supporting parts in the Class A films — by Gig Young."

Gig Young was born Byron Ellsworth Barr, and Jack seemed fixated with his career, often holding Young up as an example of what he was looking to become. By 1942, the-actor-named-Barr was under contract with Warner Bros., but his name was getting him nowhere. Warner Bros. decided to re-name him, christening him after a character he'd played in a recent movie, *The Gay Sisters* (1942). Byron Ellsworth Barr became Gig Young…and twenty years later, Jack was comparing Young's career to his own. The irony — Jack was married to a woman who got her stage name in exactly the same way. The real kick — Gig Young's success may have been solid, but not outstanding in the long run.

Jack enjoyed many away-from-the-camera hobbies. He had already proven he could handle a horse, and he loved to sail. He built radios and ship models, and tinkered with old cars. Everyone knew of his golf prowess; golf was his true love. As he figured out his next career move, as usual, Jack kept one foot on the golf course…no matter what else was, or wasn't, going on in his life.

Golf was his sanity, and being on the golf course was his sanctuary. His father, long before Jack was born, had been a caretaker for the greens at Vesper Country Club in Tewksbury, Massachusetts. Maybe Jack, Jr. learned his love of the game from his father, or he picked it up in his early adult years. Either way, there was rarely a weekend when he wasn't playing — and even then, some was for the cameras, particularly for charity events. These were promotional efforts he courted and eagerly welcomed.

The Palm Springs Golf Classic was held January 31st — February 4th of 1963. Bob Hope was honorary Mayor of Palm Springs, and he joined Jack and 382 other amateur golfers, including Lawrence Welk, Jim Garner — with whom Jack continued a cordial if not intimate relationship, Phil Harris, and Buddy Rogers. Billy Maxwell was the defending champion, heading up the 128 pros entered in the ninety-hole tournament.

Still, Jack always had to walk off the course back into reality, and he needed to make some decisions. What would he take on as his next career move? He got serious about getting out of Hollywood and, along with Donna, took necessary steps to organize an extended trip to the east coast. If he stayed in town, in such an environment, he felt he would've been forced to take work to have work, simply to be seen as still a part of the system. He was certain he would be severely limited in the long run.

Jack in front of one of his hobbies. PHOTO COURTESY JACK KELLY FAMILY PRIVATE COLLECTION

His choice to go on the road was not based solely on financial need. He claimed he had enough money in the bank to, as he put it, "lock my front door and never come out and live comfortably for four years." Clearly, though, he was paying close attention to his financial matters if he could specify exactly how many years his safety net covered. His decision focused on what Jack knew well to be the Hollywood culture. He had been a part of this world for most of his life — not only with his own career, but also as he watched how the system worked for his sister, Nancy. Jack Kelly knew how Tinseltown operated.

He was aware if an actor lived in Hollywood and didn't take offered work for any length of time, he eventually stopped getting offers, and was considered a has-been. Some were already trying to make Jack out as such.

For this reason, he and his "brain trust" — agent, business manager, and press agent — decided it best for him to change his environment. Being at work away from Hollywood for awhile could only benefit his future. He chose to take the long route to New York, stopping along the way for starring appearances in local theaters across the country. This was considered the best decision for the performer he had become.

Jack needed to re-establish himself as a Class A actor, this time without *Maverick*. He didn't think this could happen if he stayed in Hollywood, where everything he did was held up against his role as Bart Maverick. Even worse, around town he was considered an unemployed actor who'd recently been dropped hard by a major studio. Jack Kelly had every intention of beating out Gig Young for those parts in which Young currently took the lead. However, to succeed, Jack had to follow a strict plan.

He had mixed feelings about how everything had panned out. "I miss *Maverick* and I don't miss it," he said. "We had some bad luck. We sustained the ratings but there was some mix-up. I enjoyed playing the part, but there comes a time when you have to step out into the deep end and find out if you can swim. I decided the best way to do it was to work as hard as I could in stock."

Jack's bottom line — in his words? "I decided to become relatively unavailable [in Hollywood] by setting up a summer stock tour." For over five months after *Maverick* ended, Jack lived on the road. His first stop was in Milwaukee where he starred in *The Moon Is Blue* at the Swan Theater. The plan was to arrive a few days ahead of schedule to begin rehearsals with the resident company. This would become his usual routine as his tour continued down the road. "I'll know my lines by rote when I get there," he told a reporter before he left Los Angeles.

But Jack hadn't appeared in a stage production for fourteen years. Would he be rusty before a live audience? His last experience had been in 1948 when he was seen in *Time of Your Life* with a Los Angeles little theater company.

Jack proved acting on a live stage was an inherent Kelly skill. He played to packed, delighted audiences. From there, he went to Minneapolis with the same play, and then Chicago for *Under the Yum-Yum Tree*.

By September, he was in Ohio at the Canal Fulton Summer Arena in the "adult sophisticated comedy," *The Moon Is Blue*. This was called a "spicy show." Performances were held Tuesdays, Wednesdays, Thursdays, and Sundays at 8:40 each evening, with curtains going up at 7 PM and 10 PM on Friday and Saturday. Jack was working a non-stop six-night/day schedule.

This was a good role for him. In this part, Jack was "taking one more step toward stabilizing his career in the vein of sophisticated light comedy." He had returned to his roots in one more way — the man who years ago began as "comedian Jack Kelly" was once again working live audiences with his light-hearted talents. Jack said in the local paper, "I have always seemed to gravitate toward this area."

Reviews said, ""Fine acting characterizes this production. Jack Kelly, playing the lead, contributes a splendid, energetic performance, displaying real talent for this type of part. If any criticism were [sic] to be ventured it would have to be along the lines of being too energetic. The character portrayed might be a mite more plausible if it were played just one key lower. But, not withstanding, Jack Kelly adds a most enjoyable chapter to the ever-lengthening history of the playhouse." Jack worked alongside local actors, taking accolades and curtain calls with them without allowing for any special nods to his nationally-recognized star status.

Since he carried a big TV name and was fresh off the small screen as co-star in a hit TV show, Jack was seen as quite a catch for regional theaters. He was instantly recognizable and an extraordinary draw, an asset to be mixed in with homegrown talent. He had decided to play the entertainer's game with his own rules and essentially, turn it upside-down. Rather than be a mid-size fish in a big pond, Jack Kelly rewrote his career by becoming, for a time, at least, a big fish in the smaller pond… and happy to reap the rewards.

Jack discovered early on he had quite a knack for entertaining, making people laugh, and was a whiz with accents and dialects. Over the years, he used these talents not only for professional gain, but personal enjoyment. Jack's family, including Donna and, in later years, his daughter, Nicole, would speak of the fun he had tricking people, fooling them with accents and making them laugh. He'd phone a friend or family member and impersonate a foreigner, with the person on the other end none the wiser. Or go into a prolonged speech using an unusual dialect in an impeccable imitation of the real thing. Jack Kelly had come out of the womb as a true-blue entertainer.

These talents served him well as a live performer. From his earliest remembrance, he was intimately aware of how the profession, from almost every angle, operated. To take on a persona not his own was second nature. From this vantage point, Jack knew he would be able to go on to New York City, and Broadway, and "meet people and see what would happen."

At this juncture, Jack felt he had "discovered an intellectual intensity in his portrayal of satirical roles" while doing *Maverick*. Despite the serious, even melodramatic parts he had taken on in films and other TV shows, Jack always shined brightest when he played lighter characters.

Though *Maverick* was no longer in production, it had gone into syndication. This allowed Jack's visibility to experience barely a blip — different, yet constant. This helped his efforts to make his place in the entertainment world look more like he was expanding his horizons rather than saving his career. Jim Garner made a good point in a 1961 article when, speaking of his own visibility, he said he had made sixty *Maverick* shows, "which is the equivalent of thirty movies." Any actor with as many movies under his belt would be recognizable to most any viewing audience…and Jack had starred in more episodes than Garner.

Jack remained in front of the public eye on a regular basis, and the show's dedicated viewers continued to watch and enjoy him, even in re-runs. With his popularity holding bright, Jack could pick and choose theater roles in which he was most interested. Regional audiences were delighted at the opportunity to see a national TV star perform in their home town.

Able to select parts at will, Jack gravitated toward sophisticated comedy or, as one article called it, "froth with finesse." He was drawn to humor with an intellectual appeal. The story in *The Moon Is Blue* emphasized "female vulnerability," an area in which Jack had always excelled — both off-screen as well as on.

The next month, Jack was in Anderson, Indiana, with his wife, guest-starring in the lively comedy, *The Pajama Game*, with the Madison County Dramatic Players. There was a "forty-member cast opening at the Geeting Summer Theatre" in a "colorful comedy" with "twenty-two speaking parts." In addition, there was a twelve-member chorus and six dancers. This was, to date, the largest cast show ever undertaken by the Madison County Dramatic Players. Jack played the "funny, dancing and singing Hinesy." One article announced proudly how the troupe's "dauntless" director, Jon Walker, "obtained the services of Jack Kelly — the Bart Maverick of TV fame, no less!"

Skipping across the country and using his name to create a buzz proved a smart tactic. Jack and Donna had a house to themselves for their stay in town as part of their contract, including a pool for personal use. Donna, left to her own devices most of the day while Jack worked, enjoyed that pool. Jack gave the show his all, as he did everything he put his name into, and he was a local hit.

His wife was a hit, as well, especially with the press who were given extraordinary access to the glamorous Mrs. Kelly. When a reporter, Jane

Heritage, visited her one chilly morning — Jack had already left for the theater — Donna answered the door in a yellow-flowered negligee. She looked at the pool as she let Ms. Heritage in and said wistfully, "No swimming today!" Ms. Heritage said Donna was "naturally olive-skinned with dark good looks." Her skin tone was deepened from sunning, golfing, and swimming. Donna wore no make-up that morning, except "a slight touch of coral lipstick," she "moved with slow grace," and was "poised and gracious."

The reporter was taken with Donna. She continued her praise, saying Donna's hazel eyes were "large and serious" and her "dark hair waved becomingly in a length just right for down-or-up hairdos." The two women chatted over coffee about "politics, pets, housework and even a little bit of gossip."

Donna told Ms. Heritage she had been engrossed in her acting career in 1956 when Jack's name kept popping up around her. They had a mutual friend who continually insisted she go on a date with him. She finally agreed.

Jack and Donna out for the evening.
PHOTO COURTESY JACK KELLY FAMILY PRIVATE COLLECTION

This was Donna's shortened, for-the-press version of their courtship, practically by rote the same one she had given to any member of the media over the years. Almost no detail changed. She went on, talking of their life of wedded bliss. "We're serious about our marriage. Jack likes being married and he wants me with him. When other wives wonder how I'm permitted to go on location with him, I explain it's because Jack has requested it — it's not a matter of being permitted to — it's a matter of the husband's wishes."

Ms. Heritage asked about Donna's transition from actress to wife. "It wasn't easy." She'd had a drama coach — the same one who had coached

Frances Farmer years earlier — and she was serious about her acting. Donna said, "My coach told me I must learn to unwind and not take my part home with me. He said I approached acting like Farmer had in my absorption. He considered Farmer a great actress with potential not realized because she had not been offered good vehicles."

The conversation continued around many topics, and the two ladies chatted for some time. The reporter left feeling as if she'd spent a great morning with a friend, rather than simply doing an interview with a big-name stranger. This was another case of Jack and Donna keeping up appearances.

As Jack went from city to city on his stage tour, he felt confident about how things were progressing on his road to renegotiated success, but he knew he had a way to go to reach the point where he'd be in charge, fully able to pick and choose his best projects. "This stage experience will help me in the long run, financially."

He and Donna had a life which required an ever-growing paycheck. That he no longer received those regular earnings had not escaped his notice. A solid salary would've otherwise kept them in their current lifestyle without issue. He had to pay his bills, and though he wasn't broke by any means, he never wanted to be. "My wife and I like the nice things in life," he admitted to a reporter. "We're not spendthrifts and our home is not the fanciest out there, but it's beautiful. I figure it will take me twenty years to furnish it the way I want."

He gave an example, showing how his mind ping-ponged between career aspirations, material concerns, his marriage, and his ability to successfully make them all happily come together. "Take our silverware. We have only two place settings now, because the silverware we like costs $150 per place setting. I'd like to get two more but I can't afford it now. But ultimately I'll have twenty-four place settings."

Some might believe such concerns were driven solely by Donna and what may have been her expensive tastes. While they were both part of the equation, there were other points at play in this story. Jack Kelly was raised in a family which forever aspired for more. He was brought up by a mother who had looked to have the better things in life. Nan Kelly thought it crucially important to be able to afford the most current and best items in her home, as well as the best home. For as long as Jack could remember, this had been, for his mother, a major indicator of success…a philosophy which transferred into his way of thinking.

Crisscrossing his way around America, Jack played one local theater after another, building a resume completely in contrast to his recent history as a Western TV star. He never once forgot his plan, even as he enjoyed each moment of the new experience. Everyone who knew him or crossed his path could tell he had a plan. When he finally reached New York, he knew where he needed to go first.

Jack got to Broadway, post-*Maverick*, to take on a highly-visible spot in an area of the industry already known to him and his theater-savvy family. The last time he'd been on Broadway he was only ten years old, appearing with Ethel Barrymore in *The Ghost of Yankee Doodle*. Jack was a big boy this time, and he visited several Broadway producers. One was Kermit Bloomgarden, a successful industry veteran.

Sidney Kingsley was casting *Night Life: A New Drama*, to be produced by Bloomgarden, and Kingsley felt Jack perfectly fit a major role. He also understood how Jack's name, along with other TV stars added to the cast, would boost ticket sales. Jack felt the prestige of a Broadway play would pump up his adult theater resume and put a brand new shine to his image.

When he was introduced to Kermit Bloomgarden in the producer's office, Bloomgarden said in a confused voice, "Who are you?"

Jack almost stuttered. "You must know me — a top producer like you must keep in touch, and you must know that I was the star of a big television show, *Maverick*."

Bloomgarden had honestly never seen *Maverick*. He had honestly never heard of Jack Kelly. It wasn't a slight to Jack; this was evidence of Bloomgarden's taste in entertainment, and he didn't spend his time on television. He told Jack his son was a big fan and ardent follower of TV Westerns. As Jack sat in front of the other man, on the edge of his chair, waiting for a verdict on something he'd already thought was a done deal, Bloomgarden picked up the phone. He called his son to ask if he'd ever heard of an actor named Jack Kelly, or for that matter, a show called *Maverick*.

"I didn't hear what the boy told his father," Jack recalled, "but Bloomgarden offered me the part right after he hung up." Jack snagged prominent billing and a $2000-a-week paycheck, playing the part of Neil in *Night Life: A New Drama* from October to December 1962. Produced at the Brooks Atkinson Theatre, the play featured Neville Brand, a man with whom Jack was well-acquainted — "Al Capone" on TV's *The Untouchables* and the always wise-cracking Reese on *Laredo*; Carol Lawrence — Robert Goulet's wife; Barry Newman who starred on TVs *Petrocelli*, and a host of other recognizable names. Reviews called *Night Life* "a tintype about good and evil," and said, "Neville Brand and Jack Kelly, two imports from television, represent ruthless force and disenchanted respectability."

All in all, Jack's strategy had proven to be astute. The play didn't make a big splash; in fact, it was something of a flop, but the Broadway stint took him out of the Hollywood mess, a mess he was certain would have been professionally unhealthy. Jack had stayed in the game by going east. He was still an actor, and he was still acting. He was working on his terms, not amidst the dog-eat-dog life which he was sure would have sunk him if he'd stayed in California right after *Maverick*.

The move gave him a platform from which he could be re-evaluated as star material for quality movie and TV roles. This changed his known image from being Bart Maverick, to being a versatile actor of many types of roles, one of them which had been Bart Maverick. By saving face, Jack made himself a candidate to vie for the parts he wanted, not simply the parts others decided he should take on.

He was also part of a growing Hollywood "fad" of the times. A number of TV actors were courted by Broadway. Producers felt a Hollywood name was an instant draw, and while a name associated with Hollywood might not make a success, the association gave it a leg up on those without recognized cast names. And Broadway actors saw the process moving the other way…many went to Hollywood to find their way into episodic TV. Based on this common belief, if a name became known in the west coast entertainment world, they had a higher standing to return to Broadway as a bigger draw, able to demand better parts.

Since Jack Kelly had grown up in the stage world, it only took those few months for him to become "hooked" on the life again. Having been raised as a child model and stage actor, this was his background. He had no problem picking up where he had left off, despite the years in between. After he had the chance to experience Broadway as an adult, he was once more enamored, and returned repeatedly over ensuing years. Broadway was different now for him, namely because this time he, not his mother, was at the helm, directing his path. He no longer did only what he was told to be allowed to follow in his sister's footsteps.

"It was like getting religion — I never had a direction before in my life. I always drifted but now I have found something I really want to do." Jack had always been torn between the film world, TV, and bright lights of the live stage, trying to decide which felt most comfortable and offered him the greatest opportunity. He was now at a crossroads where one, or all, of those paths could take him to the next level as a top-of-the-line actor, and he was determined to keep every avenue open.

Jack still had no intention of taking on just any role. He was doggedly determined not to ever again slide into the world of "B" grade movies, a slide which would've been easy, possibly the most lucrative path he could take. With his experience, and everything he'd achieved, his name easily led the red carpet of the "B" movie kingdom right to his front door. This wasn't the type of success he wanted, though.

"Money still talks, but these days you have to increase the volume."

JACK KELLY

CHAPTER THIRTEEN

Which Way Does He Go?…
Reading The Sign Posts

When he returned to California, Jack was again able to feed his addiction to golf, and the golf course was the perfect place to nurture his love of the game while keeping his name in the spotlight by playing for charity. He was part of the Bing Crosby Golf Tournament in Monterey along with many other actors, including Bob Cummings, Ray Bolger, Gordon MacRae, Dean Martin, Ray Milland, Dennis Morgan, Donald O'Connor, his ex co-star, Jim Garner, and Jack's good friend, Desi Arnaz. Upon listing this line-up in her column, along with even more names, Hedda Hopper tongue-in-cheek commented about Tinseltown, "We're going to be mighty short of men." They all returned to Hollywood, though, and the industry suffered no loss.

Almost everything Jack did, he did with an eye toward staying gainfully employed. In early January 1963, his management announced he was being "metromanced," along with Clint Walker from *Cheyenne* fame, to co-star in a new series called *Boom Town*. This one would be modeled after the 1940 movie of the same name, with the two men taking on the Clark Gable/Spencer Tracy roles. This would have been another intriguing addition to Jack's resume, but the project was ultimately scrapped.

Another benefit in which Jack took part was the Arthritis and Rheumatism Foundation Telethon. It ran from 12:01 AM to 6 PM on Sunday, February 10th of 1963, and included many big names from TV and film. Besides Jack, the likes of Mickey Rooney, Eddie Albert, Bob Hope, Bob Newhart, and Don Rickles were featured. He was keeping his name in lights along with the best-known of stars.

He refused a guest spot on *The Ed Sullivan Show* which would've required him to do a spoof on *Maverick*. He respectfully declined, saying he wanted to stay with "modern clothes parts." He'd had enough Westerns, at least for awhile, and wasn't in the mood to make fun, even in jest, of a genre which had essentially created him.

As Jack said, his calculated efforts seemed to have "done the job." His words, "I've been getting stacks of scripts. I've got a chance to read for the lead opposite Judy Holliday in the big musical, *Hot Spot*. That would really be great for me. It would really fix things up." This was another Broadway play and though he could've never known then, it's good he didn't get the role. The play bombed with the first reviews, and the only notable name attached seemed to be Ms. Holliday's. If Jack had been with her, he would've gone down with that sinking ship.

The bright lights of the stage were always there for him now, even when screen opportunities lagged. Jack *really* enjoyed live theater, and this fact created an internal struggle. The stage was in his blood. He wanted to return not only because of potential career opportunities, but because he genuinely loved being in front of an immediately-reactive audience. But this was at the heart of where the resistance lived within him. Jack had learned a few unexpected lessons amidst his road trip east.

While he loved bright lights and live audiences, his personal preferences proved he didn't want to be on the east coast without defined work anymore than anywhere else. When that became clear, he packed his bags and returned to California. "I must say, it's better to be unemployed in Hollywood than in New York. The climate and social activities are on your side. In the East, it is cold and expensive. I was spending $1,200 a month for a hotel suite."

And that was only in New York. Expenditures — lodging, transportation, and other costs — were variables when he was on the road, more than when he was on his home turf. Jack realized while the lure of the stage was one he would often need to chase — and he did, returning to the road and the regional theater circuit year after year — the full-time lifestyle of the west coast better suited his personality, his pocketbook, and his contacts.

Once Jack was again professionally resettled in Hollywood, word got around he would star in David Susskind's "TVersion" of Arthur Koestler's *Darkness at Noon*. He had been offered "a spec" by Susskind while on Broadway doing *Night Life*. He had to keep his lips sealed until there was certainty the project would get off the ground. The controversial novel was published in 1940 and set two years earlier, during the purges of Stalin's Russia, with an anti-Stalin storyline. The project went through various Hollywood iterations over the years, most notably when openly-active Communist Party member and screenwriter, Dalton Trumbo, claimed to have blocked it from becoming a feature length film during his heyday. There is little knowledge of the evolution behind this TV movie but whatever happened, the project never came to fruition.

One addition to his resume was initially created as a ninety-minute TV special for Warner Bros. prior to the revocation of Jack's contract. As a "TV film," the project was first intended as a pilot, with the title, *Bomb Aboard — Call The FBI*. Jack was to star, with Andrew Duggan, Ray Danton, and Kathleen Crowley, who Jack knew well from her guest-starring spots on eight episodes of *Maverick*. This was considered the first non-documentary TV film to "receive an official assist" from, and the cooperation of, the FBI. Some scenes were shot on location in the FBI building in Washington.

Since *Maverick* was clearly gone, this pilot, *Bomb Aboard — Call The FBI*, looked to initially be one of the studio's attempts to get Jack right back into a series, and fill at least some of the remaining time on his contract. The creators wanted the feel of a Dragnet-style docudrama, with the action underscored through off-camera narration by William Woodson, a man who had built a career based on his bold, powerful voice.

Bomb Aboard — Call The FBI didn't make it in original format as a pilot, TV special, or TV movie. The production languished, with an overseas abbreviated version released under the title, *FBI Code 98*, which came about only after extensive re-work. One review said this was "a story based on the FBI's successful efforts to prevent a sabotage attempt." In full production as early as February 1962, there was no theatrical release until January 1963 — first in France, then in Finland in February, and soon thereafter in Sweden in the same month.

April 1964 rolled around before the production hit the United States. Even then, things were running late. The original timeline had the now "90-minute special" destined for ABC-TV in the fall of 1963 though, when it did finally arrive, promotion was calling it a movie. By the time American audiences had their chance to see it, what was left was a seriously watered-down version. The plot concerned a mad, disgruntled bomber using heightened knowledge of electronics to stay one step ahead of detection.

Posters announced, "You are looking at the hard-hitting, hand-picked heroes of the FBI moving into action. The next time you see them they will be in the bomb-ticking middle of the deadliest of all manhunts!" In early U.S. releases, as a movie, *FBI Code 98* was a second billing at drive-ins. Later in the year, there was circulation on television. Jack's name, along with Kathleen Crowley's, usually got top billing.

With such a checkered and harried past, the surprise was in how this effort ever reached a single screen. Reportedly *FBI Code 98*, along with 1959's *The FBI Story*, served as the basis for the FBI crime drama series which started about a year later, and did become a big hit.

Jack had a lot of work, loose ends and new projects, and he tried hard to consciously guide his career, now that he was independent of

Jack on left in FBI Code 98 *(1963)*. PHOTO COURTESY SUSAN KETCHAM PRIVATE COLLECTION

direct studio intervention. He felt he had a solid foothold in the industry. His name was well-known, and he was seen on television on an ongoing basis.

Still, he seemed to forever try to find his niche. A private-eye script titled, *Shadow on 59th Street*, was written by scriptwriter and author, Jay Simms. Simms had done a lot of work on the Western show front, and this piece was slated to become an independent movie starring Jack and, again, Clint Walker. Simms had earlier written film scripts in other genres, including science fiction and pseudo-horror. Jack and Walker had at times shared side-by-side movie sets, and became friends. They intended to not only head this cast, but also produce the feature film…which, once again, never made it to the screen.

Things really began to unravel in Donna and Jack's marriage in 1963. He surprised more than a few people when he showed up unannounced at Florida's Six-Gun Territory, a Western theme park outside Silver Springs on Highway 40. This was a trip Donna seemed to know nothing about, even many years later. The park opened February 2nd of that year, and Jack's visit was made on Valentine's Day.

Ad for FBI Code 98 *(1963).*

Public Relations Director, Frank McDowell, claimed to have no knowledge of Jack's plans to be there ahead of time, and told the press he "just dropped in, unannounced and unscheduled." When he was directly asked, Jack's cagey response was to say he was there "to see a friend." No details, no explanations, and no hint of the friend's identity — male or female. However, his being in Florida without his wife on Valentine's Day, not at home in California with her, was telling. As everyone knew, Jack and Donna rarely traveled without each other, and certainly not at such a romantic time of the year.

Another potential golden professional opportunity visited Jack early that year. Called "redoubtable" by Vernon Scott, Jack starred with Broderick Crawford as an insurance-investigating team in *Shadow of a Man* (1963), a segment of NBC-TV's *Kraft Mystery Theatre*. This was intended as a "test film" for a series. Both men were considered "scarred veterans of the telewars." The story was distantly related to James M. Cain's book/movie, *Double Indemnity*, and called "a cut above average." Jack took on the character modeled after the MacMurray role, and Crawford had the Edward G. Robinson part. The female lead was played by Beverly Owen in what was, to some degree, originally Barbara Stanwyck's role.

When Jack was asked why he wanted to return to television, a medium which brought him great visibility and great turmoil, his response was equally confused. Being asked this question by the press showed how far this work went to becoming a reality. Jack had already had a number of near-misses for TV shows, all which didn't get far enough off the drawing board to attract much public attention.

In answer to the question about reasons for doing TV again, Jack said he couldn't stand working fourteen or fifteen hours a day, yet in the next breath, he added, "I'm a glutton for work. I get an emotional reaction to TV which dictates my pleasures and my excitements."

He smiled like a kid, and to the reporter, he looked as if they were sharing a secret. Jack glanced around to see if anyone else was listening, then whispered, "Do you have a dog you like? Well, I missed TV like I missed a friendly dog. The friendship, warmth, and growth I get from the medium is not the same thing I get under social circumstances."

The *Double Indemnity* storyline had been altered for TV into *Shadow of a Man*. The MacMurray/Kelly murderer characterization was tempered because such a dark, sordid individual was considered not good for television audiences. Someone so shady would be considered unacceptable to TV viewers on an ongoing basis.

Jack was eager for a winner — he was in need of something to bring him solidly back to the forefront. He thought this might be the one. "I didn't think they'd dump me at Warner Bros. when they cancelled *Maverick*, but, boy, was I wrong," he said. "But I wasn't down-hearted about it. You learn to take the good with the bad in this business. And fortunately I have outside financial investments that keep the wolf away from the door."

Jack was genuinely excited about this part and the prospect of going back to episodic TV. When an interviewer reminded him stories with insurance investigator heroes had in the past been poor risks on the small screen, Jack scoffed. "It all depends on the quality of the show.... You'll see." He wanted to explain further. "The character I play isn't out of the ordinary but I'm the only actor who could play the part and give it some depth, even though ninety-nine percent of the show's success will probably depend on what the producers get for material and how they execute it."

Jack seemed relieved at the difference in casting with this show, as opposed to how *Maverick* had been put together — with two rival stars. "Brod [Broderick Crawford] and I are like night and day. We're certainly not competitors or contemporaries. The casting is perfect."

Jack and Tom Chevoor. PHOTO COURTESY JACK KELLY FAMILY PRIVATE COLLECTION

Jack's good friend, Tom Chevoor, told of being a guest on the set. He and Donna were watching Jack's taping. When the day's work was done and it was time to go home, the three of them piled into Jack's sports car, "a '58 Thunderbird, or something like that," Tom recalled. "Broderick Crawford needed a ride to the gate to get a cab. Crawford was a big guy and I was jammed into the back seat with him." This was the first year Thunderbird introduced four seats, yet still it was considered as having "a cozy rear seat." Jack was known to drive the best cars.

Well-known newspaper columnist, Rona Barrett, also visited Jack on the set. There was industry excitement surrounding this production, and media was treating the option and the stars like a sure thing. Rona announced to all who read her column that Jack "looked better" than she'd ever seen him look. She said he had a healthy tan, his eyes sparkled mischievously and his sense of humor was, as usual, sharp and on target. In her words, he had "the look of a man glad to be back at the work he knows best." Rona continued, applauding Jack when she avowed there was not "anything he can't play or do. And he is like a horse with blinders when it comes to his career. There has only been one path before him. That is the path to stardom. He is still looking for it."

Maybe this was his core problem. He was forever looking for his path to stardom. While Jack Kelly had been an immediately-recognizable name for almost his entire adult life, there was an indefinable something which continued to elude him, no matter how hard he tried, or how close he got.

This reality, unintentionally pinpointed by Rona Barrett, made it even more unfortunate *Shadow of a Man* never materialized into a series, despite all the effort and publicity put into it. Quite possibly, the darkness of the original subject matter put a pall over the show's opportunity for success, even with edits and script changes. Or maybe, as that reporter early-on had stated, "stories with insurance investigator heroes" simply weren't a good fit for TV.

Or maybe, on Jack's part, problems at home got in the way. Whatever the reason, the show didn't work out, though Jack and Broderick Crawford were considered "a delight together," and reports said they played off each other "to perfection." Jack was called Crawford's "romantic, impressionable assistant." If the try-out had been a hit, Revue Productions, in the process of being renamed Universal Television, was prepared to "crank up a full-scale thirty-week series."

The press said "6-foot-1 handsome" Jack Kelly was still doing guest spots, and miscellaneous TV roles in search of a solid, "remember-me-forever" winner. Jack took on guest spots whenever and wherever they were presented. One such opportunity came in the Spring of 1963 when he showed up on *Art Linkletter's House Party*. This was ultimately the longest-running daytime variety show, airing from 1952-1969, featuring special guests, games, and, in what became Linkletter's trademark, his uncensored, off-the-cuff interviews with young school children. Jack appeared as one of many stars who shared time with Linkletter. The show became Linkletter's legacy.

Despite growing concern over not having regular work, and rumors of marital strife, Mr. and Mrs. Jack Kelly's lifestyle didn't miss a public beat. They followed the same tempo, and their day-to-day world varied little since *Maverick* had left the public eye. Jack never stayed static. He told a reporter, "An actor has a much better chance to survive and succeed if he has true belief and confidence in himself and his abilities. If he upholds the true values he places in himself, whether it is personal or professional, then no one could, or would dare, sell him short."

Jack on set with poodle. PHOTO COURTESY JACK KELLY FAMILY PRIVATE COLLECTION

Jack and Donna lived in a ranch-style, hillside home in Brentwood with their poodles, Cinco — Jack's 1961 fifth wedding anniversary present to Donna, and K.C. and Misty. Their maid looked after the dogs when they travelled, which was often. Poodles had been a part of the Kelly family from the get-go. Donna had come into the union with dogs, and Jack quickly warmed to them.

"They were our family. He loved those dogs," she said. She explained the names of the other two. K.C. was "the name we were going to call our child — Kelly Christina Kelly, or Kelly Christopher Kelly...the initials, K. C. Kelly." And Misty "was a song he liked me to sing all the time."

They took their "family" with them wherever they could, including overseas travel. They had written a script back in the 1958-1959 timeframe about a celebrity couple's ongoing efforts to have their "little dog" transported with them to Tokyo…obviously a loosely-veiled fictionalized version of their attempts to bring along their dog when they went overseas to do *Hong Kong Affair*.

This had been a smart and profitable use of their personalized experience. They sold the script to the show, *Mr. Adams and Eve*, starring Ida Lupino as Eve, and her real-life husband, Howard Duff. The plot was a comedy, centered on the everyday life of a celebrity couple living in Beverly Hills. Lupino, who'd made headway as one of the earliest female TV directors, wanted the show based in truth, showing audiences what it might be like in the day-to-day star world. While the show only ran two seasons, it was popular, though a bit ahead of its time with a direct focus on celebrity life. The Kellys had the chance to showcase their real-life experience. Jack said about their attempts to get their dog to accompany them on travel, then and since, "We had to finally give up trying to take the dog with us, there were so many technicalities."

Donna may have had an affinity for small dogs to offer her the chance to engage her motherly instincts. She had set her mind on the pitter patter of little feet around the Kelly home ever since losing her babies to miscarriage. Jack had dearly wanted children, too, saying publicly, "I hope… God wills we have a child."

Their attempt at adoption in Hong Kong after the miscarriage attested to their sincerity. "We tried to adopt a boy in Hong Kong, a brilliant young man." Donna explained. "It was an English colony at that time. We tried but we couldn't get him. Then there was a little girl that we tried to get, but we couldn't get her, either."

Since Jack and Donna had difficulties producing natural offspring, adoption had been their next logical option. Donna said, "We visit so many orphanages and children's homes, and find that the infants are most wanted." She and Jack considered those kids which others seemed to overlook. "Our concern is the older child who, perhaps, can't understand why he wasn't chosen. I'd like to take a tween-ager, with a good mind, and give him the opportunity to become a useful individual through a good education and proper training."

While Jack had said he wanted six children, right then he must have wondered why what he always wanted seemed to be out of his grasp — whether children, a solid marriage, or the career of his dreams. As his wife publicly spoke of enlarging their reportedly happy union, Jack was privately not sure adding another person to their household was a good idea.

To take his mind off what wasn't currently happening in his home life, Jack busied himself with his many hobbies. He read historical literature, listened to "LP recordings based on show tunes," and sailed and swam. And he spent even more time on the golf course.

Jack accepted *Maverick* had ended. To stay current, he was aware he had to continue doing everything he could to see that his name stayed in the public eye. He had a wife to take care of, and a lifestyle to uphold. He loved being in front of a camera, and having an audience. He thrived on it. In a business which often easily forgot a bona fide star as soon as the word, "cancelled" entered the picture, Jack was determined to ensure he was never forgotten.

"Marriage makes a big difference in your attitude."

JACK KELLY

CHAPTER FOURTEEN

Hollywood, Politics, and Love...
Odd Bedfellows

By early Fall of 1963, it was clear that while he was still a working actor, Jack could be getting to that perilous point where The Powers That Be in the industry would go from saying, "Jack Kelly!" to, "Jack Kelly?" Columnist Erskine Johnson threw a few words his way when he asked, "What ever [sic] happened to Jack Kelly, who co-starred in all those *Maverick* television shows with James Garner? He's taking warbling lessons with a Broadway musical as his goal."

Jack was taking warbling lessons, in preparation for another stint on Broadway. One of the avenues he was following was surprising, even for the likes of the ever-changing Jack Kelly. He signed on for daily vocal instruction with Carlo Menotti, brushing up on his singing to star in a musical "before very long." Menotti was a Pulitzer-prize winning composer and operatic supporter and writer, whose works went on to be re-produced on contemporary stage and television. He may have seemed an unusual choice for Jack's musical education, but Menotti was known to coach TV and film actors making the move to musical theater, and Jack was one of Menotti's many such students.

Jack knew life could change in a split second. He was grateful he had been smart enough to secure his finances in earlier working days. As "insurance" against any wolves which might want to knock on his door, he kept active with multiple business interests in real estate, restaurants and nurseries.

When questioned if his personality was akin to Bart's, something he was still asked regularly in interviews, he would always respond, "No. I'm not as free-wheeling." Free-wheeling went out the window when he became a husband. "Before my marriage, I probably had the outlook of the Mavericks, without the guts and talent to live that way." He thought about the many ways he was different than Bart. "I'd cry up a storm if I lost as much money as Maverick does across the poker table. And there's a spiritual responsibility that we have had which is never noticeable in Maverick's life."

And keeping his marriage alive amidst uncertainty? "Marriage makes a big difference in your attitude. For instance, we have a standing rule in our house. I don't travel without my wife or she without me." This was old news, but Jack was still, in theory, serious about holding on to his self-created Kelly Rule — keeping his wife close-at-hand wherever he might go. If his union was to continue, now more than ever this was important. Still, he didn't note the times, here and there, when he made exceptions to this rule, seemingly for his own purposes.

Jack appeared overly determined to show everyone he and Donna didn't have an open Hollywood marriage…they had a solid, committed relationship. His trip to Florida earlier in the year, on Valentine's Day, put this avowed "rule" into question.

He was mum on this, and staunchly upheld how good he and his wife were together. Jack had been raised by his mother with a strong hand. His parents seemed, on the outside at least, to have had a union of convenience. This could have colored his grown-up outlook on what should, and shouldn't be, his own vision of wedded bliss. Between them, he and Donna stubbornly carried on a carefully crafted image, unity at all costs — possibly even at the cost of truth.

August 28, 1963, a day which became possibly the most pivotal moment in American civil rights history, had a public start with The March on Washington. Jack and Donna were there. By her account, they were there because it was "all his idea." She said they flew from California to Washington with friends, other Hollywood types. "That was kind of a strange day."

Jack had never hidden his social activism. People who knew Jack Kelly knew how he felt about current world events. Yet as a visible performer with strong opinions, he seemed hesitant to be counted among the politically-vocal Tinseltown crowd. Donna once told a reporter Jack didn't like to air his views because he thought they might influence impressionable youth. He was concerned that what he believed to be right and true may not be the same for younger fans who could jump on the same bandwagon simply because he was on it.

This tidbit about his political persona was in the news in early August, indicating politics were heavy on his mind. He and Donna were known to be part of a visible Hollywood contingent, albeit publicly quieter than many others. In late August this same group was part of civil rights history when African Americans, along with many others, took their concerns over equal rights straight to the steps of the government's front door.

A few months later brought about an event which became frozen in time for America, and for the world. Jack and Donna Kelly were everyday citizens, yet they were also well-known members of the entertainment community on the day John F. Kennedy was assassinated.

Ever since Kennedy came on the scene, in a big way, Jack, and along with him, Donna, dedicated much of his personal time to Kennedy's agenda. "I'm not into that kind of thing. It was all Kelly," Donna said. "That's what he wanted to do and I went along with it because he was more involved in those things than I was."

Jack sincerely believed in the man and his plans for his country. Kennedy's death, which happened in such a sudden and violent manner, tore at the fabric of everything in which Jack Kelly had ever believed. According to Donna, the emotion surrounding this event shattered the foundation of their union, hastening the beginning of the end of their marriage.

"A lot of things were going on," Donna explained. "We had the big house on Sunset Boulevard. We had friends that were...we had a very unusual life. We had Kennedy all over the house." She spoke of the celebrity bus tours so common in Hollywood. "The celebrity buses would announce, 'Jack Kelly lives here,' and 'May Wynn lives here.' Kelly used to say that when they saw our house, they would know who we were voting for. There were people coming over, Peter Lawford, and Paul Burke and his wife and children...and all the people who were friends of ours. They would stop at our house for a drink or something to eat...and stay for a couple of days." Their visitors were almost all Hollywood types.

"Then," Donna finished, "Kennedy was killed."

Even amidst this upheaval, the couple plodded on, though things were never again the same. Jack wasn't the same. So much had happened and he lost some of his spark. Though he continued to work in his chosen field, and he and Donna continued to appear together as a married twosome, something was not right...something nearly impossible to pinpoint, even while it was clearly and painfully there between them, and between him and his future.

One of Jack's credits during this period was a two-time recurring role on a *Kraft Suspense Theatre* piece titled, "Name of the Game." The storyline told of a scheme where oilman Ed Caldwell, played by Pat Hingle, offered to back Las Vegas gambler Pete Braven — Jack — with $10 million in a break-the-bank scheme. Monica Lewis and Gia Maione were in the cast. Maione ultimately became Mrs. Louis Prima, and the episode was directed by none other than a young Sydney Pollack, who went on to become an Academy Award winning producer, director, and actor. Reviews indicated "what happens after the game is sudden and unexpected."

This was an interesting role for Jack. He'd come out of a six-year stint playing a gambler well-acquainted with card games, albeit in the Wild West of days long past. The part of Pete Braven was modern, and one would think, of all people, Jack Kelly wouldn't need schooling in the art of being a card shark. Still, the part required him to be a professional on the craps table with the camera and microphone catching his every move.

Producers went all out to make sure the production was authentic. They brought in a man appropriately called "Mr. Fingers" to coach Jack. Mr. Fingers, a professional craps-shooter, taught him how to palm a pair of loaded dice, how to conceal one in a cuff, and how to tell if another player was doing the same thing.

Mr. Fingers also filled Jack in on official lingo. He taught Jack a wallet was "the okus," police were "the works," a crowd of suckers was "the tip," and an arrest was "a sneeze." During filming of the crucial craps-table scene, the unexpected did happen, and the automatic fire sprinkler went off. The table and actors were soaked. As Jack stood there, dripping wet, he made up some trade-talk of his own…in true Jack Kelly style.

"How do you like that?" he asked deadpan, surveying the scene around him. "A floating crap game." No one was surprised when Jack Kelly found a joke in an otherwise miserable situation.

Jack made sure he couldn't be forgotten by guest-starring in as many TV shows as possible. His marriage was shaky, and Jack Kennedy, the foundation of his beliefs for a better America, had been taken away. All the while, Jack's career marched on, though no matter how hard he tried, his career wasn't going in the direction in which he had originally hoped.

But he was still working. Jack played a memorable part on *Wagon Train* in a segment titled, "The Fenton Canaby Story," which aired in December 1963. The tense drama had Jack, a former wagon master, deserting his wagon train, and leaving the people he had been guiding to die of thirst.

This was a rough character. Jack took the part since it did not violate any of his "self-imposed rules about Westerns." Those rules were: 1. He wouldn't play anyone's brother; 2. He wouldn't accept a role where he was cheated by a woman; 3. He wouldn't play cards. He had made these rules after closing the *Maverick* chapter of his life. Jack stated, "No relatives, no scheming dames, and no cards. That's just the way I like it — on-screen."

The roles he was taking on were meaty, and he more than did them justice; Jack Kelly didn't do anything half-way. Yet none of these parts lasted, and this wasn't good news for his career or for his personal life. The "self-imposed rules about Westerns" were borne of deep-seated irritation. Playing someone's brother — that was obvious...being Nancy's brother in reality had overshadowed him all his life, and being Jim Garner's brother on TV, while his ticket to widespread fame, had given him more than a few headaches. Not again playing cards in a Western seemed logical, as well. He'd had enough.

As for being cheated by a woman? This brought him to his wife. One could say the rule was made to cater to Jack's nature — he was too macho and savvy to allow himself, in real life or on screen, to be cheated by a female. Yet there appeared more behind this one. Jack had never been a monk regarding his relationships with women, and had always had his pick. Still, he wasn't known to be a philanderer; while he loved the idea of being in love, he was happy with one woman at a time.

But there had been occasions when he would leave home, and Donna would wonder where he had gone. He wouldn't give her an answer when she asked, which was telling. If this was an issue for him — the cheating woman — the issue was entrenched in his concerns over his deteriorating marriage.

There was no indication Donna had been unfaithful to Jack. What appears possible is the opposite, and while there was no verification, behavior models at this stage in Jack's life indicate if anything was going awry, it was on Jack's watch. The marriage, for the world to see, still looked nearly perfect. In truth, his relationship with Donna had already survived more than its share of ups and downs.

Jo Kelly, Jack's second wife, told of an argument between Jack and Donna which came about toward the end.

"The whole day long, Donna and Tom Chevoor had been at the house. She was on the verge of leaving Jack, anyway, and Tom was trying to convince her not to go, to try and work it out. She had cooked Jack's favorite meal, corned beef and cabbage — which has to cook a long time. Jack came home from the set, sat in front of the TV, and said, 'I want a drink; I'm not ready to eat yet.' Four or five drinks later, he finally told her, his voice slurred, 'All right, I'm ready to eat now.'"

Donna wasn't happy and made her displeasure known. Jo continued the story. "So Donna says to Jack, 'All right, you want your corned beef and cabbage? Here's your corned beef and cabbage!' And she threw it all over the kitchen floor...I think Tom left about that time."

When asked directly why they finally split, Donna seemed to be at a bit of a loss herself. Their home life was growing more and more hectic, especially with *Maverick* no longer in the picture. The loss of Jack's studio contract affected their finances and lifestyle. "We had obligations," Donna explained. Money would have naturally become an issue, even though he did continue to work with little down-time.

As for politics, "I'm not trying to tell you we were politically involved," Donna qualified her earlier words, "but that had a lot to do with our life at that time. Because we were young and we were in show business and then with John Kennedy's murder…. Kennedy was charismatic; he was tremendous in our life. We did a lot of stuff people didn't want actors to do, but we did."

Their story had been overshadowed by many things which could be fatal to a marriage — work, community, finances, and family. By early 1964, the couple had quietly separated, at Donna's insistence, though they weren't ready yet to tell the world. A few months later, they officially announced a trial separation. Many in the Hollywood community — as well as Jack's fans across the nation — were shocked. The Kelly union had been regarded as one of the happiest in Hollywood, and they had taken great pains to look that way.

Murmurs of their status change, from separation to divorce, showed up in the press in March. Harrison Carroll's column, "Behind the Scenes in Hollywood" announced, "The trial separation between May Wynn and actor Jack Kelly (Nancy's brother) jelled into plans for an immediate divorce." It's interesting at this late date, after Jack's successful run on a wildly popular TV show, and after he'd had more than his fair share of appearances on other well-known television and movie sets, he was still presented as "Nancy's brother." The piece continued, "May talked to Jack in Chicago where he's appearing in *Love and Kisses*. They decided there is no use putting it off. So May will see an attorney and seek a quick Mexican decree."

The final word of the Kelly split was read in, among other places, Erskine Johnson's column. "Jack Kelly, who teamed up with James Garner for the *Maverick* series, and his wife May Wynn have decided on a permanent unhitching." The piece went on to say Jack was already dating — chorus cutie Cindy Malone of Ray Anthony's night club act. Professionally, Jack had gone off to do a stage show in Chicago and Donna was thinking of resuming her acting career.

In October, the Kelly divorce was a done deal. Jack and Donna reached an out-of-court settlement. By all accounts, Donna was not a subservient wife. She herself said she had been bossy. She was widely remembered as demanding, and she admitted to at times telling Jack what to do and when to do it. Jim Garner's daughter verified her father had problems with Donna, and in addition to Jack's drinking, Donna was part of the reason why Garner hadn't ever been comfortable enough to socialize with them as a couple. Yet Donna didn't drink much. She told of a time when Jack fixed her a vodka tonic. "I actually almost threw up. I couldn't drink it."

Cindy Malone, who dated Jack as his marriage to Donna ended.

And she adored Jack. He was, in her words, a "sweet, sweet man, a beautiful man." Her fierceness in the face of those who would speak against him or not give him his due, in her mind, had always been a form of protection. Those who were intimate with them as a couple were convinced they had once been genuinely happy.

Donna explained their troubles hadn't been specific or sudden. Issues had escalated over time. "We lost communication," she lamented, "where we were so close before. All of a sudden, everything wound up in an argument, or he would leave or I would leave."

Despite the legality of the final decree, Donna said Jack told her on the day they made it official that their divorce was meaningless. He had tried to change her mind. "We were married in church," he stated, "and you'll be my wife 'til the day I die." No matter what else was going on, Jack Kelly could not get beyond the strict rules of his Catholic faith. Divorce wasn't acceptable, no matter the marital woes.

The truth of this was brought home when Jack did an episode of *The Lucy Show* about the same time as he was handed his divorce document. The fact that he didn't want a divorce was right there on the screen in his portrayal of Detective Bill Baker, "a handsome young policeman." The character was saddled with rookie policewoman Lucy on a caper to catch "Louie, the green scarf bandit." They went on a stake-out in an unmarked police car, pretending to be lovers…parked on Lovers' Lane. The episode was titled, "Lucy Makes A Pinch."

Jack's character, Detective Baker, was a single man. Yet on his right pinky finger, Detective Baker wore a simple gold band…the same gold band worn by Bart Maverick, and every other single character Jack had played since he married Donna Lee Hickey years before.

Lucy and Desi were divorced since 1960. The friendship between Jack and Desi had weathered earlier storms, and Jack, seeing the writing on the wall, finally gave into the inevitable. He was divorced…no way around that fact. He tried to adopt a similar lifestyle to that of his friend — retreating from Hollywood, and moving to the beach.

"It's all tangled up in one word…attitude."

JACK KELLY

CHAPTER FIFTEEN

On The Horizon…
A New Kind of Cowboy

His marriage over, Jack knew he had to keep on working. He wanted to work, but he was in an emotional place where he couldn't wrap his head around everything going on. His friend, Desi Arnaz, lived on the beach in Del Mar. Arnaz was hard-drinking and forever partying, and Jack had already shown he could keep up with the best. Jack's decision to move to Del Mar and place himself in the midst of this atmosphere proved to have a negative impact on the quality of roles he was offered. According to someone who knew Jack intimately, "Alcohol pure and simple stopped Jack Kelly from becoming a big star."

Others said Jack Kelly stopped Jack Kelly from becoming a huge star. Many potentially big deals seemed to have visited him throughout his career, deals which, for whatever reason, never finalized.

Though he hadn't wanted the divorce, since reality stepped in, Jack wasted no time getting back into the singles scene. He had dated chorus girl, Cindy Malone, before the ink was dry on any sort of agreement between him and Donna, and he'd since moved on to others, including actress Karen Steele. Karen ultimately had a long career as a background character actress, and in the days when she and Jack dated, she was in about the last ten years of her career. Born in Hawaii, she became a cover girl and model, and then actress.

Karen reportedly played opposite Jack in a *Maverick* episode airing on March 30, 1960, when he had been in the middle of his "idyllic marriage." While Karen did guest-star on *Maverick* in two episodes, there appears to be no reference to her being on the show in 1960, and the show with which she is credited has her opposite James Garner, not Jack.

His romantic life was soon to take another defined turn. In trying to clear up legal matters pertaining to his divorce, Jack turned to L. Yager

Cantwell, a trial lawyer who worked primarily in matrimonial law, in partnership with his brother. Theirs was a well-established firm founded in 1896 by their grandfather under the family name. Yager Cantwell was highly-regarded amongst the celebrity community, and his client list included actors, religious and sports figures — Sonja Henie, Rocky Marciano, Ernie Banks, Charles Comiskey and Ruth Carter Stapleton,

Karen Steele, another of Jack's lady friends.

among others. Jack hired Cantwell to handle leftover divorce-related work, and Cantwell was brought on as a consultant.

Yager's brother was John Cantwell, and he himself was recently divorced — whether in spite of or due to his profession. John's ex-wife was a tall beautiful blonde named Peggy. She had a continuing good relationship with her ex-brother-in-law, and he called her one day in the last quarter of 1964. "Peggy," he said, "I'd like you to meet a man I've recently taken on as a client. I want you to meet me in Beverly Hills." Peggy couldn't resist. Since she was living in Rancho Santa Fe, down near San Diego, she drove up and met him for lunch. The "man" Yager wanted her to meet was Jack Kelly.

Yager gave her an unusual edict, especially since he had facilitated this introduction. "If he asks you to do anything further than lunch, say no." Their meeting went well and as expected, Jack asked Peggy to dinner that evening. She claimed she had other plans but he wore her down and soon visited her on her own turf in Rancho Santa Fe. This was the beginning of a years-long relationship.

Jack resumed a monogamous lifestyle, this time with Peggy Cantwell. Jack Kelly was in his heart a one-woman man. Though they never married, he and Peggy were a solid couple. Both kept personal residences, never moving in together, and each had a life of their own, separate from their union. This may have been their practice because they both had been married before and knew what they each could lose if something went wrong. Peggy didn't want to bring another man into the lives of her two young sons, who came to know him, in well-remembered terms, as simply Jack.

Peggy and Jack were an item for about five years. Many years later, she still had fond memories. He was, as she said, "a real neat guy," and she described him with the word most everyone who's ever been asked

Peggy Cantwell — she and Jack shared a long-term relationship.

has used. "He was charming... charming, charming, charming." Then she added, "He oozed charm."

Peggy talked of a time when she, her sons, and Jack went camping. "We took the kids up the Gold Coast." Jack, who had no real experience with children, was unsure how to handle their exuberance at being outdoors. The boys were deep into their determination to discover everything there was to discover about the great expanse of nature. They were young and naturally, they wanted to explore. Jack felt it necessary to first set up camp and get everything organized. Afterward, there would be more than enough time to check out their surroundings.

Peggy explained, "I was telling him kids have to be kids. When they get to a new place they want to investigate a little bit, and then they can set up camp."

One might think Jack had never been able to be a kid. He hadn't had much of a childhood, having been corralled into the perfect-kiddie mold early on. His had been a theatrical, "Hollywood" family, and he and his sister, Nancy, had never lived like most children. They were always, from their youngest days, performing in a make-believe world in front of some sort of camera. This was also the case to a much lesser degree for Carol.

However, right then, it was Jack and Peggy, and Peggy's sons, and the boys were teaching Jack Kelly how to be a child, and how to be around children. He seemed to take well to the lessons, and Peggy said he was always good with them. Jack had lived an existence without young people until Peggy and her family came into his world.

At one point during that memorable camping trip, one of her boys cut himself bad enough that Jack decided the child must be taken to the local emergency room. They all went off to the hospital and in no time, the young man was having his hand sewn up by the doctor. The nurse in charge was "stern with us but very sweet" to Peggy's son, and asked questions about how the accident occurred.

"Well, he went through this trash can. He was doing…" and Jack proceeded to explain what the child had gotten into prior to cutting himself. He went on and on, speaking in specific terms as if he were talking about an adult.

The nurse looked at him sternly and replied, "Mr. Kelly, have you never been a child?!"

Peggy thought the comment was priceless. Jack, on the other hand, was startled. He turned to Peggy and said, "I guess that's what you were trying to tell me." He had heard the lesson in her original words, and the nurse's admonition brought it home to him.

While Jack and Peggy were together, he lived in the Del Mar area, continuing to be good buddies with Desi Arnaz. He spent years there, partying and drinking heavily, and running with a questionable crowd. He had a two-bedroom apartment right on the beach.

Jack had little work of note that year. He kept a low profile and licked his wounds. Jo, Jack's second wife, talked of this period — her information secondhand from friends, and from Jack. "Jack's agent was Jack Fields," she explained. Fields was one half of the Sid Gold-Jack Fields Agency. Sid had been Jack's Best Man when he married Donna and Sid wasn't working much by then, so his partner took over.

"Jack Field's assistant told me one time," Jo said, "'Jack could've been as big a star as James Garner, but we could never *find* him.' He was always down partying in Del Mar. So…he did a *lot* of pilots but never got picked up. He didn't throw himself back into work." Jo felt it was because "he was devastated. His whole *world* fell apart. *Maverick* was cancelled and his wife left him."

This may offer understanding as to why Jack Kelly, as an actor, had repeated near-misses at superstardom over many years. He was always "thisclose"…sometimes literally, according to his agent's assistant. In some ways, many people have wondered if Jack Kelly unintentionally sabotaged his own large-scale success.

Peggy observed, "His agent didn't do a lot for him. Jack wasn't totally motivated to be fantastic in the acting business, and his agent certainly wasn't there to get him the jobs or push him. That was my opinion."

There was a "perfect storm" scenario at play. Jack lost *Maverick*. He lost his wife. His long-time agent and close friend, Sid Gold, was no longer at bat for him. And he was tired. Jack simply needed to take a break.

Jack played the father, Jeff Pringle, in Love and Kisses *(1965)... not only in the movie but repeatedly on stage.*

In 1965, Jack was cast in a movie which on the outside seemed a mismatch for him, but the storyline was one with which he was already familiar. He had played the stage version of *Love and Kisses* about the time he and Donna called it quits. The movie was based on that play, and Ozzie Nelson — of *Ozzie and Harriet* TV fame — had seen the play in New York a few years before. The original was written by Anita Rowe Block, and Ozzie adapted the story for the screen after buying the rights. Some have said the result was like a sitcom of today. All in all, with the racy subject matter, it was absolutely nothing like the *Ozzie and Harriet* series.

Jack was Jeff Pringle, father to the star character, Buzzy, played by Rick Nelson. The movie's tagline, "It's a rock n' roll riot!!" gave credence to a bizarre mixture of iconic family innocence — a la the Nelson family legacy — and a story some called "an uneasy vehicle" for Rick Nelson. The subject matter dealt with married teens living with the husband's parents. One of the quirkier parts of this production came in the form of Kris Nelson, Rick's real-life wife, who played his wife in the movie. Both were out of their teens by this time, and their squeaky-clean TV images were at war with this plot. Kris' character was a stripper...the whole production was unusual, to say the least.

This was the kind of fare Jack did well — light comedy with a touch of underlying satire. The entire production served to show Jack Kelly had moved onto another career path. He was no longer seen as a young man. Now, he took on roles which required him to act mature and carry on responsibly, even to be fatherly. As he played the part as a true-blue dad to the hilt, his flair for comedy was more than evident. Jack was hilarious, sometimes to the point of being an over-the-top riot. It was a different sort of movie for the time, but the role was a perfect fit for the often sardonic Jack Kelly. Taking on this character, despite the vehicle's lack of punch at the box office, may have been the start of something for Jack which would have brought him back to the forefront...if he had answered the phone more often when casting calls came his way.

Even as Jack's marriage had been dissolving behind the scenes, he never stopped being a popular addition to episodic TV in front of the camera. Now, with married life in his past, he continued to never be in want of steady work, and the key there was work when he wanted work...even though almost always guest-starring spots.

That wasn't the case in theater, though. When he was on a live stage, Jack was usually the star. In January 1965, he went to Philadelphia to play the Walnut St. Theatre. He was in *The Family Way*, starring with Collin Wilcox. Wilcox had played a prominent role on the big screen in *To Kill A Mockingbird* (1962). While Jack didn't do this play on Broadway, Wilcox did.

Some of his onscreen portrayals did become recurring characterizations, like private investigator Fred Piper. *Bob Hope Presents the Chrysler Theatre* was a television anthology which ran on NBC from 1963 through 1967. The twentieth episode of the first season was, "White Snow, Red Ice." It originally aired March 1964 — months before Jack's final divorce decree was announced, and on this show the Piper character debuted. The storyline had Jack/Piper smuggling a beautiful jewel thief, played by Senta Berger, from behind the Iron Curtain. Walter Matthau and Grace Lee Whitney were also in the cast.

Whitney, only a few years before her big shot at stardom, a meaty role on the series, *Star Trek*, had memories of working on "White Snow, Red

Ice," where she played a ski instructor. "We shot the pilot at a ski resort at Mammoth in the Sierra Nevadas. Senta ended up getting temporarily snow-blind, and I was in constant pain throughout the shoot." Whitney had suffered an accident on an earlier job. "When it was time for me to perform, I took my neck brace off. Between takes, I put it on again. That whole experience is kind of a blur, because I was on very heavy pain medi-

Jack and Collin Wilcox in The Family Way *on stage in Philadelphia.* PHOTO COURTESY JACK KELLY FAMILY PRIVATE COLLECTION

cation at the time. To top it off, the pilot didn't sell."

Jack's second go-round as Fred Piper was in, "Double Jeopardy," co-starring Lauren Bacall and Zsa Zsa Gabor. The last appearance of this character was in May 1966. Fred Piper had the potential to become a starring role for Jack...the possibility was there. The umbrella show was, of course, hosted by Bob Hope, and included a variety of formats — musical, drama, and comedy. Some episodes were used for potential show pilots, and if the viewing audience took to the storyline and the actors, a series was considered. This was the case with Jack Kelly in the guise of Fred Piper.

Piper, a high-flying playboy private eye, traveled by plane in "Double Jeopardy" with Zsa Zsa as his pilot, and Lauren Bacall playing exact-opposite twins. This episode was targeted as the basis for the series. If it

Jack and Senta Berger in Bob Hope Presents the Chrysler Theatre *"White Snow, Red Ice" (1964).* PHOTO COURTESY LISA OLDHAM PRIVATE KELLECTION

had survived, the title would have been *Pay the Piper*, with Jack as the jet-setting private eye who took on cases no one else could solve. Reviews said there were "moments that are just as madcap as any James Bond, 007 outing," and "some of the humor gets pretty obvious, but mostly it's diverting." This was a pilot about a pilot, and unfortunately for Jack Kelly, in the long run it did not fly.

Jack as Fred Piper with Lauren Bacall in "Double Jeopardy" (1966). PHOTO COURTESY GERI ANN SEFTON PRIVATE COLLECTION

Jack continued to do a lot of stage work. In July 1965, he was in Monterey, taking on the lead role in *The Music Man*. He played Professor Harold Hill for three weeks at what was called the Monterey Wharf Theatre.

James Drury happened to be in the audience one evening. "A friend of mine was writing for the show and I went to see it." He was surprised to see his old acting buddy leading the cast. "Robert Preston...that was his signature role. Preston did it for years all over the country and he did the movie. He was wonderful but I don't think he was as good as Jack. Jack was a better *Music Man*. He had the character in the palm of his hand. We were mesmerized. I sat there with my mouth open. I never knew he could sing. He could sing like an angel."

While Jack was for the most part now making his living as a guest-star on other people's TV shows, interspersing theater when he was offered a good part, he and Peggy were firmly ensconced as a couple in Del Mar's social life. Everyone knew they were together, and they were invited to many insider parties and local events. According to Peggy, they were separately invited to become members of La Costa Country Club and Resort, near Carlsbad, by Merv Adelson, legendary TV producer.

La Costa was hailed as the resort to end all resorts, "the ultimate international watering hole." By the time the first guests arrived in the Summer of 1965 — and Jack and Peggy were part of this exclusive group — the La Costa name had already become synonymous with excellence, setting a new standard for resorts. However, La Costa's name was also marred by the arguable fact it was built and grown by investors known to have Mob connections.

"La Costa was a place where a lot of celebrities came. Golfing professional celebrities, movie industry celebrities, wealthy people…a great spot and a lot of fun when it first started," Peggy explained. "There were rumors some of the people who were big in La Costa were original Mafia members." She stressed she never knew the truth. She had no personal awareness either way.

"There were a lot of Las Vegas people in the formation of La Costa. Merv Adelson was the biggest one. I don't think Merv had ever been in the Mob," she added, but "he had connections." She recalled one of his connections. "I can't remember the guy's name. He was a darling man, from Las Vegas…kind and nice, and he had this lovely wife. I didn't picture him as what someone from the Mob to be but, of course, I had no experience. You have a picture of someone but maybe they're not like that at all. These people can be good family men, good friends," meaning people who were involved with the Mob, "but that's separate from what they do for their work."

La Costa was never the typical country club. "If you live in a community and belong to a club," Peggy observed, "you just see the people in the community. This club had people from all over the world."

Late that summer, Jack did another live theater tour. He made his fourth appearance in *Goodbye, Charlie* at the Canal Fulton Summer Arena in Massilon, Ohio. His character was a west coast playboy whose best friend, Charlie, is murdered by a jealous husband. When Charlie is reincarnated as a girl, Jack's character is forced to deal with a whole new set of issues, not the least of which is being attracted to his old friend in a new, transformed body. The plot was complicated and entertaining, and Jack thoroughly enjoyed the part. He also appeared at the Arena at various times in *The Moon is Blue*, *Come Blow Your Horn*, and *A Thousand Clowns*. He obviously liked the area, and the theater.

He and Peggy made a trip to Canada while he was on tour. They stayed at what Peggy called "a lovely bed-and-breakfast." She remembered how much Jack enjoyed the setting, and the overall concept. "He would've loved to have done something like that," she observed. He even told her as much, saying, "We ought to open a bed-and-breakfast." They played a lot of bridge on their trip, with the woman who owned the place where they stayed. In the back of Jack's mind, it seemed, he was always thinking one step ahead and often, his thoughts included the dream of opening his own restaurant or a related establishment which entertained, and fed, the public.

In the midst of his touring, TV appearances previously filmed never stopped showing. *Kraft Suspense Theatre* was an anthology series, and its episode, "Four Into Zero," was a "cliff-hanging tale" which starred Jack in a unique adventure about a million-dollar journey, the story of an ex-ski instructor married to a wealthy heiress. Jack's character concocted a million dollar money-making scheme which turned sour. Martha Hyer was the female lead. Reviews said this show had some "very tense scenes."

He did another *Kraft Suspense Theatre*, almost back-to-back. Starring with Kathryn Hays as his wife, Jack played a jinxed race car driver. His character brought bad luck to all who crossed his path. Titled, "Kill Me On July 20th," this episode was called a "weird tale" by the press.

There was always time for a golf tournament in Jack's schedule, and the Annual Redlands Country Club professional-amateur golf tournament was right up his alley. He, along with other Hollywood notables such as John Agar, actor/producer, and Sol Biano, Warner Bros. head casting director, enjoyed the spotlight with 250 other golfers, all hosted by Professional Jerry Krueger. While Warner Bros. had, in some ways, thrown Jack under the bus by dumping him before the end of his contract a few years earlier, he was not averse to professionally socializing with the studio's top brass. True to his nature, if he could get his name in the newspaper by enjoying a game of golf, Jack was quick to jump at the opportunity.

With the summer at an end, Jack helped close out Indiana's stock straw hat season with Avondale Playhouse's *The World of Suzie Wong*. He took the lead of Robert Lomax. This show ended their twelfth season, presented nightly, except for Saturday, when Jack had to do two performances. He was called "a familiar face to Indianapolis audiences," since he'd starred there in *The Moon Is Blue* in 1962 when he "set attendance records" for the theater, and *Guys and Dolls* the year before at Starlight Musicals. When the curtain came down on his final performance, he packed up and returned to California.

The next year, Jack's Fred Piper character got his last chance at visibility, though an actual series had already been nixed. The episode, called, "One Embezzlement and Two Margaritas," required Jack to play tennis. This was one sport which, the papers indicated, according to Jack himself, he had "never played in his life." To practice, he took a racket and a can of tennis balls to a backboard on the lot. On his first swing, he hit the ball into a small drainpipe hole in a nearby wall. "Why," he lamented, "can't I do that in golf?" Jack appeared as Fred Piper in a total of five episodes, spanning 1964-1966.

This is when Jack took up tennis. He and Peggy played regularly at La Costa, and wherever else they had the chance.

Jack had created a new norm for his career, and he would always return to stock theater when the weather turned warm. In the summer of 1966, he went back once more to the Canal Fulton Summer Arena, this time for *The Tunnel of Love*. The story featured a suburban couple that had remained childless after five years of marriage, and they tried to adopt a baby. Their effort was complicated by a loud-mouthed neighbor and over-enthusiastic social worker who announced she was pregnant. Even though considered a "light comedy," this storyline had a heavy theme and may have brought up emotional baggage for Jack.

Yet he didn't have a lot of time to think about his past. He and Peggy were socializing at every turn, and they enjoyed the life they created together. They became comfortable with each other's family and friends. The summer brought a special dinner hosted by Peggy's mother and stepfather, Mr. and Mrs. Lloyd McDonald, at the McDonald home in Arcadia, California, in honor of friends, Mr. and Mrs. Henry Anastasia. The McDonalds were high-visibility and the event was mentioned in the society column of a local newspaper. Jack was said to be a resident of Pacific Palisades, and in addition to this dinner, Jack "entertained with cocktails and dinner for the visitors" the Sunday before.

As he and Peggy grew increasingly closer, he continued to relate well with her sons. "He was a lot of fun with them," Peggy recalled. She told of one trip they took to Mexico…the two of them, five boys, and five surf boards. In addition to Peggy's three kids, they brought two of the boy's friends along. Everyone had a great time.

Peggy said Jack loved baked potato skins. "We'd go into a restaurant, and he'd say, 'What I want you to do is bake this potato, and then take out all the potato and do this, that and the other,'" explaining to the staff how he wanted the potato prepared, and then re-baked in the skins, with all sorts of good stuff added on top. Peggy laughed. "Now, baked potato skins are popular but then, nobody knew anything about them." She hesitated and added, "As if he invented them."

Jack's TV stints never stopped. In fact, they didn't even slow down. Though he may not have found another starring vehicle with his name attached, he had become adept at keeping himself on the small screen. One such appearance had him acting alongside Jack Klugman, Juliet Mills, and Jeannette Nolan, again in a *Bob Hope Chrysler Theatre* episode. This one was "Time of Flight." There was a touch of science-fiction combined with a contemporary murder mystery in the storyline.

Jack played private detective, Al Packer, hired to protect Klugman's character, hoodlum Buddy Markos. Packer, aka Jack, saw his client gunned down and as he reported the murder to the police, the "corpse" began to move, and to talk — but he was no longer talking as Markos. A *Time* magazine notation said this show was about "two murder victims that won't stay dead." An ad touted, "A hoodlum is gunned down. A man breaks his neck. Another man is electrocuted. A private eye discovers the *unearthly* reason why these men cannot die." Quite a melodramatic plotline.

By 1967, Jack's guest appearances were still as plentiful as his stage work. These two factions had come together as the core of his career, and he was no longer determined to reach for the golden ring in movies…or on TV. His current career course didn't offer him the never-ending star's life, like when he was on *Maverick*, but it was a good existence.

Whenever he wanted a job, one was there. Along with Lee Grant, he starred on TV in "Deadlock," an *Adventure Theatre* segment. The story featured a woman who used a pistol and a bottle of nitro to bluff her way into a police precinct, turning it into a waiting room for death. She held everyone hostage as she anticipated the return of the cop who killed her hoodlum husband. Others in the cast were Tige Andrews and Percy Rodrigues.

Another set of gigs was somewhat reminiscent of his days on *Maverick*. Jack guest-starred on *Laredo* in 1966 and in 1967. The show in 1967 was called "Enemies and Brothers." His old stage friend, Neville Brand, in his regular part as a Texas Ranger, went up against Jack, who played a notorious outlaw who happened to be the brother of the Rangers' Captain Parmalee, aka Philip Carey. The problem…the brother was thought to be dead, and Jack played him very much alive. The show was always humorous, and the quirky nature of its personality fit Jack's acting style quite well.

He wasn't specializing in any one type of role. Whatever the script called for, he did it. When his management came to him with a guest spot on the weekly TV show, *Please Don't Eat the Daisie*s, he went for it. The episode was "Remember Lake Serene? (1967)." He was a happy bachelor whose life was complicated when neighbors wanted to do some matchmaking. Stephanie Powers was the other guest star in this innocuous story.

In-person appearances continued to keep him current. He was still widely known as Bart Maverick, an easy factor on which to capitalize. In May 1967, Jack was an honored guest at St. Marks Catholic Church in Encinitas where he awarded prizes at an annual two-day fiesta. He was always willing to help out the Catholic Church, and this was the sort of opportunity which aided the community while also keeping him in the public eye. Such an occasion made him feel pleasantly nostalgic.

Jack had somewhat forsaken his Church since his divorce. Going to Mass regularly had become a thing of his past. This happened not because he no longer cared, but because he cared too much. His solid, indoctrinated Catholic upbringing taught him a divorced person could not easily be part the world in which the Church revolved. Catholic guilt was so engrained in him, he felt unworthy.

Little theater in communities around the country took up a lot of Jack's time these days. He was enjoying the interaction with young and seasoned local actors who truly loved the craft. The experience was rejuvenating, giving him a chance to once again act for the pure joy of acting. He also did some directing. In May 1967, he worked with a troupe in San Diego from the San Dieguito Little Theatre. The material was old hat for Jack. Once again taking on *Love and Kisses*, Jack was a big hit with his co-workers. All in a day's work, he would joke with them, shouting out direction. "Remember, now, it's a comedy, not a wake!" or, "More energy, schmucks!" And then when they proved their merit, he heaped on the praise. "Hey, you did it! I'm proud of you!"

After the show wrapped, they presented him with a plaque which read, in part, "Love and Kisses…and much admiration for being enough of a gambler to take a Maverick cast, brand them actors, and round them up into putting on a pleasingly palatable play! Thank you for all you taught us." This sort of direct interaction kept Jack Kelly coming back to work day in and day out.

Jack, far left, directing Love And Kisses *in Del Mar (1967).* PHOTO COURTESY JACK KELLY FAMILY PRIVATE COLLECTION

In November, *The Bob Hope Show* hosted the "Shoot-In At NBC (1967)." A variety show, there was an all-star cast including Don Adams, Steve Allen, Jack Carter, James Drury, Bobbie Gentry — the only female in the bunch, Raymond Burr, Doug McClure, Cameron Mitchell, Don Rickles, Dale Robertson, Danny Thomas, Buddy Hackett, Paul Lynde, Jack Palance, Larry Storch, Phil Carey, and Forrest Tucker. The premise had television's cowboys up against television's comedians — Jack was, literally, both. A lot of group appearances and silly skits were packed into forty-seven minutes.

James Drury told of one skit which featured him, Jack Kelly, Jack Palance and Bob Hope. He, Jack, and Palance played "three villain cowboys, what we called 'dog heavys.' We were dressed in real rough clothes, guns hanging off us. Bob Hope was chipping off his putting green into the woods. We emerged, our mouths full of balls." He laughed as he remembered. "We had put three or four ping-pong balls — supposedly golf balls — in our mouth, and we spit them out at Hope's feet."

The shtick had Bob Hope shooting balls right into their mouths as they walked through the woods. "We were [supposed to be] real unhappy. A funny bit. Jack Palance and Jack kept each other in stitches. Palance was a great storyteller. We all then went to dinner together. We were there the one day, and it was a great experience."

Jack kept busy, and when Fall of 1968 rolled around, he was again playing in Ohio at the Canal Fulton Summer Arena. He had come to know this place fairly well, and managed to mesh his interest in the area with his social activism. In his off hours, he toured his surroundings. One spot which caught his attention was the local jail. He toured the Stark County Jail with the sheriff, and met with deputies and dispatchers, managing to turn the visit into a photo opportunity and press piece. Called a "free-swinging showman," Jack revealed in the resulting article that he had years ago been a "special deputy in Los Angeles." He also said he was "considering another television series in which he'd be starring in a northwest lumber camp production."

Jack, upper left corner, part of all-star cast in "Shoot-In At NBC" (1967).

Jack and Peggy never considered marriage even though they had an exclusive relationship. "I was not interested in getting married until my children were pretty well grown." She kept her own place, and he lived nearby. This seemed the perfect arrangement…until late in 1968. They'd had issues between them before, but always worked them out. This time, Peggy recalled, "Jack was in the Midwest doing little theater. I didn't go because my kids were still with me; then they left to go with their dad."

While Jack was gone, Peggy continued with her social life. "I was at La Costa one night and this gal said she was going on a cruise." The lady was a friend of hers, an older single woman with a lot of money. Peggy offhandedly commented how she'd always wanted to go on a cruise.

"My friend said, 'This is a three-day cruise out of San Francisco. I'll call and ask if you can share my suite.' She did, we went, and I didn't tell Jack I was going." Since she and Jack lived independently, and this would only be a few days, she didn't feel the need to check in with him. "We had a great time." Afterward, the crew asked both women to go on to the next port. Peggy's friend had an appointment in San Francisco and had to return home. Peggy had no immediate responsibilities; she continued on, telling her friend to "call Jack and tell him that I'm gone." The trip lasted another week for Peggy.

She was enjoying herself, and when she was invited, again by the crew, to go for free from Seattle back to Los Angeles, she couldn't pass that up. When the adventure was finally over, Jack met her at the ship to take her home. "All the crew members, the people on the ship," she remembered, "I knew well by this time. They said, 'Peggy, can't you go farther with us'?"

This familiarity seemed completely normal for her by then, but didn't sit well with Jack. On their ride back, she said he ranted and raved. "He was so jealous." She recalled he grabbed her arm and tore her sleeve in the process. "I said, 'Y'know, the whole time we've been together, I have never done anything but be with you. This time, I did something fun for me. It was nothing you should be upset about. I wasn't screwing around with anybody. I was just enjoying my life." Peggy had had enough. Jack had a jealous streak, and she didn't want to deal with this anymore; she didn't want to deal with him anymore.

So Jack left the country. He spent nine weeks in Sardinia, Italy, and Spain, filming his first movie in quite some time. What came out in November in Italy, titled *Commandos* (1968), never had an in-the-moment debut in the United States. Jack even commented, "This film was so outstanding, it has, to this day, never been selected for exhibition in theaters in the United States." He wrote this in an article in 1981, but he was wrong. Throughout the next year-and-a-half, the movie found its way to theaters in Spain, France, West Germany, Sweden, Finland, and even Norway. In 1972, under the same name, *Commandos* came to American movie houses in at least Iowa, Utah, and California, debuting to no better than lukewarm audiences.

He played the part of an inexperienced captain who, along with a "hardened commando sergeant," Lee Van Cleef, led a small group of American soldiers ordered to take over an Italian base in North Africa. One review stated, "The acting can best be described as inconspicuous — neither outstanding nor glaringly bad."

During his trip, Jack said he "flew over Austria, Switzerland and other

Jack and Lee Van Cleef in Commandos *(1968).*
PHOTO COURTESY MIKE LUSCOMBE PRIVATE COLLECTION

locales I cannot pronounce," and he "enjoyed a Paris airport coffee shop for five hours on a layover caused by two blowouts." He also "became as intimate with the countryside as one can get from 28,000 feet." His words indicate the experience was as forgettable for him, as it was for moviegoers.

In early 1969, Jack guest-starred on *The Name of the Game* in the first of two episodes. This one was titled "The Inquiry." Gene Barry was the star, accused of pilfering funds from the Army. Sporting a rather unusual-looking thick mustache, ostensibly to make him appear serious and official, Jack played Barry's attorney, defending him in front of a Senate Subcommittee.

Starting in 1968, there seemed to be some time when Hollywood forgot Jack Kelly...or possibly more appropriate, Jack Kelly forgot

Hollywood. He was on TV on a regular basis, but in reruns. He made few public appearances, and for the most part, stayed away from the theater. Jack burrowed into his home in Del Mar and made himself relatively inaccessible. When he did work, he was usually on a live stage somewhere. When he and Peggy became serious years earlier, he had rented his place on the beach. Now that they were on the rocks, he needed to again re-

Jack on the beach. PHOTO COURTESY JACK KELLY FAMILY PRIVATE COLLECTION

evaluate his personal life even more than his professional world.

In October, a rare movie role, *Who Rode With Kane* (1969), starring movie legend Robert Mitchum, came Jack's way. Soon re-titled, *Young Billy Young*, the picture was expected on American screens in October. Jack played John Behan, a dark, sadistic man, a change from his usual light, easygoing film appearances. He was quite believable, though, and his part in this movie, carrying the heavyweight name of an icon of old Hollywood, was a feather in Jack's cap.

Jack Kelly in Young Billy Young *(1969).*

"I will always take care of you, Baby."

JACK KELLY

CHAPTER SIXTEEN

Movin' On…
As The World Changes

Little did Jack Kelly know how his life would change once again, and once again, because of a woman. In the Summer of 1969, on his way home from a theater gig, he attended a 4th of July party on the beach in Playa del Rey. There he met a saucy, dark-haired beauty named Jo Ann. Though she was over ten years his junior, the attraction was immediate on both sides.

Jo, as she was usually called, admitted later she'd had a crush on Jack Kelly as a teenager in high school. At the time they met, she was engaged to marry another man, and she lived in a rented duplex on the beach. She and a group of friends were at her place getting ready for the big holiday party, being thrown by Frank, her landlord. At that moment, in the downstairs apartment, Jack and his good friend, Dick Mordigan, were visiting with Frank.

Jack's friend, whom everyone called Mordigan, lived in a big home in the Hollywood Hills. Jack was known to stay with him often — convenient if he was doing a gig, or auditioning, or coming and going from a theater engagement. Jack and Mordigan had stopped at the duplex on the beach, on their way to LAX to pick up Jack's luggage.

Jack didn't want to make the stop. Mordigan coerced him. Jo explained, "When he came off this dinner theater thing he flew to San Francisco to go fishing with Mordigan, then they went back to Mordigan's house."

On the way to get the bags, Mordigan said to Jack, "Let's stop at Frank's. It's the 4th of July." Jack said he was too hung over, and not interested. Mordigan insisted. "You've got to get your luggage, anyway. Playa del Ray [Frank's place] is a few minutes from the airport. Let's stop. We'll have a beer, a hot dog, and then go get your luggage."

Mordigan was driving, and they did stop. When they caught up with Frank, Jo said he told Jack, as she later heard the story, "Have I got a girl for you! Let's go downstairs and collect the rent." Moments later, Margo, one of Jo's girlfriends, came running into her room where she was getting dressed. It was about 7 o'clock in the evening. "Jo! It's Jack Kelly," Margo said excitedly. "He's in your living room. You've got to come out and meet him!" Jo said Margo gave her a pointed look and added, "But stay away from him. I want him."

Jack and Jo Ann Smith on the beach. PHOTO COURTESY JACK KELLY FAMILY PRIVATE COLLECTION

Jo didn't stay away from Jack, and he didn't stay away from her. "We went out onto the beach," Jo finished, "and proceeded to have fun with all the party people." She and Jack dated all of six weeks.

Jo was certain he was still seeing Peggy during the sum total of their whirlwind courtship. Jack seemed to have been confused, unsure as to where he wanted his private life to go. He hadn't made up his mind between the two women. The incident with Jack and Peggy after he had picked her up from her summer cruise and brought her home had really been a blow to him.

Jo explained how she knew he hadn't completely cut his ties with Peggy. "After the 4th of July, but during that period, I had a date with Jack, and he stood me up. When he finally showed up the next day, he said he'd been with Peggy."

His words were defiant. He told Jo, "Yeah, I was with Peggy and I made love to her that night. And you know what? I made love to her the next morning."

Jo stared at him. "I was twenty-nine years-old, literally in love with this man," she continued. "I didn't know how to respond. He wasn't 'my man.' I was just dating him."

Jack and Jo Ann Smith on the golf course. PHOTO COURTESY JACK KELLY FAMILY PRIVATE COLLECTION

And she was still technically engaged to someone else. Jack knew this. Her fiancé was in the Cayman Islands for the entire summer, where there were no phones. She couldn't get hold of him, and had to wait for his call if she needed to have a conversation. She didn't yet know if there was any reason to change her status because she couldn't tell what Jack was going to do. He held his cards close to his vest, and hadn't given her solid indi-

cation of his intention. Jack wasn't sure what Jo was going to do. They found themselves in something of a stand-off.

Not long before Jack and Jo had met, he had tried out for a part as a game show host on national network television, and when they got together, he still hadn't learned if he would be selected. When his relationship with Jo came to this fork in the road, he needed to make some choices.

"He was auditioning for *Sale of the Century*. He did not know when he was auditioning that they would, 1. Hire him, and 2. Take the show to New York City. So when he got the job and realized they would send him to New York, he had to make a

Jack and Jo just before ceremony…ring appears to be on his left pinky finger in preparation. PHOTO COURTESY JACK KELLY FAMILY PRIVATE COLLECTION

decision. 'Am I gonna marry her and take her with me, or will I have a long-distance affair?'" Jo surmised, "Jack, knowing he was leaving, loved me and wanted to take me with him."

Jo told of how this finally resolved. They had been to a golf tournament in which Jack had played and were on their way home. "The weekend he proposed to me was August 10, 1969. We were in the back of the limo, and it was a Sunday. He was hemming and hawing and telling me he loved me, saying he's not a rich man…this and that." Jo had a feeling something was coming.

"I said, 'Jack, Jack, do you have something you want to ask me?' And he said, 'Yes, will you marry me?'"

Jack and Jo both had loose ends to tie up alone before tying the knot together. He told Jo he had to break the news to Peggy. This proved that up until only days earlier, he'd had some sort of relationship with her. Jo explained, "Jack told me, 'I went to see Peggy. I looked at her and said I have something to tell you.' Jack told Jo that Peggy replied, 'You're getting married, aren't you?' So she *had* figured out there was somebody else."

Mr. and Mrs. Jack Kelly leaving church after wedding. PHOTO COURTESY JACK KELLY FAMILY PRIVATE COLLECTION

And Jo's fiancé finally called on August 16th. This was the day she and Jack prepared to leave for Las Vegas, where they would marry that afternoon. When she explained to the now-other man she was getting married to someone else, he asked, "When?" She said, "Well...today." That was the last time they ever had contact.

Jo and Jack went to Las Vegas, said their, "I do's," and had a nice wedding dinner with friends. Immediately afterward, they returned to Los Angeles.

"We flew home that night," Jo explained. Jack was due the next day in Florida, to be on set for a production with Jill St. John and Robert Stack, so they got to Los Angeles, and stayed the night near the airport. The next morning, they were on a plane again. Jack had a part in *The Name of the Game*, his second for this series, this time alongside St. John, who played his wife. Stack had the lead. The episode, titled "The Civilized Men" (1969), was set in comfortable times for Jack — the old West — with a storyline centered on cattle-rustling. He and St. John were a couple involved in dark times when several cases of food poisoning showed up on a ranch.

Jack on location with Jo for "The Civilized Men" (1969). PHOTO COURTESY JACK KELLY FAMILY PRIVATE COLLECTION

Within a few months of their marriage, the couple set up home base in New York City. Upon their return from Florida, Jo had gone to Del Mar and packed up Jack's apartment — "got rid of some stuff, put other stuff in storage" in Jo's words — and did the same thing for her place. When they got to New York, they stayed at the Hampshire House where they lived for about a month while they looked for a home. Jack was very familiar with the management.

Jo said they stayed in the "same suite Jack and Donna stayed in when they were there doing some kind of a promo thing. They must've been there for quite awhile because there was chicken wire around the balcony." The chicken wire had been put in place specifically for their poodles, to give the dogs some outside space.

Jack and Jo did find their own home. They rented a two-bedroom,

Jack and Jo on boat. PHOTO COURTESY JACK KELLY FAMILY PRIVATE COLLECTION

two-bathroom co-op from one of the heads of Singer Sewing Machine, who was in Argentina with his wife on an extended stay. They paid $500-a-month rent. They didn't have a car and would rent one if they needed to drive out of the city.

Jack had been named the star of *Sale of the Century*. This was different for him, though it did hark back to his early days as an announcer and live performer. Jack's return to his hometown of New York City didn't go unnoticed by the press. He was featured in an article titled, "After Long Absence…Jack Kelly Back Home At Last." The piece heralded his return to his birth state. He announced he'd now live in Manhattan with "his wife, the former Jo Ann Smith."

The article went on to say Jack returned to California as often as he could "to fish for salmon and striped bass." There was a determination in the piece to paint him as "an avid outdoors fan," explaining he was "co-owner of a cabin cruiser" and he liked to "get away to Mexico for outdoor camping." Jo explained the truth of this. They didn't own the cabin cruiser. They leased it from actor Jack Jones' father, Alan. "We rented a boat from Alan Jones, maybe a twenty-footer, and took it out to Long Island for the summer so we could party."

Jack in promotional picture. PHOTO COURTESY JACK KELLY FAMILY PRIVATE COLLECTION

Sale of the Century was produced in Studio 8H at the NBC Rockefeller Studios in New York City, and debuted on September 29, 1969. The concept came about after Executive Producer Al Howard lamented over how hard it was to find a real bargain. The thought morphed into a national game show in which contestants were asked easy questions. When they responded correctly, they earned a few dollars. The gimmick was simple — after delivery of the right answer, contestants exchanged money for expensive prizes offered at extreme discounts.

This wasn't the sort of thing Jack was best known for, but he was really in his element, chatting up guests and letting his naturally engaging personality shine. He had his name on the marquee. The opportunity gave him the best of both worlds. He was again bringing in a regular paycheck, and he held onto the gig for almost two years, until August 23, 1971, when he was officially replaced by Joe Garagiola.

Sale of the Century took over a spot previously held by a game show called *Personality*. Monday through Friday, 11 AM — 11:30 AM, Jack showed up on the TV screens of homes across America...mostly watched by appreciative housewives.

Some TV viewers were confused by the turnaround in Jack's persona. One reader of Hy Gardner's "Glad You Asked That" column said, "Jack Kelly...is an accomplished actor. So why'd he become MC of a give-away show?"

Gardner's answer was on target. "Doing a show like *Sale of the Century* offers other rewards. It gives Kelly daily network exposure, a chance to display his own personality, and it keeps his name box-office for guest spots and perhaps a lucrative nightclub act."

Working around his taping schedule, Jack continued to do public appearances; in fact, this was encouraged. He and Jo were in Long Island for one such event, staying in a rented home. Tom Chevoor visited, going into town with them to watch show tapings. In the evening and on weekends, they all enjoyed their leisure time on Long Island.

Tom's younger brother was running for State Representative, and he invited Jack to speak at a political rally in their family's hometown of Watertown, Massachusetts. Jack eagerly accepted, and he and Jo went to Watertown for the rally. Tom's brother didn't win the election but as Tom put it, "That wasn't Jack's fault."

About this time Jack took a side trip to Lowell to delve into his roots. He had never spoken much to anyone — not his wives, not his friends — about his family history or the dynamics. He always seemed to act as if he didn't care about the past, his or anyone else's. Not long after he and Jo married, she spoke to him about her early family life. He looked at her and said, "Why are you telling me this?"

Jo was confused. "Well, we're married. I wanted you to know about me."

He replied point-blank, "I don't care. I don't care anything about your past. I just care about from this day forward."

Jack and Jo out on the town. PHOTO COURTESY JACK KELLY FAMILY PRIVATE COLLECTION

His desire to go to Lowell and look into his family's story showed that he wasn't as immune to the past as he might want others to believe. He took that day trip, solo, but when he returned to Jo and friends, he was tight-lipped, with little to share. He did mention the house in which he'd lived as a child, saying, "My mother used to have different colored bottles in the windows, and they glistened." The house no longer stood, but the trip had affected him, and jarred his long-buried recollections.

He and Jo had moved to New York figuring they would be there for some time. The East Coast celebrity social life was a good fit for them, and they always had something on their calendar. Soon after they settled in, they were helping Mr. and Mrs. Robert Alda celebrate their wedding anniversary at the Inn of the Clock in the city's Twin Towers, near the U.N. They kept a weekend home in the Hamptons, and enjoyed private time there whenever they could get away. And they saw Nancy.

Jack had lived his life well. He knew how to be a part of high society, in fact he was good at it, and he had no intention of changing now. Whatever Jo needed, she had immediately. She called him her "Candy Ass Cowboy." She told a story of when he came up behind her one day, put his hands on her shoulders, and firmly stated, "I will always take care of you, Baby."

Jack meant those words. Jo said he always took good care of her, and never slighted her in any way. After they married, he turned over all of their financial operations to her. He was making a good salary as a game show host, and Jo was, as she put it, "frugal." She said Jack received $1500 per diem each week, which they lived off while she made sure his entire salary was banked.

Jack had celebrity tastes and an accompanying lifestyle to uphold. He wanted to make sure Jo had everything she needed or wanted, and always looked the part of the wife of a well-known TV star. One particular perk was a traveling hairdresser who came to them as they needed her. Phyllis Della "trimmed the locks" of the rich and famous, and Jack and Jo were among her clients. One night, the couple went to Danny's Hideaway in New York, and with them was Phyllis, their "curvy, beautiful guest." They were close for a time, not only as an employer of sorts, but also as friends.

Danny's Hideaway had been a favorite haunt of Jack's in New York for a long time. Jo said Danny "loved Jack. Danny loved celebrities, period. Whenever there was a celebrity appearing in town, Danny would host a huge dinner for the celebrity and all the celebrity's friends...and always Jack Kelly. Always. One time we were at dinner with Don Rickles, Frank Sinatra, Shelly Winters, Jack Dempsey...all kinds of celebrities. Danny would always invite us, and then we'd go to wherever the celebrity was appearing — Waldorf Astoria, or the like."

Danny, christened Dante Charles Stradella, weighed 130 pounds and stood a few inches over five feet tall. His was one of *the* places to be seen in New York City. There were three four-story buildings, with eleven dining rooms which seated 300, two separate kitchens and two completely stocked bars on different levels. A sixty-foot awning topped the front of the complex, proclaiming this was "The Home of Danny's Hideaway and His Inferno; His Music Room; His Menu Room; His Key Room; His Nook." Celebrity photographs lined the walls and in most of those photos, along with the well-known…was Danny.

The world in which Jack and Jo lived wasn't always rosy. They partied often, and they partied hard. He had lived this way for many, many years, long before Jo came into the picture, and the lifestyle had slowly been catching up. After one weekend of heavy drinking, Jo became livid. His behavior was erratic, and when he was under the influence of alcohol, Jack was sarcastic, biting, and sharp-tongued. These weren't his finest moments.

Jack didn't drink at all that Monday, attempting to make up for his behavior of the last few days. He didn't touch a drop. On Tuesday, he started his day as he usually did, but he didn't feel well. Suddenly, his world turned upside…and he had a seizure, the first of many over the

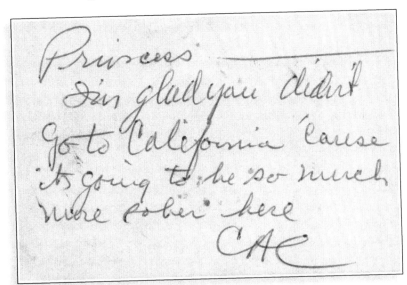

Jack's written apology to Jo. PHOTO COURTESY JACK KELLY FAMILY PRIVATE COLLECTION

following years predicated on alcohol consumption. Jo said the episode came and went, but each additional period proved more of a concern. Every seizure seemed to follow a period where he decided he would no longer drink, at which time he would suddenly stop consuming.

With everyone around him, Jack minimized any health concerns, and forever stayed busy — pilots, guest appearances, and promotional efforts. There was something always going on and most often, Jo was at the side of her "Candy Ass Cowboy." He was 44-years old, effectively middle-aged but still attractive to the opposite sex. Successful in his chosen — or more aptly, chosen-for-him — profession, he happily settled into his new marriage with a beautiful younger woman.

Jo didn't hide her feelings; Jack usually did. While they were somewhat opposite in how they approached issues, they loved each other, and were seen as a good match. His first wife hadn't been able to share with him the one thing he had always wanted. Peggy, the lady with whom he spent a number of years after marriage, had not wanted to make the commitment with him.

But now...Jo was pregnant. Jack was going to be a daddy; finally he'd get the family he had always desired. Jo told of the day she learned she was going to have a baby, and how Jack reacted. "I had a doctor appointment. When I came home, he was lying on the couch. In pain. He had done his two shows for the day [*Sale of the Century* tapings], and was on the couch, fully dressed because he couldn't get out of his clothes — he was in so much pain."

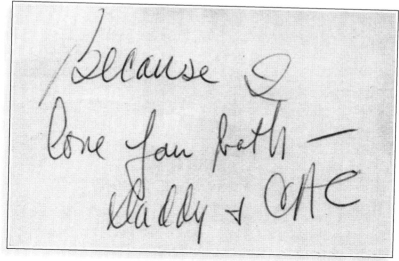

A note from Jack, "Daddy" and "CAC," to Jo and their not-yet-born baby.

Jo realized her husband had had another seizure. Seizures had become somewhat routine. Most had been physically painful yet didn't require him to seek immediate medical attention. Symptoms usually included agitation, trembling, confusion and varying degrees of physical discomfort. Jo had learned how to calm him, and this time, once she made sure he would be okay, she sat down next to him and quietly told him they were going to be parents. "He looked up at me with this cock-eyed grin. He couldn't even get excited about the fact I was pregnant because he was in so much pain from the seizure."

Jack *was* excited. He recovered from that particular incident, not again thinking twice about it, and threw himself full-force into becoming a daddy. It was what he had always wanted.

NBC's *Comedy Theater* was revived in early 1971. The part originally held by Bob Hope fell to Jack. In this short-lived iteration, there was no fresh material. Programs were from Hope's old show; Jack hosted "reruns of reruns" as a summer replacement. The first show re-aired "Wake Up, Darling," starring Barry Nelson, Janet Blair, and Roddy McDowell. This was first shown in 1964 under the title, *Bob Hope Presents the Chrysler Theater*. The 1971 newspaper review wasn't kind, saying the effort really wasn't "worth all that air time."

While he was "busy hosting a daytime game show," Jack had a guest stint at the card table as a disreputable cow town doctor on the popular buddy Western, *Alias Smith and Jones*, in an episode titled "Night of the Red Dog (1971)." The formula for this weekly show followed closely the line-up Jack pioneered years earlier with Jim Garner. His character was a heavy loser at cards, something of a turnaround on his earlier *Maverick* years. For Jack Kelly, the man, he broke his own rule of never again playing cards onscreen.

Roundabout this time Jack's tenure on *Sale of the Century* abruptly ended. Official reasons for his departure indicated he was "going to return to films and television drama," and "complete several projects which require him to travel frequently to California." Or so the press was told. Essentially, Jack was going back to Los Angeles to resume his acting career.

Probably more to save face for the show's brand than to save Jack Kelly's public persona, the truth was never revealed. He had been a big hit with Al Howard in the beginning, and they remained on friendly terms until a sudden verbal altercation changed everything. They were at a party. Jack was drinking. The next morning, he woke to a painful sobriety, wondering what he'd done wrong. A swift change in his status, as well as words from his wife who'd been with him when the fiasco occurred, gave evidence to what had been, at least, an unfortunate evening. Once again, alcohol had derailed Jack's success.

When reports discussing his departure from *Sale of the Century* reiterated he'd turned over the position to Joe Garagiola to go on to bigger

Nancy Kelly Caro, Kelly Caro, Warren Caro. PHOTO COURTESY KELLY CARO ROSENBERG PRIVATE COLLECTION

and better opportunities, press follow-ups responded, "So far the only thing Jack has been doing is TV commercials." They noticed he hadn't signed any new contracts. Not even Garagiola reportedly knew why Jack was out. He explained, "I can only remember a meeting with Al Howard and Willie Stein and we talked about the show and what they expected."

Nan Kelly Yorke, Jane Walsh, Nan's sister, and Bill Kelly. PHOTO COURTESY JACK KELLY FAMILY PRIVATE COLLECTION

The damage was done. Jack was fortunate insofar as having absolutely no public flack follow his departure from his foray into game show TV. Since Jo was pregnant, things needed to be different. He should've been on top of the world and, in many ways, he was. He was going to be a father. This was what he had always wanted.

Jack didn't have many extended family worries anymore. His mother had settled well into her new suburban lifestyle, remarried to a younger doctor husband, and enjoyed her society world and the local women's club. Nancy was a mother herself. Though she'd had to rearrange her life since she had a child, she still acted.

Carol was also married; she no longer looked to the spotlight to support her. Bill, well, Bill was doing what he'd done most of his life — not much, but this was no longer Jack's main concern. Bill was looked after by their mother, when he needed looking after, though he was known to visit Jack now and then. Some things didn't change. He usually showed up when he was in need of money.

Jack had, after many years, finally begun to realize the intimacy his own personal family life could offer him. This was something which, through experience with parents and siblings, and to some point with Donna, had always eluded him. Now he was at another crossroads. If he could only shake his predilection toward alcohol as his way of handling stress and change, he could possibly have it all. Easier said than done, for a man practically raised on the bottle.

This was a bittersweet period for Jack. He had a child on the way, and he was in the midst of another transition. He knew alcohol was not his friend, and he really wanted to do right by his family. His intent was genuine.

"We tend to shoot blame at every target except ourselves."

JACK KELLY

CHAPTER SEVENTEEN

Cowboy Husband, and Father…Finally

On the sixth of November, 1971, a daughter, Nicole, was born to Jo and Jack in New York City. This was the purest, happiest of days for them. The idea that Jack had created a new life amazed and delighted him. He had believed a child would never be in his cards. This one daughter was a far cry from the six kids he and Donna had said they would have…but that didn't matter. Nicole was so much more special because she was his one-and-only. Jo had told him she would have one child for him, and Nicole was that child. She was his baby, the fulfillment of a dream. He felt as if God had finally smiled down upon him, in the form of this precious little girl. He had another chance to get it right.

Once Nicole was part of his life, Jack had a renewed sense of purpose. Everything he did from that point on, and everything he had done to that point, was part of his daughter's legacy. Having a child never slowed his pace. He and Jo were a married couple and a business team — she taking on the role of his personal manager. She organized him, personally as well as professionally, handling his promotional needs, and making sure he was seen as receptive to his fans.

He still had a lot of fans. When people wrote asking Jack for an autograph, Jo would make sure he signed a stock photo, or if a photo was sent with the request, he signed that. Jo took care of all the mailings, and she kept everything moving. The rest of their business operations — real estate, mostly — also continued to grow under her careful direction.

Jo and Jack had moved back to California. When Nicole was only six weeks old, she met her Aunt Nancy when her parents flew with her to Washington, DC, where Nancy was appearing in a play. She was divorced, back at work, and had her own daughter. Jack and Jo took

Nicole backstage and left her with stagehands as they sat in the audience. Afterward, they briefly socialized as a family.

Jack continued to be well-regarded and in high demand. He had unintentionally made a long-running career of being a guest star, with a regular sideline of summer theater. While he came quite close a number of times to starring in another series — with no less than five known pilots thrown

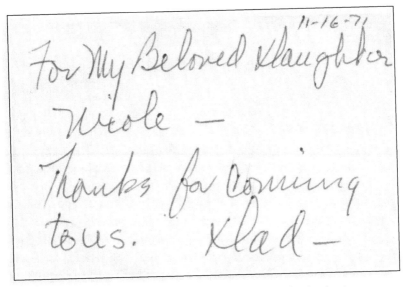

Card from Jack to daughter, Nicole, nine days after her birth.
PHOTO COURTESY JACK KELLY FAMILY PRIVATE COLLECTION

out to test the waters between 1955, even before *Maverick*, and 1978 — none of them made the mark.

What may not be well known is how pilots were used in early television, and how the concept evolved as TV matured. "Unsold Pilots on Television, 1956-1966," from a website titled, *Television Obscurities*, explained how pilots were test episodes used to sell potential shows to advertisers and networks, but the bulk of them never became series. This made the process a crap shoot for both the people who put out the money to produce the pilots, and actors who took the chance at stardom through what was only a whisper of a possibility, but nowhere near a sure bet.

The sad truth is what traditionally happened to unsold pilots...usually nothing. In early days, it was "commonplace for the networks to run summer replacement series made up entirely of unsold pilots." This was one reason TV anthologies became popular. They gave the industry an opportunity to make use of what would otherwise have been lost time, talent, and resources. *G. E. (General Electric) Summer Originals* came out in 1956, and The *New York Times* announced, "The problem of what to do with 'pilot' or sample films of projected television series that previously have failed to sell has been solved."

However, as the website indicated, "Broadcast television is a commercial industry. Money is put in and money is expected to come out." Due

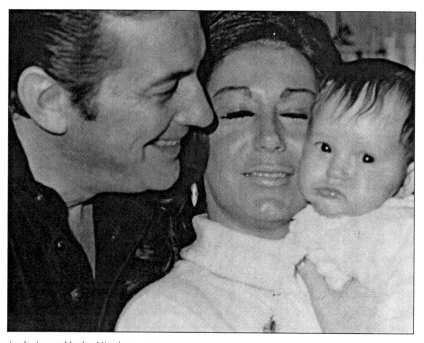

Jack, Jo and baby Nicole. PHOTO COURTESY JACK KELLY FAMILY PRIVATE COLLECTION

to the cost of airing shows even as fillers — writers, directors, actors and others involved received royalties each time a show was seen — it ultimately became cost-prohibitive to use them in any fashion, and batched failed pilots slowly stopped being a part of everyday television.

These pilots each began as a hopeful opportunity every time one came about for Jack Kelly, but ultimately they were but a reminder of another "almost there" with every airing. Still, he'd done quite well for himself despite twists and turns. He was seen regularly on most all the nighttime TV shows, and his activity, past and present, regularly brought in healthy paychecks. Between that and residuals from *Maverick*, Jack and his family were financially well-situated. As long as *Maverick* was shown somewhere on a TV set, or in any other way, Jack Kelly was making money, and his visibility was assured.

When Nicole was not quite two months old, Jack was seen on *Ironside* in "Cold Hard Cash (1972)." He and Barbara Rush played parents of a daughter kidnapped under strange circumstances. She was an "aging movie star" and Jack was her ex-husband. Along the way, they learned "some truths about themselves." His acting in this may have been deepened by the awareness he was now the father of a girl child. His TV show daughter was played by Kay Lenz in her first major role. She was a success and, as a result, was cast as the lead opposite William Holden in the Clint Eastwood film, *Breezy* (1973).

Jack became violently ill when Nicole was about eighteen months old. Jo took him to the hospital, where it was found he had a congenital defect in the veins in his brain. He was in grave danger, and doctors wanted to do immediate brain surgery to alleviate the pressure. Jack flat-out refused.

His medical team agreed to wait it out. They impressed upon Jack the importance of being examined every year

Jack and Jo with Nicole. PHOTO COURTESY JACK KELLY FAMILY PRIVATE COLLECTION

for any changes in his condition, and he good-naturedly agreed. Since this was a birth defect, and had never before been an issue — in fact, he had to this point never even known the problem existed — a watch-and-wait approach was deemed sufficient. If the concern grew in size, an operation would be unavoidable.

So Jack returned home. A few months after this upheaval in his life, he was acting as if nothing had ever happened. Jo stayed home with nearly-two year old Nicole in the summer of 1973 as he returned to the road for regional theater gigs. Alongside actress Gale Storm, he worked with Florida State University acting students during their summer play, *Affairs of the Heart*.

Jack said, "We feel fortunate to get back into the grassroots — back where it all begins." He enjoyed these one-on-one, in-person connections. "It matters not if we communicate the knowledge while sitting on the grass outside the theater, backstage or on stage. Through our contact with students, we can expose some of what they will find in a realm quite well populated."

It was Jack's opinion show business had become "frail," and the entertainment world was in a "peculiar shift." There was no longer any solid footing. "Once a big name, such as Clark Gable, meant a big drawing card and security, but that was before television came along and people chose to push a dial instead of going out and paying the price of a theater ticket." Live theater gave him a chance to get away from the dial and share his experience and maturity with young actors, people who at some point could become stars. Jack had a sense of accomplishment and pride at being part of this process. He felt his experience would benefit up-and-coming actors, and this was itself a legacy. He in some ways had added the role of "teacher" to his resume.

Peggy Cantwell remained fond of Jack long after their split. If not for his moments of difficult behavior, she may have tried to make a life with him. Instead, she married a dentist, Dr. Jerry Jones, and Jo and Jack visited them a few times in Del Mar.

Jo said, "We went down to their house and partied with them, and we lost Nicole." She laughed. "She was about three, and they had a big spread. They lived in Rancho Santa Fe. Big sprawling house with lots of land. We were out wandering around in the back somewhere and, all of sudden, I couldn't find Nicole. She had wandered off." Obviously they found their daughter — her being "lost" was an overstatement, more about the size of the property than a commentary on a missing child.

Peggy also spoke of this period. "Jo and I saw each other a couple of times. Once, we were going to have lunch and she said, 'I hope you don't mind but I invited Jack.' Of course I didn't mind. It was nice to see him again. He was sober then. We had a lovely luncheon; it was fun to see him. I thought he was adorable." They socialized a number of times, she and her husband, and Jo and Jack. "When they came down, we had dinner and played tennis together."

Jack had picked up tennis…no longer the "one sport" he didn't play. He had started playing in earnest with Peggy at La Costa. She explained about their get-togethers, "Jo was a heckuva tennis player. She could concentrate so well. I was always kind of jealous. I loved tennis but I was not…she really focused."

Summing up their meetings, Peggy finished, "It was…a good relationship. Not a close relationship. They lived up in Orange County, and I lived in San Diego County."

Jack had something in his personality which endeared him to almost every woman who'd ever known him. No matter what had gone on between him and any one of these women, each continued to think well of him, and he of her. While not forgetting his shortcomings, each lady seemed ready to forgive him. Even Donna didn't hold a grudge. She remarried...to another Jack. She couldn't get away from that name. And she, like Peggy, didn't give Jack Kelly the forever heave-ho from her life.

Jo said, "We all stayed friends — Jack and I, and Donna and her new husband, Jack Custer. We used to go to their house and have dinner, and they'd come to our house. Finally, Jack said to me, 'Would you stop socializing with those people? She *drives* me crazy!'"

Two beloved women in Jack's life weren't his wives, or girlfriends, or any sort of romantic connection. They were his sisters, Nancy and Carol. Though they didn't have a deeply close relationship, they had always genuinely cared for each other, making the effort to see each other when their busy schedules allowed.

Jack did see Nancy on occasion after Jo and Jack had returned to California, though Jo was never sure of when or how those meetings came about. He never spoke of them with her, never made any noise over them. She was not included. She felt Jack didn't like to mix certain members of his birth family with his home life. Donna had much the same impression when she was married to him. Nancy and Jack spoke on the phone, keeping in touch enough to at one point consider doing a TV series together. While they plotted an idea and a storyline, the effort never came to pass.

Jack and Carol would see each other off and on. Jo said she would come to their house at Christmas, and Nicole clearly remembered her visits as she grew older. They weren't frequent, but Carol seemed to have a deeper desire to hold onto familial ties.

Jack had moved his family to Huntington Beach in 1972, putting down solid roots. They ended up there "almost by accident," when he and Jo visited friends and fell in love with Huntington Harbor. Before they knew it, they'd bought a home with the money that had been banked from Jack's work on *Sale of the Century*.

On Mother's Day that year, Jo's first Mother's Day, Jack gave her a card, "For My Wife," which proclaimed with flowers and a beautiful sentiment, "This Is Love." He wrote in his own hand, from his heart, "May you always know my only wife — how much you make my only life — a place to love and true endure our love, our, child, forevermore!" He signed it, in true Jack Kelly fashion, "That says a lot for a CAC [Candy Ass Cowboy]."

About the same time, Jo went to real estate school and made "very successful investments." They continued to put their money in local real estate interests, each managing their business with their strongest skills — Jack contributed "packaging, seeking out investors and management." Jo did the "buying, selling and handling tenant negotiations." Jack credited her with "tremendous energy to make their business and personal lives

Portrait of Jack and Jo. PHOTO COURTESY JACK KELLY FAMILY PRIVATE COLLECTION

a success." Jo had worked in public relations prior to their marriage, and Jack saw her drive as a "component of her character."

He had his finger in many pots; Jo ran their day-to-day efforts while he continued acting, doing voiceover work, and playing the business field in a variety of ways. His many interests finally brought Jack to the point where he considered acting almost an "avocation." He was a partner in a construction-design firm which had earned "good returns for the past ten years." Regarding his acting career, he said, "If a super job came along for an ongoing role in a series, I'd have to think seriously about it. But there are so many other things in my life." He added, "I don't have to act for the rest of my life."

In the Fall of 1972, he appeared with Jason Robards and Stella Stevens in "The Dead We Leave Behind," an episode of an anthology show, *Ghost Story*, hosted by Sebastian Cabot. Stevens' character was bored with her forest ranger husband, and took up with neighborhood men, while becoming addicted to their new TV. They argued; he killed her. She haunted him via the TV set. Jack played a character simply called "the motorist," yet his part was important because he was the man with whom the wife had her most notable affair. When "the motorist" showed up at the ranger's cabin seeking shelter on a stormy night, after the wife's untimely death, her husband killed him, too. The infamous William Castle, with his William Castle Productions, known for shock-factor features, was at the helm.

While the love between Jack and Jo never died and continued through the rest of his days, and after — even now she gets a tear in her eye as she remembers him — their relationship was admittedly stormy, almost from the get-go. Jack's drinking was most often at the core. His stint in the hospital had not been enough to put the fear of mortality at the forefront for him. He had again picked up the bottle. For awhile, Jo drank with him, and they had wild and wonderful moments, but also times which bordered on manic. As they became too familiar with how substances affected them, together and separately, the fun wore off bit-by-bit.

Still, people in general loved Jack Kelly. Everyone seemed to enjoy his lively and jovial company and had great things to say about him. Negatives entered the picture only after Jack added alcohol. Drink made him acerbic and sometimes verbally unkind.

This behavior became more and more of a concern, and eventually got to where Jo stopped drinking. She realized alcohol wasn't good for her, as a mother or as a wife. In all areas of life, alcohol seemed to cause only grief. This conscious change in her created a rift with Jack, who continued to drink heavily.

Finally, things reached a crescendo and Jo couldn't take anymore. She demanded Jack move out of the house and into one of their empty rental properties. She couldn't live with him like this. Not too much later, he seemed to be his old self again, and Jo once more saw the man she married. They reconciled; he returned home. This cycle repeated itself, again and again. Jack would get beyond drunk and once more, Jo would demand he leave. She said about this period in their lives, "I moved him in and out of the house seven times." Despite everything, Jack never lost sight of his love and responsibility for the two females who were most dear to him, females who had become his one true family.

It wasn't as if Jack didn't know he had a problem. He knew, and he tried to do better. When he was aware he was getting out of control, he'd allow Jo to direct his activity, and he'd tell her each time, "Okay, kid, I won't stand in your way." He would walk out the door, going to whichever rental home Jo had readied for him. He'd live away from his family...until she called him home again. The situation ultimately made them a family divided — together in most everything they did involving Nicole, even going on elaborate vacations. Yet they no longer were able to live in the same house.

The *Mystery Movie of the Week* offered new and established actors the chance to get, and keep, their names and faces in the public eye in uncomplicated fashion. *Faraday and Company*, one of four revolving shows which aired every week under the *Mystery Movie of the Week* banner, was one of the title shows. Faraday was a private detective imprisoned in a South American jail for twenty-five years for a crime he didn't commit. Once freed, the plot put him in convoluted scenarios. In December 1973, Jack was a guest star in an episode titled, "Fire and Ice." Faraday was played by Dan Dailey.

Some things never changed. Jack continued to take on TV guest spots while also doing regional theater whenever a project appealed to him. Despite the drama behind the scenes in his personal life, Jack still always got more work. He rarely ever had a problem when he stood in front of a camera, or on a stage.

Banacek, with Victoria Principal and Sterling Hayden, was another 1970s TV series in which Jack guest-starred. The plot for "Fly Me — If You Can," which aired in February 1974, was built around a missing airplane forced to make an emergency landing at a remote airstrip. When the landing caused a rather unusual problem, the solution formed the basis for the storyline.

In late 1974, he received word he'd been selected for "a super job…for an ongoing role in a series." He would start the year playing Lt. Ryan, the new police captain, in an already ongoing series, *Get Christie Love*.

This was a shot in the arm, and good for his aging screen alter-ego. The synopsis for the episode in which Jack debuted said, "Christie (Teresa Graves), already on the wrong side of new police captain Jack Kelly, wors-

Jack, Jo and Nicole on one of many family vacations. PHOTO COURTESY JACK KELLY FAMILY PRIVATE COLLECTION

ens the situation with her unorthodox way of hunting a thief who shoots policemen." This was called "one of the better shows of the season," and in discussing Jack's character as part of the regular cast, commentary indicated, "Jack Kelly should be a good addition." He did ten episodes.

His quirky sense of humor followed him into his middle years, and never left for a single moment. Almost anything to which he put his name ended up with an amusing angle. He couldn't help himself. Jack was always happiest when he played a character with a funny side. One episode of *Get Christie Love*, airing that summer, had Christie jetting to London, back home, and then to Zurich, all because someone forced Ryan, Jack's character, to do *something*…something which was intentionally never defined.

The write-up for this "nutty story" said, "Get Christie Love! is very funny, often on purpose." In some ways, there was a *Maverick* quality involved — otherwise serious storylines intentionally lightened through eccentric characterization. In addition to Teresa Graves as the star, Eric Christmas, John Astin, Steven Keats, and Wilfrid Hyde-White made up the cast.

The winter holidays found Jack enjoying the extravagant light display on Naples Island off of Long Beach. The Christmas Boat Parade, a long-standing tradition, was cause for, as a headline said, "parade parties and more parade parties." The houses around the island put on some of southern California's best displays. One of many parties was co-hosted by a local man, Bob Kerivan. Well-known names who attended the fete, in addition to Jack and Jo, were Priscilla Presley and her then-beau, Mike Stone.

Jack and Nicole in her bedroom. PHOTO COURTESY JACK KELLY FAMILY PRIVATE COLLECTION

In late 1976, Jack played a part on *Hawaii Five-O*. A story of old-fashioned murder, it told of Jim, a man who'd escaped from prison determined to prove his murder conviction was false. Jack Lord as McGarrett eventually uncovered a witness and a "rat's nest of hatred and conspiracy." Yet another solid guest-starring performance for Jack Kelly on major nighttime TV. This had become his career.

February 1977 brought one of a few mini reunions with Jack's *Maverick* co-star. Jack had a lively, if not large, role in Garner's show, *The Rockford Files*. He played a bad guy in "The Becker Connection." He and Garner had only one scene together, and while a reviewer called it "great casting," there was little interaction between them.

In September, he was back, and his on-screen play with Garner in "Beamer's Last Case" was again only one scene, and Jack's part in the story-line was secondary. Pairing Jack and Jim in meaty scenes seemed a logical publicity tool, for the show as well as the actors. That their previous public history wasn't in the least bit exploited is telling. This omission speaks loudly to the private difficulties that had always been between them.

A little over a year later, there was an intentional effort to capitalize on the *Maverick* brothers as a pair. More than twenty years had passed since the series first hit the airwaves. *The New Maverick*, a TV movie/pilot, tested broadcast waters in September 1978. An ad said, "*The New Maverick* once again transforms the Old West into history's most light-hearted poker game." The plot was based on the story of Ben Maverick,

Charles Frank, Jim Garner, and Jack in The New Maverick *(1978).* PHOTO COURTESY MIKE LUSCOMBE PRIVATE COLLECTION

nephew of Bart and Bret. Played by actor, Charles Frank, he was handsome and charming, like his uncles, and the ladies couldn't get enough of him…like things used to be back in the days when his uncles rode through town after town on their way to their next poker game.

Jack revived his role as Bart, but two decades in between gigs was a long time. There was a new generation in charge of the TV landscape — the remote control, and the official programming — and everything had changed. Tastes had refined along with advancing technology, and TV was now operated in and around an entirely altered reality.

Not the least of the problems for such a show as *Maverick*, new or otherwise, turned out to be the fact that the original stars were considerably older. Antics they would've been a part of in the early days did not easily translate into the current lives of two guys who were each 50-plus years old. Even though a review stated "reuniting Garner and Kelly for the movie return of *Maverick* was a logical move," *The New Maverick* did not become a series.

Jack, Nicole, and Jo on a cruise. PHOTO COURTESY JACK KELLY FAMILY PRIVATE COLLECTION

Jack's mother, most often known as Nan Kelly Yorke, died in late October 1978 at the home she shared with her husband in Ventura, California. Jack was over 50 years old, and had lived all his life with his mother's shadow looming large. He managed well to mitigate Nan's influence on his day-to-day decisions as he aged, but her lasting impression on the man he had become was still there, and always would be. This was also true for his sisters and brother, and their reactions to their mother's passing spoke volumes.

The Kelly siblings came together one last time at their mother's funeral. Carol, according to Jo, "totally flipped out and lost it." She and Jack, and Carol and her husband had been friends, seemingly without major concerns between them. As far as Jo knew, Jack never saw Carol again after the funeral. Bill was staying at a local motel, and Jo drove him there when

312 A MAVERICK LIFE: THE JACK KELLY STORY

the ceremony was over. She said, "He didn't work and I gave him money." Nancy had, at one point, said of her mother it was like "sucking on the stone breast." The children, even as adults, and the mother seemed to have had a love-hate relationship. With Nan gone, they were left to deal with their loss in their own private manner.

In true Jack Kelly fashion, he quickly, and seemingly unemotionally, closed that chapter of his life. Work was, as usual, always there, and he found himself part of another TV show. The decades-old *Hardy Boys* books had been made into a series the year before. That Fall, Nancy Drew, star character of the books which featured a young heroine in the same sort of adventures, co-starred with the boys. Soon after, they were combined into one regular series, the *Hardy Boys/Nancy Drew Mysteries* (1978). Jack was taken on to play CIA operative, Harry Hammond. It wasn't a big role but it was recurring, enough to give him additional regular work and brand his name to the show until late 1978.

Jack was involved in a charity holiday event at Christmas with members of the I.O.I.'s Children's Village U.S.A. project at the Wilshire Country Club. Three hundred and two guests welcomed the one-and-only Santa Claus. Jack "bought silver champagne bucket, tray and goblet worth two hundred dollars." He wanted the collection as a Christmas present for Jo, and he was happy to be able to make the donation for such a worthy cause.

The next year, a solid example of the march of time was evident when Jack was one of many "old school" Western-type actors who took part in *When The West Was Fun: A Western Reunion* (1979). This was a whimsical TV get-together for popular Western series and film players since the beginning of early television. The show was pure nostalgia...and by showcasing stars of yesteryear in today's evolving medium, the differences in the world of entertainment, then and now, were boldly evident.

Jack, top row with no cowboy hat in
When The West Was Fun: A Western Reunion *(1979).*

"A city the size of Huntington Beach can't be managed by the inarticulate trappings of a prehistoric pecking order such as an appointed Mayor."

JACK KELLY

CHAPTER EIGHTEEN

Turning Point...
Look To The Horizon

Jack soon found himself again at the point of reinvention. He wasn't sure which road to take, or even in which direction he should go. He was in no financial difficulty — everything he'd done, not the least of which was the original *Maverick*, had been well-handled from a business standpoint, and he and his family would likely never have money problems.

Yet similar to when *Maverick* ended and Jack was forced to regroup and review, to decide where and how he should make his next move, he was again negotiating his future. Jack could have continued to take on guest roles on episodic TV to ensure his name stayed at least moderately current. He could be assured of going on in perpetuity in TV's rerun Heaven, and residuals would keep him, and his wife and daughter, warm and cozy.

But Jack had gone this route for years. It wasn't enough anymore. He was bored. This work no longer satisfied or fulfilled him. He did some soul-searching, looking deep inside himself. In no time, he was able to lock onto what he saw as his solution. Jack had held onto his personal convictions, and they would become the springboard to his next chapter.

Since he and Jo had bought and sold real estate for years, Jack was deeply entrenched in the liveliness of southern California politics. He knew what it took to get a permit, change an opinion, and shmooze the right person. He'd learned well how to get work done in and around Huntington Beach. People continued to like him, and naturally gravitated toward him. In turn, Jack genuinely cared about others. He believed he had the area's best interests at heart, and knew if he put himself into the local political mix, he could make a difference, and become a key player.

In 1980, at the ripe old age of 53, and after already nearly that many years in some form in the public eye, Jack Kelly changed audiences. Campaigning with the slogan, "Let Maverick Solve Your Problems," he ran for, and won, the first of two four-year consecutive terms on Huntington Beach's City Council. Not only his work on TV and in movies, but extensive local exposure, made him nearly a shoe-in.

He distributed brochures in the design of cards from a poker deck, and The *Press Democrat* said he "taunted council incumbents with the slogan, 'Call Their Bluff.'" A Huntington Beach article pegged Jack as "a hard-drinking but personable sort whose good-old-boy approach made him popular." Another said Jack Kelly was a "man who takes on new turf as a way of life." As always, he seemed to thrive on diversity.

Regarding his work in real estate, Jack said, "That's the only thing I know a little bit about," and his knowledge served him well. For a time, he also owned the local newspaper, the *Huntington Beach News*.

The people of his town eagerly welcomed former Hollywood star and local personality, Jack Kelly, into City Hall. By the time he was elected to the Huntington Beach City Council, Jack and Jo had socked most of their finances into local land holdings, as well as other well-placed investments. This new position in Jack's life didn't carry with it a weighty salary, which speaks to

Jack Kelly note urging local political involvement for young people. PHOTO COURTESY JACK KELLY FAMILY PRIVATE COLLECTION

his real desire and determination to take on, and become part of, his local government. He wasn't doing it for the money.

Jack felt as if all of their businesses required three people to manage. Jo was the real Business Manager, not only for their professional operations but also for Jack, the man, as he morphed into a professional bon vivant, a public personality with multiple faces. Politics, real estate, voiceovers, still the occasional TV and theater role…and father. Jack Kelly had become a new man.

He was foremost a public personality. That was his overall profession, and as a sub-title, he was a Huntington Beach politician. The first apparent mention of his name in City Council meeting notes — the first of many — came on April 21, 1980, when it was indicated Jack Kelly was "elected as member of the City Council...for a full term of four years." Those same notes went on to state Jack "thanked his family, his committee,

Jack Kelly, 1983. PHOTO COURTESY LISA OLDHAM PRIVATE KELLECTION

and citizens who supported his candidacy." This was the start of a lively relationship between the man previously best known as TV's *Maverick*, and the citizens, politicians, and business people of Huntington Beach, in particular, and California at large.

Jack was a vocal champion of real estate and business causes in and around his city. In favor of building up the area, he worked to bring in money to advance the community. Oftentimes, this meant he was at war with preservationists who believed Huntington Beach was becoming too commercialized; Jack Kelly was, in many instances, seen as the root of that problem.

This didn't bother Jack much, though. He was "bored" with political infighting from the day he took office, according to Richard Barnard, the then-Huntington Beach City Administrator. Barnard indicated Jack "wanted to see action on street sweeping and trash collection and city services so citizens could see what they were getting out of their government."

Not everyone held this opinion. Even years later, Jack Kelly was remembered for his feet-in-the-sand voting record. "The city fathers of Huntington Beach have been RUINING this once beautiful beach town for close to thirty years," an anonymous resident stated bluntly. "Going all the way back to when Jack Kelly and Harriet Wieder were on the council there has been some sort of warped vision of turning downtown into Miami Beach west. No vision was used for preserving the past, rather it has been [a case of] bulldozing the past, and bring on the tourists. There is no uniqueness to downtown anymore. It is over-crowded, dirty, and not much different than the beaches in L.A. County."

Jack clearly had his detractors, but he had more than his share of loving supporters. He had always been known to hold an opinion, or three or ten, and he was never one to shy away from sharing his ideas, with absolutely no concern over what others thought…especially in relation to area redevelopment. One person said about him, "While sometimes reckless in terms of showing his feelings for what he loved and his disdain for what was not right…he did do it his way."

And by doing things his way, Jack was having a revival as a public persona. An article in the *Orange County Register* in early 1981, gave a well-rounded look at his life, post-TV star. Jack said he was involved with "the pursuit of eclectic endeavors" and the article reflected on "a funny coincidence" how Jack's *Maverick* character, who had always been "running into unprecedented situations," was not unlike Jack himself.

As the show, *Maverick*, had evolved in its day, the character of Bart Maverick had melded into the reality of the actor who played him. As

Jack's life moved away from the TV screen, the obvious became clear... the two personas would never fully separate. He said about himself, "I have an unarticulated desire to be my own man. I eventually found it unproductive to constantly see the same people and hear the same things."

Years before, Jack had invested in desert property, never dreaming such an activity would become anything more than a sideline. During his acting heyday, he was always pursuing choices which would allow him "to be in the Museum of Modern Art and eat a hot dog with sauerkraut at the same time." This was Jack's way of saying he wanted to always be able to enjoy the best of both worlds. He and Jo had become "successful real estate entrepreneurs." They created a company called August II, "a firm involved in property management, buying, selling and financing."

Jack gave in to a nostalgic offer in early 1982. Jim Garner had contractual obligations after *The Rockford Files* left the air, and a show was developed to capitalize on his *Maverick* fame. *Bret Maverick* was on the air in 1981, lasting for two seasons. Ratings were decent, yet the network unexpectedly canceled all future shows after the second go-round. Jack appeared as Bart Maverick in "The Hidalgo Thing," the season's last show, in a sentimental brotherly reunion. He had been slated to return in a regular, recurring role.

Jack really didn't need the show. He had politics in his life now. In 1982 alone, he was cited repeatedly on record regarding a large number of development and property issues. The first was in July when he motioned the Huntington Beach Redevelopment Agency to approve the sale of property in the Warner/Goldenwest Project Area for renewal. Then in December, he recommended that "white papers" include information that property adjacent to, and within, the Talbert-Beach Redevelopment Project Area be designated as industrial. These were only a few such notations.

He was the subject of the following comment, "Time and again, Kelly is the lone vote for or against an issue." Jack wouldn't disagree, saying of himself, "I'm Mr. 6-1," in regard to his voting record. "But I can't worry about that. I figure every time I push the button to vote, half the people are going to love me and half are going to hate my (expletive) guts.'"

Despite semi-retirement from being in front of the camera as an actor and performer, Jack hadn't given up on Hollywood. He'd proven this with his recent *Maverick* stint. An occasional guest spot still enticed him, primarily because he didn't want his name forgotten in the national arena. In early 1983, he showed up as himself in an episode of *The Fall Guy*, titled "Happy Trails." This was no more than an "I'm still here" appearance, giving him a chance to have fun, ham it up and be back in the TV spotlight again, something Jack always enjoyed.

About this time, City Councilman Kelly motioned to approve and authorize an Underwriting Agreement. This was with Stone and Youngberg/Merrill Lynch White Weld Capital Markets Group for single-family and multi-family mortgage revenue bonds on area property. He also motioned to adopt a resolution for an agreement to provide for the development of senior citizen condominiums and rental housing on sites within the Talbert-Beach Redevelopment Project Area. Jack said he was "so pro-business it's funny," also calling himself a "social liberal."

Bill Kelly and Walsh relative, possibly Samuel or William. PHOTO COURTESY JACK KELLY FAMILY PRIVATE COLLECTION

This idyllic period wasn't to last. Maybe a month later, on April 6th, Jack was at home watching TV when the phone rang. Carol was calling to tell him that their brother, Bill, had committed suicide. He'd taken a shotgun, put it in his mouth, and pulled the trigger — a drastic move made by a drastically unhappy man. Jo was in Hawaii, and Jack called to give her the news. She asked if he needed her, if she should come home; he told her not to worry. Jack avowed he'd take care of everything…and he did.

William Clement "Bill" Kelly, known on his Social Security card at the time he died as Jay O'Kelly, lived in the Tarzana area at the time of his death. He was cremated, and his ashes scattered in the ocean off of Long Beach, California, on April 27, 1983, by his brother, Jack Kelly. An official "Certificate of Burial at Sea" was presented to Jack, with the entire ordeal being a private affair. Jack displayed little emotion to his immediate family throughout, from beginning to formal end.

Jo made it known Jack had loved his brother, he'd cared deeply for Bill…but keeping his deepest emotions inside had always been Jack's way. Little was said about Bill or how he had died from there on out. Bill Kelly was gone, and what minimal amount was known about him during his life, this is how he remained in death — something of a shrouded mystery. With no wife and no children to mourn or remember him as time marched on, William Clement Kelly has stayed an enigma, known only to immediate family no longer around to speak

Bill Kelly, Certificate of Burial at Sea, April 27, 1983. PHOTO COURTESY JACK KELLY FAMILY PRIVATE COLLECTION

his name. Jack jumped back into work, as if he'd never left it, serving as Huntington Beach's Mayor Pro-Tempore starting that same month, through November.

During Jack's growing visibility as a local politician, he continued to hide his private demons. His campaign manager would see to it he was kept away from alcohol when he needed to be, during the times he was running for office. After he won his election, there were those who ensured he remained well-behaved and on the mark for public appearances.

The reality was not that folks didn't know Jack Kelly drank. Folks simply didn't know he drank as much as he did, or what happened when things got out of control. Yet his family knew. And Jack knew, too. He was, and always had been, aware he had a serious problem.

September 16, 1982, was Jack's 55th birthday. That morning, he uncer-emoniously walked into Jo's room — they lived in the same house, but had separate bedrooms — and announced, "I'm not going to drink any-more. I'm quitting."

Jo had heard this before, and she answered with the first thing to enter her mind, "This is your birthday."

"Yeah, a good time to stop."

Jo didn't believe he would, or could, go cold turkey, and stay sober. Even if he did stop, as he had in the past, he would start again. There had never been any Alcoholics Anonymous meetings in his plans, or any professional inter-vention. She knew Jack's intentions were good. He wanted to stop, but he wanted to stop on his own. She felt this was unwise. He still had the aneurism ticking away in his brain. He still had no intention of seeking medical atten-tion. Jack was doing the right thing, yet he was trying to do it the wrong way.

The intent was important, though. He seemed more focused this time. What Jo hadn't known then, and didn't know until years later, was that Nicole had written her father a long letter.

Nicole recalled what brought this about. "He never seemed to be drunk until the evening… He never spoke badly to me, even when he was drunk. He and my mom would fight and…it was always words that hurt us, but the words, to me, were embarrassing stories or questions, or he would be lethargic and slower to talk. He seemed different and it was such an obvious difference…like he was in his own world and almost numb to anything or any conversation and it was that, that embarrassed me."

Nicole's reminiscence explained how she had been the only one able to get through to Jack. "I don't remember ever even being yelled at by my dad. I only remember a few times he was really even upset with me, and I would do anything to make everything okay. I could not stand to have my dad upset with me."

When she wrote her letter, she was desperate. "I remember being sad and disappointed. He had this one line. I knew instantly he was drunk when I heard these words…like something out of a movie, the same words every time. I could ask him a question or make a comment, not realiz-ing he was drunk, and he would say, 'Whatever's fair, kid, whatever's fair.'"

These words never made sense to Nicole, and she would know when she heard him say this, that something was off kilter. "My heart would sink, and I would walk away. He wouldn't even notice I was gone, or had abruptly ended the conversation. I took it personally. How could he do that to me? I know it had nothing to do with me, but I didn't think it was fair. As amazing as my dad was and as wonderful as our relationship was, this didn't seem to fit."

Her letter to him came after one such incident. "I remember he had upset me the night before his birthday. And while I don't remember what it was, I might have had friends over and was embarrassed again. I remember thinking, 'I am done with this and I am the only one he will listen to.'"

So Nicole did what she had to do. A nine-year old girl decided to perform an intervention, though she had no idea this was what she would

Portrait of Nicole and Jo. PHOTO COURTESY JACK KELLY FAMILY PRIVATE COLLECTION

accomplish. "I remember thinking it being a milestone birthday [and it] seemed appropriate to me to write the letter." She loved her father dearly, she knew he loved her more than anything else in the world, and something had to be done to save him from himself.

"In the letter I told him how I felt; I was scared he was going to die and I couldn't live without him...I didn't want to have friends over anymore because he embarrassed me, and I didn't want to be around him when he was drunk. I also told him how much I loved him and if he couldn't stop for himself, could he do it for me?"

He was drunk when he went to sleep that night. Nicole sneaked into his room and left the letter so he would wake up to read it in the morning, on his birthday, before coming downstairs.

That next morning was when he showed up in Jo's room, sober, and made his announcement to her. And he stayed sober for years.

In November, 1983, Jack once again made big headlines, not only locally, but around the country. Variations on the same story proclaimed, "Bart Maverick, brother of James Garner's Bret Maverick, has a new role… as Mayor of the seaside town of Huntington Beach, California."

Jack had taken the natural step up from City Council. He handily won the election to become Huntington Beach's mayor. When Jack was asked by reporters if he would now make politics his life, he nonchalantly responded, "Ask me that in a year." Being a local mover and shaker had become an occupation which fit his personality, as if this was what he had been moving toward in all those years past.

The man who used to be *Maverick* was again on the top of the heap. He was regularly in the news over the next few years — if not entertainment news, then the local political detail. He was effecting change, a lot of it. Jack Kelly reveled in being in the know, being part of a group molding the world in which he lived, rather than only someone who moved

Jo and Jack, her "Candy Ass Cowboy." PHOTO COURTESY JACK KELLY FAMILY PRIVATE COLLECTION

within a world created by others. Politics had always been in his blood, and now he was in the thick of it in a big way within his community, and southern California at large. Even James Garner made an off-handed comment about how Jack had become firmly ensconced in his high-visibility California gentleman persona. "He owns all of Orange County," Garner stated, only somewhat in exaggeration.

Repeatedly championing the redevelopment of Huntington Beach, in specific, Jack wanted to bring in more business. "This used to be a sleepy little seashore town," he said. "But not anymore." Discussing the city's image as a "bedroom community," Jack said, "We've got enough bedrooms now. More of them aren't going to help this city keep pace with its needs.

Commercial development — wisely-planned, of course — will provide a much bigger tax base with far less drain on public services."

He was also often on top of the city's growing traffic issues. "There's no getting around it. We have massive traffic circulation problems." Jack was usually seen to be at war with the environmentalists, not because he didn't believe in preserving the environment, but he felt their methods hindered essential area growth for economic purposes. "In a word, the ecology forces have stymied development."

Jack was also sometimes in a fight with those who wanted to preserve the Huntington Beach that once was — seemingly uninterested in any potential of the city of the future. In response to folks who bemoaned the loss of certain landmark locations, such as "the hallowed Golden Bear bar," he said, "Despite all the development, there really isn't any discernible difference down along the Pacific Coast Highway."

Two years later, 1986, brought yet another term as Mayor for Jack Kelly. Life was good. He continued on much the same political path, widely supporting, and being supported by, forces strongly behind development and forward-movement. Called "Huntington Beach's Maverick Mayor," Jack was in attendance at the dedication of Manning Park on Delaware Street, thanking everyone for being a part of a celebration to honor the city's first mayor, Ed Manning. Huntington Beach had come a long way since its incorporation in 1909.

That Christmas, Nicole gave him a deeply personal and special present. Their relationship had tightened beyond anything they'd had between them in the past, and they were as inseparable as a father and daughter could be. She had been carefully holding on to clippings of her dad's career for years. Many had been collected by a news service. Other pieces, Nicole saved herself. She arranged them in a large photo album, working hard to make sure it was ready for the holiday.

At the end of the organized news pieces and photographs, she included a personal note which said, in part, "This album will be passed down from generation to generation of our family... This book is very special to me and I hope it means just as much if not more to you... Oh, I suppose you feel like a star now!!! Well you are! I want you to know that to many people you are still a big star, but no one thinks of you as a bigger star than me... I love you more than words can say and I am so proud to be you're [sic] daughter..." Nicole ended her note by titling it, "The Life of Jack Kelly" and then wrote, "Your one and only daughter, Nicole Kelly."

Indeed, she was his one and only daughter. Nicole and Jack had forged an unbreakable father-child relationship. For him, being a star meant little in comparison to the love shown him by his fifteen-year-old daughter. The part of "father" was one he'd reached for from his earliest adult years. Now he had the title, and worked to ensure that it remained his starring role.

Jack meets with President Reagan and Dave Baker. PHOTO COURTESY JACK KELLY FAMILY PRIVATE COLLECTION

With all of Jack's political visibility came wide-scale scrutiny and public accountability. Things which might have made little difference to him as a TV star were given much more examination in his conspicuousness as a politician.

In 1988, out of the Mayor's office and back on the City Council, Jack Kelly was fined $4,000 by the Fair Political Practices Commission on two counts of improper financial disclosure. He was accused of failing to make public the purchase and resale of an area apartment building.

To his credit, Jack took his knocks without backing down. He admitted to the omission, saying boldly, "I did it, I'm sorry, it was a mistake, and I paid dearly for it." He attributed the situation to a simple bookkeeping error.

In later years, Jo cleared up misconceptions. "I was the real estate broker and Property Manager. That fine was over a tax deferred exchange. We did nothing wrong." Her assessment of what happened boiled down to,

"I guess the Fair Political Practices Commission wanted to make a politi-cal statement. I met with those people and laid out all the paperwork to show them there was no wrongdoing. I thought they understood what a 1031 tax deferred exchange meant; clearly they didn't."

By quickly and openly owning up to everything and not trying to hide any bit of the mess, Jack kept his career, and his image, on an even keel.

Mayor Jack Kelly in cowboy hat. PHOTO COURTESY JACK KELLY FAMILY PRIVATE COLLECTION

The people of Huntington Beach, in general, seemed to like him even more for his candor. He barely missed a beat, and thoroughly enjoyed the lively discussions which ensued. And no matter the issues between him and Jo privately, she was quick to defend him in the court of public opin-ion, saying there was no one more honest on God's earth than Jack Kelly.

Often it was hard to decipher whether people really agreed with what Jack said and did, or simply shook their heads in amazement at his bra-vado, shrugging and ultimately giving in to him as part and parcel of life in their beach town. Much of the pseudo-mystique, and acceptance, could be attributed to his often sarcastic, yet well-honed, sense of humor, which continued to serve him well in his public and press interactions.

One anonymous writer said Jack "held court from a booth at Maxwell's, the steak-and-red-leather restaurant at the base of Huntington Beach pier, and gave five-minute ad lib speeches in council meetings as one long run-on, jargon-laden, stream-of-consciousness sentence — kind of James Joyce meets Norm Crosby with a touch of Huey Long…" and "…he went with his ego and bluster, reliable pro-development vote and

Jack hugging Nicole. PHOTO COURTESY JACK KELLY FAMILY PRIVATE COLLECTION

undeniable rough charm, and he told great stories…"

Jack considered running for Orange County Supervisor, intending to turn around the hoopla surrounding the fining incident. He told the press he had everything figured out — it was not unusual for Jack to have his tongue rock-solid planted in his cheek. When asked about how the slight scandal might affect his chances to win, he replied, "I will just step up and say, 'I'm Jack Kelly, the thief who was in bed with the producer of [those] buildings, and I was fined $4,000 for purchasing one of his homes. Any other questions on that issue?"

Instead of running for Orange County Supervisor, Jack took on another term with the Huntington Beach City Council. "City Council decisions require 'biting the bullet' and 'shooting from the hip,'" he stated. "Government leaders need to be the 'lead riders.'" Since he was known as the ally of business and builders, the other side of the coin showed him as the bane of slow-growth proponents.

He was one of the top vote-getters in Huntington Beach's election history, proving that he hadn't lost a bit of his charm, or a drop of his influence.

There was no way to ignore Jack Kelly's presence in and around town. No matter what people thought of him — as a politician, an actor...or as a man, few, if any, truly disliked him, even if they didn't care for his politics, and even as they raised their eyebrow at some of his often-outrageous antics.

Jack opening special Christmas gift from Nicole, a scrapbook she made for him (1983).
PHOTO COURTESY JACK KELLY FAMILY PRIVATE COLLECTION

Jack, without apologies and possibly without awareness, openly wore an old-school, when men-were-men-and-women-were-dames sort of persona. He regularly got in a fix as times changed, and as women's roles became more advanced. Jack spoke to male worker-types with words such as, "Howya doin', handsome!" and to women he would say, "Hiya, baby doll!" He'd call a woman, any woman — no matter her public status or lack thereof — "sweetheart." He freely told a female reporter about his kissing technique with a particular "broad" at a social gathering, only asking that the reporter withhold his kissee's name, but not that she withhold the story. He didn't care if she publicly related how he told his side of the tale... which of course that reporter did write about.

Jack Kelly remained a well-known TV personality, and now he was a well-known politician. Most people forgave him his old-fashioned attitudes because he had come from that era, and he was guileless in how he communicated. In all fairness to him, his manner with women, a reporter suggested, may have been nothing more than simply a product of a bygone era. He was what he was, and at his age, he wasn't likely to change.

Jack was confounded at the suggestion some women found expressions such as "baby doll" and "sweetie" sexist. "I have no recollection of rejection of it [referring to a woman as 'sweetie'], but then maybe they just don't tell me," he said. "I would say there's some merit if someone were to think it was condescending, though it's not meant to be. I don't get up in the morning thinking about who I can hurt."

A consensus of women who were asked how they felt about his unabashedly chauvinistic ways — or depending on how one perceived it, old-fashioned — was split down the middle. Some were downright appalled. One woman who did business with the city said Jack approached a client as she stood next to her, remarking openly about the size of her breasts. His secretary said he used to happily talk to co-workers about her nice rear end, using more descriptive terms.

On the other side of the argument, Westminster City Councilwoman Joy L. Neugebauer served alongside him on the Board of Directors for the four-city Public Cable Television Authority. She said of Jack, "I find him knowledgeable, well prepared and intelligent. In fact, he's charming. In conducting meetings he gives credence to what I say, whether he agrees or not."

Another, Harriet Wieder, covered all the bases with her thoughts. "I have a good working relationship with Jack. The kernel of Jack's behavior is sexist... If he ever called me Wieder-babe, God, I'd punch him!... He has chutzpah, unadulterated gall. He's flagrant, and people are so shocked that he gets away with it. He's a good ol' boy, and he keeps getting the vote."

He did keep getting the vote. Only after two consecutive terms on the Huntington Beach City Council did Jack finally leave to once again become a private citizen, and then only because city law would allow him no more unbroken time in the same office. Otherwise, Jack would've continued doing what he was doing for the town and the people he loved. The law, while not allowing more than two consecutive terms, did not forbid continued service after a break of four years. Jack had every intention of returning to his office in the City Council building.

When he was no longer a political force, Jack, who rarely put the brakes on much of anything he said publicly even when he was in office, was completely free to say whatever he cared to say, and to whomever he cared to say it.

He was interviewed by Nancy Wride, a *Los Angeles Times* Staff Writer, about a month after he left the Huntington Beach City Council. She said he "smoked Marlboros and had graying brown hair," and though he was a four-decade Democrat, he had recently re-registered as a Republican. In talking about his way of doing the city's business, he told her, "I'm a nonconformist, flamboyant [expletive], but hey, this isn't a solemn court with...red ermine collars and powdered wigs. It's only politics!"

Indeed, Jack was well known for his colorful free-flowing language; he had even used the word "caca" at public meetings...a safe if not genteel word, only a little less acceptable than others he could have uttered. In reminiscing over his long and varied, character-driven career, Jack exclaimed, "Ah, [expletive] it. I'm too old to worry about rejection and losing. I mean, so what? I guess if you really researched it with a jewel loupe [life], I did it my way." Regarding *Maverick* in particular, he was philosophical. "Let's face it; the character was not like playing *The Hunchback of Notre Dame*." He seemed amused. "I'm a realist. Life goes on."

"If custom T-shirts were in vogue when the Titanic got crushed, one could have been inscribed, 'What a dumb place for an iceberg.'"

JACK KELLY

CHAPTER NINETEEN

Ridin' Off Into The Sunset…
With A Smile

Life did go on, though it had changed drastically from those old *Maverick* days. He was married to Jo, and she was a completely different type of wife than Donna. In many ways, both women seemed to rule his household. Donna was more traditional. Jo was clearly the Kelly family Business Manager. Jack was the front-man, the wheeler and dealer, while Jo was most often behind the scenes, figuring out how to finance and organize everything, and keep the wheels turning.

In an interview with both Jack and Jo, where Jo spoke of Jack's days as Mayor, she said she ran the household from daily upkeep to finances, while he was "playing golf and playing Mayor." Jack followed up with, "My wife is an exceptional manager, and she's a broker. So I don't have quite that much to do with the real estate once we buy it. I snag deals."

Some things hadn't much changed for Jack. Not really. He ignored his medical issues, refusing to have his aneurism checked. Ever. When Jo would periodically nudge him, he would respond, "Yeah, kid, I gotta do that. I will. Don't worry about it. I'll go." He never did.

Instead, he continued to enjoy life much as he always had — with gusto and a hint of abandon. Often off the cuff. Jack Kelly was still a whiz in the kitchen, and he loved every minute he could spend there. He did almost all the family cooking, freeing Jo of any real culinary duties. He remained exceptional at what was clearly one of his genuine talents. According to Jo, he had a "free-form style" and he would "throw incongruous ingredients together." The end was always, in her words, "magic."

He rarely kept his recipes anywhere but in his head. Only a few survived over the years. In particular, he made a dish he called, "Chicken Diable":

1 tbsp butter or margarine
½ cup honey
¼ cup prepared mustard (Spicy Brown Gulden)
1 tsp salt
1 tsp curry powder
6 chicken breasts split and boned

Melt margarine or butter slowly over low heat, blend in honey, mustard, salt and curry powder to a smooth sauce.

Lightly grease large baking dish. Dredge chicken breasts in sauce mixture. Arrange in bottom of casserole and spoon over remaining sauce. Leave the skin on…and "let it play around in the fiery graveyard."

Bake 45 minutes at 375 degrees.

Turn temperature to 500 degrees but keep careful watch at this point and remove as soon as chicken gets a quick coat of crisp brown.

People regularly raved about Jack's salads. One of his favorites was Caesar. He considered eggs to be "his Waterloo" and omitted the usual "coddled egg." Instead, he added generous dustings of parmesan cheese to keep the salad from becoming dressing-logged. He said this was an "instinct" thing, and he did it "ad lib." He went "soft on olive oil, heavy on fresh lemon juice," and he advised to "taste as you go on." Next, he added a tablespoon of oil to the juice of one lemon, a pinch of garlic powder, and salt and pepper. The crisp, dry salad greens were tossed first with the dry seasonings, and then the lemon juice. Jack added only enough parmesan to coat the greens, tossing the salad again, and drizzling on oil until the cheese soaked in. As he predicted, not a drop of dressing ended up in the bottom of the bowl.

Kelly family life had evolved. The relationship between him, Jo, and Nicole, as a unit of three, stood out to everyone who witnessed them together — whether close friends or casual acquaintances. No matter what was between Jo and Jack as a couple at any moment in time, whether they were personally together or apart, as parents they were united in their love for their child. They believed Nicole would benefit from all they did "in this life. She was the single most important person between them," and they were in agreement over whatever they had to do ensure she had the best of everything they, as her parents, could give her.

Jack said, "Our contribution to the world consists in how well we prepare Nicole to handle the things she is given in life."

Jack at home in the kitchen. PHOTO COURTESY JACK KELLY FAMILY PRIVATE COLLECTION

Nicole never felt as if her parents were separated. She knew the reality, that they were not a traditionally married couple, but they spent a lot of happy time together — whether having dinner at the house or at a restaurant, or going out for official city events, and even taking extended vacations out of the country — so in her mind, whether or not Jack and Jo lived in the same house or apart, she saw the three of them as a cohesive family unit.

Jack was philosophic about how he'd lived to this point. "Life experience changes from day to day. It's how you react to what you encounter that matters." He considered the experiences he'd had with Jo to be valuable, everything good and everything difficult. Each moment came together to "utilize even the negative experience, because out of that usually comes something of value."

An entertaining story of the time came from Nicole. She was in her last years in college, taking a class on the evolution of film — as a medium which had been influenced by what went on in society over the years. Her professor showed students five different movies. One was *The Commies Are Coming* (1962).

Nicole knew nothing of this film. The teacher explained about how "the main character was this guy who has a dream. And in his dream, in his entire world, he's the only left who isn't a Communist. Everyone else is. They're all trying to get him. His wife, his kids, the whole thing."

She waited for the film to roll, like everyone else. "I'm sitting in my class, watching, and the lights go down. There's this guy in the bed, asleep, and the scene's blurry. It's really bad blurry to make it look like a dream, and then all of a sudden it gets clear…and it's Daddy!"

Ever since Jack had reacted to her heartfelt letter in such a positive way, Jack and Nicole had been having dinner together every week, sometimes twice a week, just the two of them. They would go out to one of a few of their favorite restaurants, take over a regular booth or table, and eat and talk for hours. Nicole had come to expect these get-togethers as a regular part of their relationship, and she cherished the chance to have her father all to herself.

After class this particular evening, the two of them had dinner together. "So, Daddy," she spoke conversationally as they sat down at their table, "I saw this really great film in class today. I wonder if you've ever heard of it?"

Jack responded with interest, "Hmm? What was it?"

"It's called *The Commies Are Coming.*"

"Oh my God!" he exploded. "I thought that movie was buried somewhere. Who would've ever…I didn't think anyone would ever mention that to me again!"

"It was so funny!" Nicole laughed as she remembered the moment. Jack went on to tell his daughter he'd had to do the movie. The studio gave him no choice. He was a contract actor and in those days, whatever came his way he had to take on, or else he would be considered in breach of contract.

Jo spoke well of her husband, no matter what was going on between them, and she always managed to be a bit playful while at the same time offering a personal point-of-view. "Jack is twelve years old," she said at one time. "Everybody takes care of him. In my next life I want to come back as Jack Kelly… The best thing that ever happened to Jack is me, and if he was real honest, he'd admit it."

Jack knew he had it good, and he usually did admit this to anyone willing to listen. While most knew he loved his wife, even as they slowly drifted apart as a couple, there was no one who did not notice how he absolutely adored, and was devoted to, his daughter. Nicole was everything to him. She was his shining star, the one accomplishment in his life of which he continued to be in awe. He would leave her notes on a regular basis, in places so she would easily find them. One such note was indicative of all the others: "Riddle of the day!! Guess who I love? The correct answer is my greatest reward…"

Jack wasn't resting on his laurels. He continued with a host of business ventures which Jo usually oversaw; being an entertainer remained high on his list. His natural talent for voices and accents was put to solid financial use between stints on the Huntington Beach City Council. Depending on the format and areas of broadcast, some of the ad campaigns he did carried potential to earn him upwards of $100,000 for twenty-five or thirty

Jo, Nicole, and Jack on vacation. PHOTO COURTESY JACK KELLY FAMILY PRIVATE COLLECTION

minutes of work...not a bad deal from any angle. The talent was natural for him, requiring little effort or time, and Jack always walked away with that solid chunk of change. All part of a day's work.

He explained, "I do great dialect, great Italian. I do a Jew better than a Jew." He went on to say without conceit he believed his voice had "the rich quality of Max Von Sydow." Jack thought there was purity to voiceover and radio work which wasn't found in other forms of performing. "It's a niche where age and beauty have no importance."

He thought much about this these days. Jack was over sixty. He was beyond the dashing, handsome roles he had taken on before and after *Maverick*, and Bart himself was but a distant memory. Now he was a businessman through and through, and a father and a husband. His life had definitely changed.

Jack Kelly had well managed the transition, yet he was in many ways a product of a bygone era. One person commented, "Like your uncle who still wears Brylcreem, Kelly has a personal style that often seems frozen in his acting prime — that era of blond furniture and brown liquor, when women were flattered to be called dishes, dames and skirts. His conversations ring of a Frankie-Dino rat-packer, with a Marlboro twist." Jack had been part of that "Frankie-Dino rat-packer" generation, the world in which he had matured and lived most of his formative days.

Now he found himself in the middle of an often flat-for-him, brave new world.

Jack had a chance to take one more walk down Hollywood's Memory Lane. The TV movie, *The Gambler Returns: Luck of the Draw* (1991), had him revive Bart, albeit now many years older. While maybe something of a downer, remembering the virile and dapper fellow Bart had been, Jack had a symbiotic cohort when Jim Garner came along for the ride. The *Maverick* brothers were together again, if only for a brief moment in time. Viewers enjoyed the chance to see them revisit the roles which made both of them famous.

There was one very special part of this experience for Jack. Nicole, a student at Golden West College in Huntington Beach, had a walk-on role as a saloon girl escorting Maverick to the poker showdown. Even though her part was eventually left on the cutting room floor, father and daughter loved the opportunity to work together in front of the cameras.

This return to his roots was little more than a blast from his past, and Jack knew it for what it was. "It was just a ball being together with all those old-timers," he said in an article in the *O. C. Register*. "It was a super fun piece." He wasn't going to give up his political world to go back to the bright lights of Hollywood.

In 1990, Jack ran for, and won, a third term on the Huntington Beach City Council. This go-round wasn't set to expire until 1994. The people proved they still loved Jack Kelly by putting him back in office. They believed he had a continuing vision to make their city better. This was something of which Jack was immensely proud and in the long run, seemed to mean more to him than any role he'd taken on in front of a TV or movie camera.

This revived-yet-again public exposure directly and intimately involved him with his local community at a level which acting had never truly afforded him. Being among the people was in some ways akin to being on stage with a live audience feeding off his every word, and that was where Jack had always thrived.

One experience had become a full family affair every 4th of July. With Jack on the Huntington Beach City Council, he rode in the city's Independence Day Parade. A car carried him, Jo and Nicole along the parade route, and he'd sit on the top of the seat, smiling and waving to residents

Jack and Nicole on the set of The Gambler Returns: Luck of the Draw *(1990).* PHOTO COURTESY JACK KELLY FAMILY PRIVATE COLLECTION

on both sides of the street. Jo and Nicole were usually beside him, waving along with him...smiles all around. Nicole remembers vividly. "There were some great BBQs and a wonderful Huntington Beach fireworks display in the evening."

January 1991 started a lively period for Jack; some might say a rather embarrassing period. A delegation from Anjo, Japan, one of Huntington Beach's sister cities, came to town for a visit. During a Council Meeting, Mayor Peter Green, Anjo Mayor Shuji Iwatsuki and others from the delegation, exchanged bows as Green accepted a check for $93,000 from Iwatsuki. The money represented funds raised in Japan for Huntington Beach's Municipal Pier reconstruction project.

As he watched events unfold, all was well until, in true Jack Kelly fashion, he turned to Councilman Earle Robitaille and casually commented in a low voice, "How could guys who bow that much ever bomb the [Pearl] Harbor?"

No one reported hearing the comment in Council chambers, but the off-camera remark was audible in the meeting's cable TV broadcast. Once

Jack and cast on the set of The Gambler Returns: Luck of the Draw *(1990), James Drury second from left.* PHOTO COURTESY JACK KELLY FAMILY PRIVATE COLLECTION

the comment was publicly aired, there was no way to retract his words. Jack refused to apologize, discounting his aside as "just another cheap, smart Kellyism, and it's backfired on me."

The Mayor explained, "He was elected by 20,000 people…and I think he needs to be responsive to them. But I can't reprimand Jack Kelly for being Jack Kelly…That's the person Jack is, and voters should know who he is and expect Jack to be Jack." What Jack called a "Kellyism" was electronically omitted from the videotape before a copy was mailed to the Japanese delegation. Still, they learned of the hoopla through the grapevine.

Because they did find out, and because the press was determined to make certain Jack's gaffe was well-circulated, he had no option but to finally back down. "If I have offended people who have claimed such offense, I would certainly hope that you would attribute it to carelessness

and thoughtlessness rather than to any moment of prejudice or bigotry..."
Jack stated to fellow council members in a brief prepared statement. "I
would hope you would accept my apologies."

He went on to say his remark had been nothing more than "flippant,"
never intended to insult the Japanese. "One thing that I cannot express
more appreciatively is affection for the citizens of Anjo with their excep-

Mayor Jack Kelly, with Jo and Nicole in an earlier 4th of July Parade. PHOTO COURTESY
JACK KELLY FAMILY PRIVATE COLLECTION

tional generosity," he said. "They made an incredible gift to help us build
our new pier." He added that "while inopportune and flippant," his comment "was not meant to be disrespectful to our guests. As a matter of fact,
it was nothing more, in my mind, than an expression of ironic humor."

And his words had been definitely an expression of Jack Kelly-type
humor. Few were surprised at such a remark from him, and most would
have sloughed it off if not for the potential international issue. Jack realized this, and he knew it was in the best interest of his city and state to
do the inevitable and own up to his jokester self getting the best of him
at the worse possible moment.

After Jack made his public apology, Mayor Green, who'd known Jack
for six years, released his own statement in his friend's defense. Jack was,
he said, "absolutely not capable of uttering a deeply felt racial slur."

Eventually the sideshow went away. With the unusual political brou-haha finally behind him, Jack happily went back to the stage in a local performance at the Huntington Central Park Amphitheatre. He por-trayed an alcoholic father in *A Teenager Is*, a play about the problems youth often faced in a dysfunctional family dynamic. Featured in a sepa-rate scene in this play was Jack's daughter, Nicole. The subject matter was, in some general ways, close to home for both of them.

In the Fall of 1991, after a full month of community and City Council haggling, an official nickname was given to Huntington Beach. The City Council agreed "Surf City" would be the best title for marketing the com-munity to a larger arena. By a 6-1 vote, the Council appropriated $2,500 to copyright the name. Officials said they could even see possibilities of merchandising a line of Surf City beach clothes and accessories. Ron Hagan, Director of Community Services, said, "The media have been calling us Surf City for years." He felt the time had come to capitalize.

The lone vote against the new tagline came from Jack Kelly. He was afraid the city might get carried away by the glitz of the concept. "I don't think there's sufficient support for it in the community," Jack said. He was overruled, and the nickname was made a part of the city's marketing plan.

The Surf City vote was only one of many issues, small and large, seem-ingly insignificant yet clearly crucial, in which Jack was a part in those days of service to his beloved Huntington Beach. This was his life — local politics, golf, and his family. What had been his Hollywood world years before had become little more than a memory and, now and then, a quickly-passing reflective pang.

There had been a long battle ongoing about the Huntington Beach Pier between folks who wanted the area preserved as it always had been, and those looking toward a more business, proactive way to attract visitors and locals. The original pier had been badly damaged, and con-demned, thanks to a 1988 storm. Four years later the pier was finally fully rebuilt.

Jack was part of the pro-business, forward-looking group. An article explained, "For civic leaders, business owners, and residents, the reopening of the pier is a giant step toward the economic and spiritual rejuvena-tion of downtown Huntington Beach," which, despite his distaste for the name, was now officially and loudly being called "Surf City." The article brought Jack into the discussion by saying, "Councilman Jack Kelly said he has heard the nostalgic pining of those who complain that downtown has lost its soul…"

"The place was falling apart," was Jack's response. "It was dingy. It was dark. It just wasn't attracting people...We had nothing to attract anybody unless you wanted to buy a surfboard." He managed to add the jab to the town's new nickname, while making his point over financial and developmental benefits afforded the city with the reopening of the new pier. Everyone always knew what Jack Kelly thought. He never hid his

Jack and Nicole on Nicole's birthday, November 6, 1991. PHOTO COURTESY JACK KELLY FAMILY PRIVATE COLLECTION

opinion, or skirted an issue.

Jack had not had a drink in years. He felt well, and he was generally happy. He had been living in one of the Kelly rental homes, not in the house with Jo and Nicole. Though this was a source of some sadness for him, he had come to terms with the lifestyle. He had been in the rental house for some time. He had dinner with Nicole for her birthday that year. The love between them had never been deeper.

On Valentine's Day, 1992, Nicole gave her father a card which said on the front, "Happy Valentine's Day, Dad...A woman's heart always belongs to her father." The inside read, "You're the only man I ever met who could afford it." This was a cute "Cathy" cartoon, but despite the light-hearted sentiment, was a representation of many cards she'd given him over the years. Every one included a sincere handwritten message, and would say, "To my #1 man!" She always told him how much she loved him in glowing terms.

Jack Kelly had a heart attack on April 28, 1992. He was rushed to the hospital, and his previous medical history finally came back to haunt him. This time, he couldn't hide from the truth. He wasn't healthy, and hadn't been for awhile. Doctors decided to do bypass surgery a few days later. Jack came out of the operation in relatively good condition, and hoped the bad stuff was now behind him for good. Jo brought him back to the family home, and he began his recuperation with his wife and daughter surrounding him.

All was going well when his doctor gave Jack a bit of friendly advice. He told him that a glass of red wine with dinner — a glass, nothing more — would do his heart good. This practice, the doctor said, would help him relax, and cause him no harm. Jack had started to feel much better, though those closest to him saw him as only a shadow of the man he'd once been.

Once he was again self-sufficient, Jack returned to his bachelor house. He wanted Nicole to move in with him but she was a young lady, with her own life, and his place didn't afford her a decent amount of space. She had been living with her mother, and then in her own condominium.

Left to his own devices and with no one to whom he had to answer on a daily basis, Jack took his doctor's words to heart. He began to have a glass of wine with dinner. At first, there was no issue. The wine did seem to help him, and as Nicole said, "He didn't change with wine, the way he did with hard alcohol. He actually got a little relaxed, maybe even happy or silly… or at least not mad or lethargic like before." While drinking was drinking, the wine didn't have the same harsh negative effects on his behavior.

She and her mother, however, were not happy with the fact that Jack's doctor, knowing his history, had suggested he pick up any sort of alcohol again. They tried to talk Jack out of drinking anything. Wine had never been his drink of choice, according to Nicole. It had most often been scotch.

Alcohol, any alcohol, wasn't a good idea for Jack Kelly. He had done well until now, staying sober for so long, but when he started again, his body embraced the practice. One glass of wine turned into two, then three…then a bottle. Nicole would try to talk to him but, in his mind, as she put it, "…he had a 'legitimate' green light and while he didn't defend it in any angry manner, he would blow it off as no big deal."

Nicole, and Jo, never forgave that doctor.

Jack stayed in contact with some of his old Hollywood friends. Donna spoke to him on rare occasion. They still shared mutual acquaintances and on one evening, she and Jack were at the same dinner party, at the home of Paul Burke. Jack and Jo were living separate lives.

"Kelly was upset," Donna remembered. A group of them were playing cards after the meal. "He looked at me and said, 'I can't do this anymore,' and he got up and walked out of the room."

Jack had loved the women in his life, every one of them, with all his heart. He was a true woman's man, and he seemed to care deeply and completely. Donna was worried about him.

Not long after this dinner party, maybe a few months, Jack suffered a massive brain aneurism. He was home, and he was alone. The birth defect discovered those twenty-plus years earlier likely combined with the heart ailment and his heavy drinking to finally do him in. He was rushed to Humana Hospital after Jo found him unconscious. When Jo and Nicole reached the hospital, he had already been x-rayed, and the doctor showed them the results. The blood vessel burst, and the blood had flooded his brain. He was brain dead. This was the end, and his family knew it.

Jack Kelly received Last Rites from the Catholic Church and was taken off life support, and on November 7, 1992, it was announced to the world that he was gone. Tom Chevoor's wife, Mary Ann, recalled the moment she heard. "It was really bizarre because I was getting ready to go to work and the radio was on. It said, 'Jack Kelly is dead.' And I thought, 'On Nicole's birthday.'"

Earle Robitaille had been fishing in Mexico. When he returned to the office, someone said to him, "Did you hear about Jack Kelly?"

"No," Earle replied. "What did Jack do now?" Jack was always up to something, and Earle was sure there was another "Kellyism" in the news. The fact that Jack was dead was nowhere near what he expected.

Donna remembered having being concerned when she saw Jack last. "He didn't look well." When she heard the news of his passing, she, like Earle Robitaille, had a humorous thought, but only after the shock wore off. "I remember making a comment that this was typical Kelly," she laughed. The presidential election had recently occurred. "He'd make sure he got that vote in."

Carol's son, Michael, came to Jack's funeral service to represent the family, and told Jo, "My mom prefers to grieve in private."

Nancy didn't attend but sent flowers to Nicole, and she called. Nicole said this was the first time she remembered ever talking to her Aunt Nancy as an adult — and it was also her last.

Not only those closest to him mourned in their own ways the loss of this, at times, larger-than-life man, but the city of Huntington Beach as a whole was devastated. Flags were lowered to half staff at City Hall on the order of Mayor Jim Silva, who said, "This is a very sad time for all the citizens of Huntington Beach," and then he added, "Jack loved this city like no one else."

City Administrator Michael Uberuaga said of Jack, "He called it the way it was. He didn't politic, he just told it the way he saw it, and I think that is a real value in politics today."

A memorial service in Huntington Beach's City Hall was attended by about 500 people. Roger Work, former executive with the Huntington Beach Co., said, "He rode hard, was a straight shooter, loyal as a friend and never backed down from a fight."

The owner of the Waterfront Hilton Beach Resort said of Jack, "He was colorful, controversial and straight-talking." He went on to compliment his friend. "He also had one of the greatest vocabularies of anyone I've ever known." Quite a com-pliment for a Candy Ass

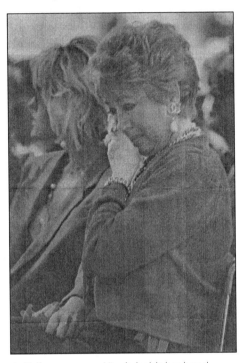

Jo Kelly mourns as Nicole holds her hand.
PHOTO COURTESY JACK KELLY FAMILY PRIVATE COLLECTION

Cowboy who may have never received an official high school diploma.

Kaye MacLeod was a citizen of Jack's beloved hometown, and worked with him when she spearheaded the bicentennial celebration. She said Jack was "very, very patriotic." She remembered his voice when he deliv-ered speeches. "His voice was great and the kids loved him."

The most loving tribute came from Nicole. As her mother sobbed, Nicole said her dad "always did what he believed was the very best thing. He was my best friend. I loved him more than anything in my life."

A few words written about Jack's friend, Merv Adelson, in a 2003 article in *Fortune Magazine*, seemed to mirror how Jack Kelly had taken in his world. "Along the way he meets mobsters and movie stars, presidents and kings. He marries glamorous women. He lives in beautiful houses. He becomes rich and powerful — or so it seems."

Jack Kelly had done most of those things. He did it his way...a Maverick life.

Nicole gives her father's eulogy at his memorial service. PHOTO COURTESY JACK KELLY FAMILY PRIVATE COLLECTION

Jack Kelly salutes in one of his daughter's favorite pictures of him. PHOTO COURTESY JACK KELLY FAMILY PRIVATE COLLECTION

Films

1939: *The Story of Alexander Graham Bell*.........Banker's Son *(uncredited)*

     Young Mr. Lincoln ....Matt Clay as a Boy *(uncredited)*

1949: *Fighting Man of the Plains* ....Cattleman *(uncredited)*

     Holiday Affair...................................... Drunk on Train *(uncredited)*

1950: *Peggy* ....Lex–O.S.U. Player *(uncredited)*

     Where Danger Lives... Dr. Mullenbach

     The West Point Story........................ Officer-in-Charge *(uncredited)*

1951: *Call Me Mister*............................... Marching Soldier *(uncredited)*

     New Mexico .... Private Clifton

     People Will Talk ....Student in Classroom *(uncredited)*

     Submarine Command...Lt. Paul Barton

     The Wild Blue Yonder ....Lt. Jessup

1952: *Bronco Buster*.. Photographer *(uncredited)*

     Red Ball Express...Pvt. John Heyman

     No Room for the Groom..Will Stubbins

     Sally and Saint Anne .... Mike O'Moyne

1953: *The Redhead from Wyoming* .... Sandy

     Gunsmoke (Movie) .... Curly Mather

     Law and Order..Jed

     Column South..Trooper Vaness

     The Stand at Apache River... Hatcher

     The Glass Web.. TBC Engineer *(uncredited)*

1954: *Drive a Crooked Road*..Harold Baker

     Magnificent Obsession .... First Mechanic *(uncredited)*

     The Bamboo Prison.. Slade

     Black Tuesday .... Frank Carson

1955: *The Violent Men* ....De Rosa, Parrish Rider

     Cult of the Cobra..Carl Turner

     Double Jeopardy ....Jeff Calder

1955: *The Night Holds Terror* .... Gene Courtier
        To Hell and Back.. Kerrigan
1956: *Forbidden Planet* .... Lt. Jerry Farman
        Julie..Jack (co-pilot)
        Canasta de cuentos mexicanos (movie short)..... ("Canasta" segment)
1957: *She Devil* .... Dr. Dan Scott
        Taming Sutton's Gal .... Jugger Phelps
1958: *Hong Kong Affair* .... Steve Whalen
1961: *A Fever in the Blood*.................................... Dan Callahan
1962: *Red Nightmare (movie short)* .... Jerry Donavan
1963: *FBI Code 98*.. Robert P. Cannon
1965: *Love and Kisses*... Jeff Pringle
1968: *Commandos*.. Captain Valli
1969: *Young Billy Young* .... John Behan
1976: *The Human Tornado* .... Captain Ryan
1978: *Spawn of the Slithis* ....Radio Announcer *(voice work)*

Television

The Ray Milland Show: Meet Mr. McNulty
        "Swimming Problem" (1954)...
They Rode West .... Lt. Raymond
Stories of the Century
        "Clay Allison" (1954).. Clay Allison
The Pepsi-Cola Playhouse
        "This Man for Hire" (1954)..
        "Girl on the Drum" (1954) ....
        "The Sound of Silence" (1954) ....
The Star and the Story
        "Safe Journey" (1955) .... Detective
Hallmark Hall of Fame
        "Patrick Henry" (1955)...Patrick Henry
City Detective
        "Man Down, Woman Screaming" (1955)...................Tom Arthur
Cavalcade of America
        "Sunrise on a Dirty Face" (1955)........................... James E. West

TV Reader's Digest
 "My First Bullfight" (1955) ....Sidney Franklin
Kings Row (1955)................................Dr. Parris Mitchell *(starring role)*
Dr. Hudson's Secret Journal
 "The Score Card" (1956) ....Dr. Bennett
 "Carolyn Bennett Story" (1955) ....Dr. Bennett
 "Dr. Bennett Story" (1955)..Dr. Bennett
Jane Wyman Presents The Fireside Theatre
 "Scent of Roses" (1956) ....Gilman
 "Kristi" (1956) .... Rayburn Stone
Strange Stories
 "This Man for Hire" (1956)...
Frontier
 "The Hostage" (1956)..
 "The Return of Jubal Dolan" (1956) ....Jubal Dolan
 "The Hunted" (1956)...
The Millionaire
 "The Fred Graham Story" (1956)............................Fred Graham
Schlitz Playhouse
 "Explosion" (1956)...
State Trooper
 "Jailbreak at Tonopah" (1956).............................. Johnny Bledsoe
Lux Video Theatre
 "Just Across the Street" (1957) ....
The Ford Television Theatre
 "The Idea Man" (1957).. Hal Jeffers
Gunsmoke
 "Jealousy" (1957) .... Cam Durbin
Sally
 "Sally Tries to Say No" (1957) ....Tony Rhodes
Maverick (1957-1962) ....as Bart Maverick *(starring role)*
Studio 57
 "Explosion" (1958)..
Sugarfoot (1958)...as Bart Maverick *(walk-on)*
Kraft Mystery Theater
 "Shadow of a Man" (1963) ....Sam Greenlee
Wagon Train
 "The Fenton Canaby Story" (1963) ....Fenton Canaby
The Lucy Show
 "Lucy Makes a Pinch" (1964)....................... Detective Bill Baker

Kraft Suspense Theatre
      "Kill Me on July 20th" (1965) .... Tony Camion
      "Four into Zero" (1965) .... Charles Glenn
      "The Name of the Game" (1963) .... Pete Braven
Daniel Boone
      "The High Cumberland: Part 2" (1966) .... Second Horseman
Batman
      "The Cat and the Fiddle" (1966) .... Jack O'Shea
      "Hot Off the Griddle" (1966) .... Jack O'Shea
Run for Your Life
      "Baby, the World's on Fire" (1967) .... Harry Bevins
Laredo
      "Enemies and Brothers" (1967) .... Bart Cutler/Frank Parmalee
      "The Deadliest Kid in the West" (1966) .... Lance Mabry
Please Don't Eat the Daisies
      "Remember Lake Serene?" (1967) .... Bob
Bob Hope Presents the Chrysler Theatre
      "Deadlock" (1967) .... Detective Ray Baker
      "Time of Flight" (1966) .... Al Packer
      "One Embezzlement and Two Margaritas" (1966)
            .... Frederick Piper
      "Double Jeopardy" (1965) .... Fred Piper
      "White Snow, Red Ice" (1964) .... Fred Piper
The High Chaparral
      "The Doctor from Dodge" (1967)
            .... Doctor John Henry/Holliday
The Iron Horse
      "Dealer's Choice" (1967) .... Logan
The Name of the Game
      "The Civilized Men" (1969) .... Creighton Howell
      "The Inquiry" (1969) .... Frank Fowler
Alias Smith and Jones
      "Night of the Red Dog" (1971) .... Dr. Chauncey Beauregard
Marcus Welby, M.D.
      "Solomon's Choice" (1972 .... Actor
Circle of Fear
      "The Dead We Leave Behind" (1972) .... Motorist
Ironside
      "Cold Hard Cash" (1972) .... Bobby
      "Tagged for Murder" (1967) .... Johnny Corman

Faraday and Company
    "Fire and Ice" (1973) ....Coleman
Banacek
    "Fly Me — If You Can Find Me" (1974)...................Lou Wayne
Chase
    "Out of Gas" (1974) ....
Toma
    "Joey the Weep" (1974)...
McCloud
    "This Must Be the Alamo" (1974) ....Manny Donner
Lucas Tanner
    "Look the Other Way" (1974)...................................Ted Lefferts
Get Christie Love!
    "I'm Your New Neighbor" (1975).............................Arthur Ryan
    "A Few Excess People" (1975) ....Arthur Ryan
    "A Fashion Heist" (1975) ....Arthur Ryan
    "From Paris with Love" (1975)...............................Arthur Ryan
    "The Big Rematch" (1975) ....Arthur Ryan
    "My Son, the Murderer" (1975) ....Arthur Ryan
    "Murder on High C" (1975).....................................Arthur Ryan
    "Our Lady in London" (1975)...................................Arthur Ryan
    "Too Many Games in Town" (1975) ....Arthur Ryan
    "The Deadly Sport" (1975)..Arthur Ryan
Ellery Queen
    "The Adventure of the Lover's Leap" (1975)
        .... Attorney J. T. Latimer
The Family Holvak
    "The Tribute" (1975)..George Iverson
The Bionic Woman
    "Claws" (1976).. Charles Keys
    "The Martians Are Coming, the Martians Are Coming" (1978)
        .... Ray Fisk
Hawaii Five-O
    "Let Death Do Us Part" (1976) .... Jim Spier
Quincy, M.E.
    "Visitors in Paradise" (1977) .... Peter Devlin
The Rockford Files
    "Beamer's Last Case" (1977) ....Ralph Steel
    "The Becker Connection" (1977)............................ Alex Kasajian

A Double Life (1978, TV Movie) .... Walters

Vega$

    "High Roller" (1978) .... Merle Ochs

The Incredible Hulk

    "The Waterfront Story" (1978) .... Tony Kelly

The New Maverick (1978, TV Movie) .... Bart Maverick

Sword of Justice

    "A Double Life" (1978) .... Walters

Flying High

    "The Vanishing Point" (1978)...................................... Reynolds

The Hardy Boys/Nancy Drew Mysteries

    "Defection to Paradise: Part 2" (1978).............. Harry Hammond

    "Defection to Paradise: Part 1" (1978).............. Harry Hammond

    "Scorpion's Sting" (1978)................................. Harry Hammond

    "Dangerous Waters" (1978) .... Harry Hammond

    "Search for Atlantis" (1978) .... Harry Hammond

    "The Last Kiss of Summer: Part 1" (1978) .... Harry Hammond

    "Arson and Old Lace" (1978) .... Harry Hammond

B.J. and the Bear

    "The Murphy Contingent" (1979)................................... Nichols

    "Detective Finger, I Presume" (1981) .... Capt. Jim Dryer

Bret Maverick

    "The Hidalgo Thing" (1982) .... playing Bart Maverick

The Fall Guy

    "Happy Trails" (1983) .... Bart Maverick

The Gambler Returns: The Luck of the Draw (1991, TV Movie)

    .... Bart Maverick

Sources

Interviews/Correspondence:

Barilla, Bette. Interview with the author. 2011.

Cantwell, Peggy. Interviews with the author. 2010-2011.

Chevoor, Tom. Interviews with the author. 2007-2011.

Chevoor, Mary Ann. Interviews with the author. 2007-2011.

Drury, James. Interview with the author. 2011.

Economakis, Peter. Interview with the author. 2011.

Ford, Peter. E-mail correspondence with the author. 2011

Garagiola. Joe, E-mail correspondence with the author. 2011

Garner, Gigi. E-mail correspondence with the author. 2010.

Garner, Nicole Kelly. Interviews with the author. 2007-2011.

Garner, Nicole Kelly. Personal correspondence with father. 1980s-1992.

Kelly, Jack. Personal correspondence. 1980s-1992.

Kelly, Jo. Interviews with the author. 2007-2011.

Maross, Michael. Phone contact with the author. 2009.

Moore, Sir Roger. Interview with the author. 2011.

Palmer, Gregg. Interview with the author. 2011.

Pall, Gloria. E-mail correspondence with the author. 2010.

Robitaille, Earle. Interview with the author. 2011.

Rosenberg, Kelly Caro. Interviews with the author. 2009-2011.

Van Doren, Mamie. E-mail correspondence with the author. 2010.

Wynn, May. Interviews with the author. 2007-2011.

Newspapers:

Abilene Reporter News [TX]
Albuquerque Tribune [NM]
Anderson Daily Bulletin [IN]
Anniston Star [AL]
Arcadia Tribune [CA]
Arizona Republic
Associated Press [AP]
Avalanche-Journal [TX]
The Bee [VA]
The Berkshire County Eagle [MA]
Blizzard, Oil City [PA]
Blytheville Courier News [AR]
Bradford Era [PA]
Bridgeport Telegram [CT]
Cedar Rapids Gazette [IA]
Chicago Tribune
Clovis News-Journal [NM]
Colorado Springs Gazette-Telegraph [CO]
Corsicana Daily Sun [TX]
Cumberland Times [MD]
The Daily Inter Lake [MT]
The Daily Review [CA]
Daily Telegraph [WV]

Dunkirk Evening Observer [NY]
Edwardsville Intelligencer [IL]
El Paso Herald-Post [TX]
Eureka Humboldt Standard [CA]
Evening Independent [OH]
Fairbanks Daily News-Miner [AK]
Florence Times Tri-Cities Daily [SC]
Frederick News-Post [MD]
Gastonia Gazette [NC]
Gettysburg Gazette [PA]
The Record [PA]
Hammond Times [IN]
Harrison Daily Times [AR]
Hutchinson News [KS]
Independent [CA]
Independent Star-News [CA]
Indiana [PA] *Evening Gazette*
Intelligencer [PA]
International News Service [INS]
Kingsport Times [TN]
Kokomo Morning Times [IN]
The Lethbridge Herald [Canada]
Lexington Dispatch [NC]
The Lima News [OH]
Long Beach Independent [CA]
Los Angeles Examiner [CA]
Los Angeles Herald & Express [CA]
Los Angeles Times [CA]
Las Vegas Daily Optic [NV]
The Lowell Sun [MA]
Miami Daily News-Record [OK]
The Milwaukee Journal [WI]
The Modesto Bee [CA]
Nevada State Journal
News-Palladium [MI]
North Adams Transcript [MA]
Northwest Arkansas Times
Oakland Tribune [CA]
Ocala State-Banner [FL]
Orange County Register [CA]
Pasadena Star-News [CA]
The Post Standard [NY]
The Press-Courier [CA]
Press-Telegram [CA]
Progress-Index Petersburg [VA]
Provo Daily Herald [UT]
Racine Journal Time Bulletin [WI]
Redlands Daily Facts [CA]
Reno Evening Gazette [NV]

Salinas Journal [KS]
Salt Lake Tribune [UT]
San Antonio [TX] *Express* [TX]
San Antonio Light [TX]
San Diego Reader [CA]
Sandusky Register [OH]
Sarasota Journal [FL]
Simpson's Leader-Times [PA]
Star-News [CA]
Stars and Stripes, European Edition
Stars and Stripes Newspaper, Pacific Editions
Syracuse Herald-Journal [NY]
Times Record [NY]
Tipton Tribune [IN]
Traverse City Record-Eagle [MI]
Tucson Daily Citizen [AZ]
United Press [UP]
United Press International [UPI]
The Valley News [CA]
The Vidette Messenger [IN]
Winnepeg Free Press [CANADA]
Winona Daily News [MN]
Wisconsin State Journal
The Yuma Daily Sun [AZ]

Various Writings of Columnists and Nationally Syndicated Writers:

Bacon, James.
Barrett, Rona.
Budge, Gordon.
Carroll, Harrison. "Behind the Scenes in Hollywood"
Connolly, Mike. "Mr. Hollywood" and "Notes From Hollywood"
Cook, Ben. "Hollywood Film Shop"
Denton, Charles.
Fidler, Jimmie. Fidler In Hollywood. "Idol Chatter"
Finnigan, Joseph.
Fiset, Bill.
Gardner, Hy. "Glad You Asked That"
Goode, Bud.
Graham, Sheilah.
Handsaker, Gene. "Glimpses of Glammerville"
Hopper, Hedda. "Hollywood Today"
James, Frances. "TV Close-Ups"

Johnson, Erskine. "Hollywood Today" and "In Hollywood"

Kaufman, Dave. "Short Cut"

Kelley, Willis B. "On The Air"

Kilgallen, Dorothy. "Voice of Broadway" and "Broadway"

Manners, Dorothy.

Maxwell, Marilyn. "Here's Hollywood"

Noglee, Pat. "Writing on Air"

Parsons, Louella. "Louella Parsons In Hollywood"

Ricketts, Al. "On the Town with Al Ricketts"

Sampas, Charles G. "Sampascoopies"

Scott, Vernon.

Scout, TV. "TV's Best Bet by TV Scout"

Sullivan, Ed. "Little Old New York"

Thomas, Bob. "Hollywood"

Vernon, Terry. "TV Tele-Vues"

Weinstock, Matt.

Wilson, Earl. "It Happened Last Night"

Winchell, Walter. "Winchell on Broadway"

Magazines and Periodicals:

Boxoffice

Community Connection. Huntington Beach, CA

Movieland

Movie Stars Parade

TV Guide

TV Listing

TV Radio Mirror

Websites:

Ancestry: *http://www.ancestry.com*

Glamour Girls of the Silver Screen: *http://www.glamourgirlsofthesilverscreen.com*

Huntington Beach City Council: *http://www.huntingtonbeachca.gov*

Internet Movie Database: *http://www.imdb.com*

Museum of Broadcast Communications: *http://www.museum.tv*

Newspaper Archive Database: *http://www.newspaperarchive.com*

Orange County [CA] Government: *http://egov.ocgov.com/portal/site/ocgov*

The Tall Dark Stranger There: *http://jackkellytribute.blogspot.com*

Television Obscurities: *http://www.tvobscurities.com*

About the Author

Linda Alexander grew up with the '70s entertainment scene. After doing the hustle and watching *The Mod Squad*, she began writing about entertainment characters who engaged her imagination. Linda has published five other books — three nonfiction and two novels, the most recent, the biography of Golden Era film star, Robert Taylor, *Reluctant Witness: Robert Taylor, Hollywood, & Communism*.

Her newest book, *A Maverick Life: The Jack Kelly Story*, is the biography of TV and 50s film star, Jack Kelly, published by BearManor Media in late 2011. She teaches non-credit writing courses for her local community college, and co-hosts with Debbie Barth "The Three Wise Girls," an internet entertainment radio show.

Index

Walsh, Mary Ann (aka Ann or Nan) (mother) 21-22

Walsh, Samuel (uncle) 320

Walsh, William (uncle) 23

Waring, Fred 42

Warner Bros. 79-80, 83, 96, 100, 110, 113-115, 125, 127, 129, 134, 136, 140-141, 146, 151, 154, 158-159, 165, 167, 170-180, 187, 189, 191-193, 200, 202, 206, 208-216, 219, 222-223, 226, 239, 242, 269

Warner Bros. Archives 11

Warner Bros. Library 146

Warner Bros. TV Legal Department 12

Warner, Jack 152, 172-173, 180, 211-212, 214-215, 217

Washington, D.C. 239, 250, 299, 368

Wayne, John 125, 141, 206

Weaver, Dennis 53

Webb, Jack 142, 216

Weinbaum, Stanley G. 102

Welk, Lawrence 226

Western Airlines 78

Westminster, California 330

West Point Story, The (film) 44

Westward No (theater) 217

Wheeler, Michelle 12

Wheeler, Randal 12

When The West Was Fun: A Western Reunion (TV) 312-313

Where Danger Lives (film) 43-44

White Squaw, The (film) 89

Whitman, Stuart "Stu" 53, 113

Whitney, Grace Lee 264, 265

Who Rode With Kane (film) 277

Wieder, Harriet 330

Wilcox, Collin 264-265

Wild Blue Yonder, The (film) 45

Wild Goose (nightclub) 81

Willes, Jean 89

William Castle Productions 306

Williams, Johnnie B. 184

Wills, Chill 49, 136

Willys Jeep 183, 185

Wilshire Country Club 312

Wilson, Earl 70, 142, 152

Winchell, Walter 71, 81, 92

Winters, Shelly 291

Wizard of Oz (film) 84

Wizard of Oz (radio) 25

Wood, Natalie 102

Woodell, Patricia 216

Woodhead, Tim 12

Woodson, William 239

Woolf, James 212, 213

Work, Roger 346

World of Suzie Wong, The (theater) 270

World's Most Beautiful Girls, The (film) 58

World War I 21

World War II 45, 54

WOR-TV 191

Wouk, Herman 133

Wride, Nancy 330

Wyman, Jane 82

Wynn, May 10, 67, 70, 89, 92-94, 96, 100, 103-104, 106, 123, 136, 152, 154-155, 221, 251, 254

Yates, Herbert J. 46

Yorke, Nan Kelly (mother) 296, 311

Young Billy Young (film) 277-278

Young, Gig 226, 228

Young, Loretta 37, 60

Young Mr. Lincoln (film) 37

Young, Nell Lynn 11, 148

Yuan (film) 104

Zanuck, Daryl 33

Zimbalist, Efrem, Jr. 181-182, 184, 187

Reluctant Witness: Robert Taylor, Hollywood, & Communism, published in 2008 by Tease Publishing LLC, is the exhaustive biography of Golden Era movie star, Robert Taylor. He was officially called "The Man With The Perfect Profile" by MGM, and some considered him the most beautiful man to ever grace the movie world. Yet there was more to him. He was complicated. He saw history — movie history and world history — and he was part of both.

He loved, literally and on screen, some of the most beautiful and glamorous women during the most glamorous era of the Silver Screen. His very public involvement in Hollywood's pre-McCarthy era Communist hysteria made him the only visible and well-known star whose appearance before the House Un-American Activities Committee cameras was widely leaked to the press. By the time he got there, Washington, DC was in a state of hysteria. Much has not been told about his part in this period, and what has been examined, has often misrepresented the truth.

Reluctant Witness: Robert Taylor, Hollywood, & Communism reveals striking new details and outlines the facts of that tumultuous period in American history ... and Robert Taylor's part in it. The book gives a vivid likeness of the flesh-and-blood man behind the image, and Taylor's son, Terry, said about Linda Alexander's portrayal of his father, "No better author to write it."

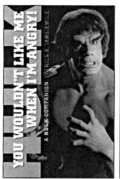

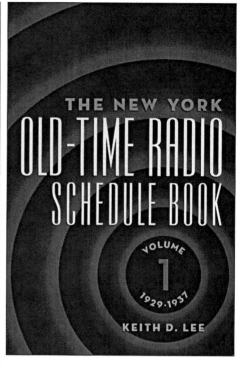

CPSIA information can be obtained at www.ICGtesting.com
Printed in the USA
BVOW010933050613

322478BV00010B/330/P